THE NATIONAL TRUST
COUNTRY HOUSE ALBUM

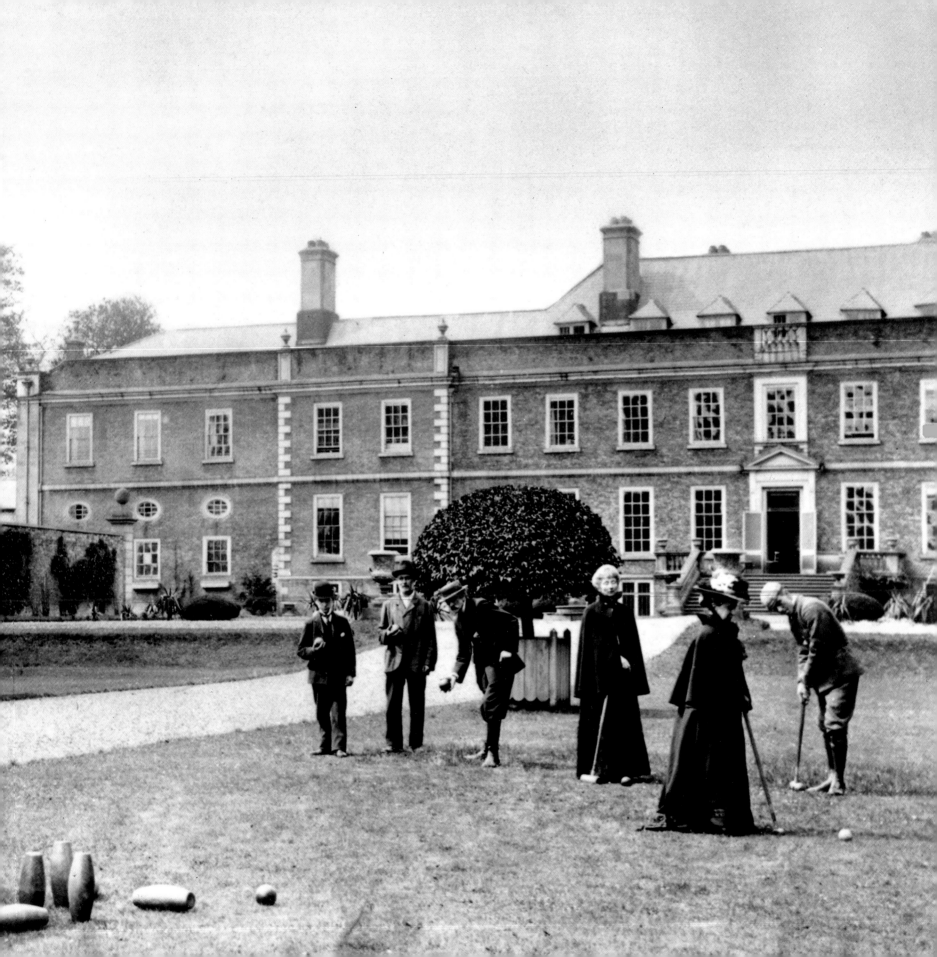

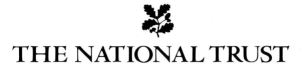

THE NATIONAL TRUST

COUNTRY HOUSE ALBUM

CHRISTOPHER SIMON SYKES

PAVILION
MICHAEL JOSEPH

Published in association with
THE NATIONAL TRUST
36 Queen Anne's Gate
London SW1H 9AS

First published in Great Britain in 1989 by
PAVILION BOOKS LIMITED
196 Shaftesbury Avenue, London WC2H 8JL
in association with Michael Joseph Limited
27 Wrights Lane, Kensington, London W8 5TZ

Designed by Louise Brody

A CIP catalogue record for this book is available from the British Library

ISBN 1 85145 201 X

10 9 8 7 6 5 4 3 2 1

Printed and bound in Italy
by Arnoldo Mondadori

Frontispiece: The front lawns of Erddig

CONTENTS

INTRODUCTION

I was brought up surrounded by photographs. My mother kept marvellous snap albums which chronicled her extremely busy social life and provided after-dinner entertainment for the endless guests who always seemed to be staying with my parents, and who were amused to see their faces appearing on page after page. I particularly loved the books which covered her childhood, since I had never known my grandfather, who died the year after I was born. He appeared as rather a dashing figure, always sporting a bow-tie and often surrounded by glamorous theatrical friends such as Noel Coward. I came to know him well through the pages of these books. The walls of my mother's bathroom were another source of endless amusement, covered as they were from floor to ceiling with framed photographs of family and friends. In the attics and cellars there were huge wooden chests, the contents of which included glass plates going back to the time of my great-great-grandfather, tin box after tin box of celluloid negatives exposed by my grandfather in his first Kodak on his travels abroad, and album after dusty album from the pages of which stared out the faces of long-dead uncles, aunts and cousins. Loose prints seemed to be stuffed at the back of almost every drawer in every room of the house.

One photograph held a particular fascination for me. It was very faded and hung framed on the wall behind the door of a distant loo. It showed my great-uncle Christopher, a tall and mournful-looking man with a beard, standing alongside a rather youthful Prince and Princess of Wales, the Queen of Denmark, the Duke of St Albans, and two shadowy unknown men in the grounds of his house in 1869. In the background is a curious contraption on wheels with a small funnel poking out of the top of it, and the Prince of Wales' feathers painted on its side. Closer inspection reveals it to be the photographer's cart in which he carried all his equipment. In the windows of the house behind, faces are pressed against the glass watching the scene before them. As I used to stare at this oddly-assorted group, no figment of an artist's imagination, but a scene recorded by the camera just as it was, I was invariably overcome by that profound sense of nostalgia that is so often attached to photographs of people no longer living, or buildings which have long since disappeared. What were they thinking about?, I wondered. What did they do next? Who was the man peeping out from behind the Prince's shoulder? What became of him? It was these feelings which inspired me to gather all this material together to create a fascinating pictorial record of our family from the earliest days of photography up to the present day.

Great-uncle Christopher with the Prince and Princess of Wales.

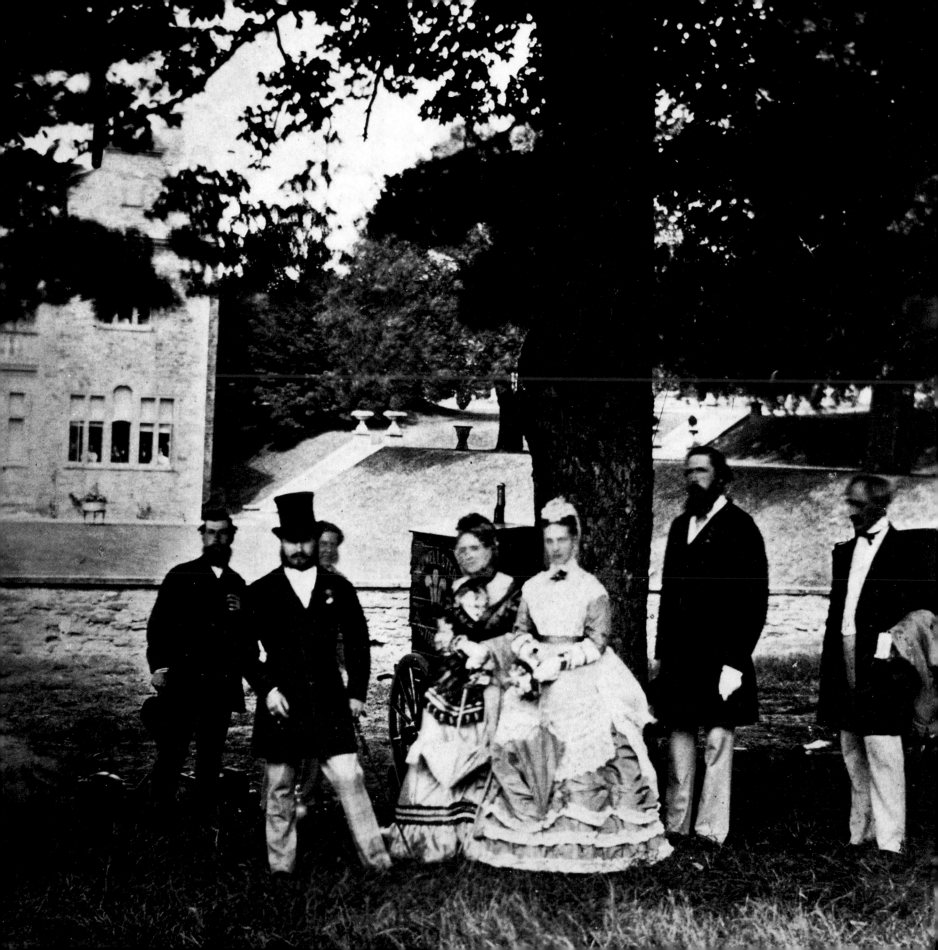

In this book, which is a celebration of the work of the earliest photographers over one hundred years after the invention of the art was officially announced, I have attempted to make a similar record of various different families as they lived in their country houses, before handing them over to the National Trust. The English country house can in many ways claim to be the actual birthplace of photography, the earliest photographic negative in existence being of the diamond-latticed windows of Lacock Abbey, a beautiful Gothic house in Wiltshire. This was the home of William Henry Fox Talbot, grandson of the second Earl of Ilchester and Whig Member of Parliament for Chippenham, to whom must be given much of the credit for the invention of the process as we know it today. Educated at Harrow and Trinity College, Cambridge, he was a scientist, a mathematician, a botanist, but above all an inventor. It was while on the Grand Tour of Europe in August 1833 that Fox Talbot became obsessed with the idea of fixing the images cast by a Camera Obscura with which he was attempting to sketch some Italian landscapes. He began experiments using paper sensitized with silver chloride, and within a year he had made his first photograph. This picture of the windows of Lacock Abbey was taken with a tiny two-and-a-half-inch square camera nicknamed 'the Mousetrap', and the pictures it created were no bigger than an inch square.

The collection of photographs by Fox Talbot at Lacock is well known, but there are other more obscure collections which have come to light after years of gathering dust in the back passages and distant corners of country houses. These were the work of gifted amateurs, such as the Hon. Hugh Annesley, who took the marvellous shot of breakfast at Ickworth, and Sir Edmund Verney who kept his own darkroom at Claydon. Many of them were women who were inspired by Talbot's invention, first shown to the public at the Great Exhibition in 1851, to abandon their watercolour brushes and their needlework, and experiment with the new art. The most famous of these was Julia Margaret Cameron, but there were others such as Lady Lucy Bridgeman, a daughter of the 2nd Earl of Bradford, who travelled extensively round the great houses of England. She took a series of superb photographs, for example, at Scotney Castle as early as 1853, which include some charming informal studies of Mr and Mrs Edward Hussey and their children on the steps of the house, and a remarkable interior of Mr and Mrs Hussey seated in the drawing room. Lucy Bridgeman's work has remained unknown because, unlike Julia Margaret who exhibited her photographs, she merely pasted hers into albums which were passed around family and friends. As more and more people took up the hobby, it soon became *de rigueur* for families to keep such albums, and they form a remarkable social document of the life that was lived in England's great country houses, recording as they do, in painstaking detail, the daily activities of their inhabitants.

I spent countless happy hours pouring over such collections. There is nothing, neither words nor the most detailed or atmospheric painting, that can evoke the past so powerfully

Opposite above: Study of a man in the cloisters of Lacock Abbey by Fox Talbot, below: George Bernard Shaw giving a child a demonstration of his Leica.

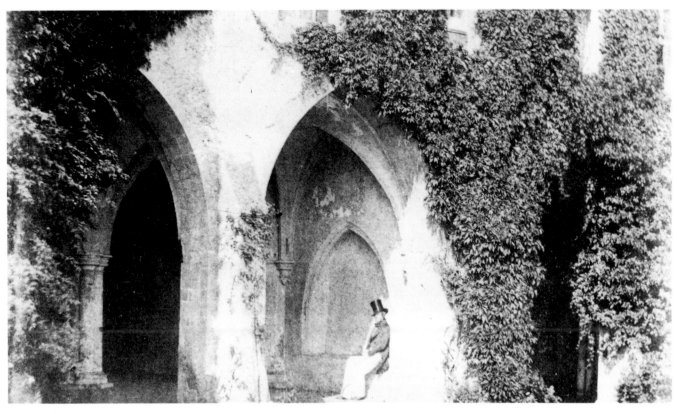

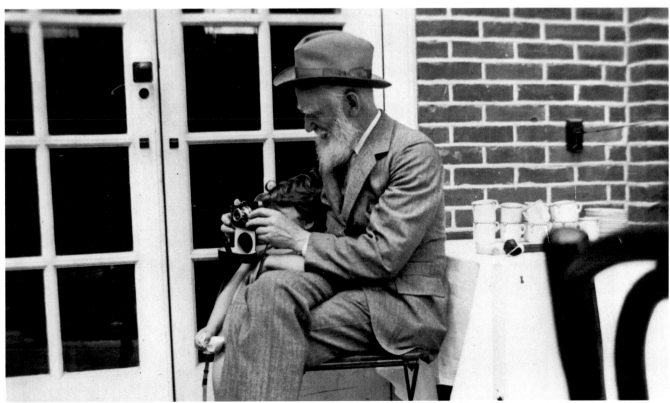

and so completely as a photograph, and in spite of the fact that I was usually shivering in inhospitable storerooms, I was soon lost in another world, a world in which the houses we have come to know so well as public visitors were filled with the to and fro of endless guests in pursuit of pleasure. They came to shoot, to race, to play tennis and croquet and cricket, to hunt, to conduct courtships. They came to be amused and they stayed for weeks, waited on hand and foot. Servants were invariably recorded by the early photographers, perhaps because they made such obedient and uncomplaining sitters. At Petworth, Mrs Percy Wyndham kept a book dated 1860 and bearing the title 'All The dear Servants at Petworth When I came there', and in the 1880s and '90s a local photographer, Walter Kevis, took group pictures of all the different household departments. Perhaps the most celebrated collection of servants' photographs, however, is from Erddig, where over the years the Yorkes treated their staff almost as family. The result is a wonderful collection of photographic portraits chronicling their comings and goings over a century. At Polesden Lacey, Mrs Ronnie Greville also kept a faithful record of her servants, and here one sees for the first time the appearance of the chauffeurs and mechanics who had begun to take over from the coachmen and grooms.

One of the most fascinating series of albums that I discovered was at Wallington, the Northumberland seat of the Trevelyan family. They are of particular interest in that they cover the period from the 1890s up to the 1950s. The pictures taken by Lucy Bridgeman and Lord Craven were all taken on cumbersome cameras using large glass plates and very long exposures, but in the early 1890s the George Eastman Company of America introduced the revolutionary Kodak camera, a small wooden box with a fixed-focus lens which gave sharp definition to everything beyond a distance of eight feet, and had only one speed and a fixed stop. The camera could now be taken everywhere and anybody who could 'Pull the string – turn the key – press the button' could take a photograph. The Trevelyan family albums perfectly reflect this new approach to photography. They are filled with an engaging succession of 'snaps', such as that of Mary Trevelyan mending a puncture, which instantaneously bring the house and family to life, and remind me of the work of the great French photographer, Henri Lartigue. Lartigue came to mind too when I was researching the work of Bernard Shaw, who was a very keen photographer and had his own darkroom at Shaw's Corner. Using a variety of cameras, from the quarter-plate mahogany and brass field camera of early days to the more up-to-date Leica, invented in 1925, he recorded the day-to-day life of his family and friends in a series of snapshots which have a rare freshness and immediacy about them. As an enthusiast he had no doubt read the advertisement for one of the new cameras which advised 'A collection of pictures may be made to furnish a pictorial history of life as it is lived by the owner, that will grow more valuable every day that passes.' The photographs in this book are a tribute to all those who took heed of these words.

Mary Trevelyan mending a puncture.

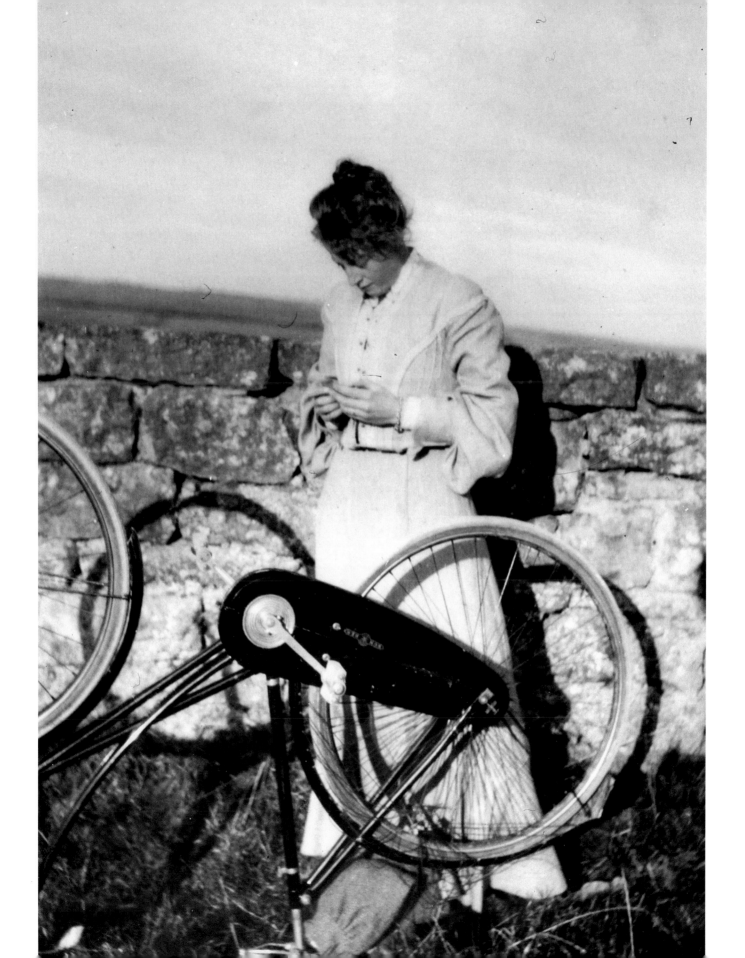

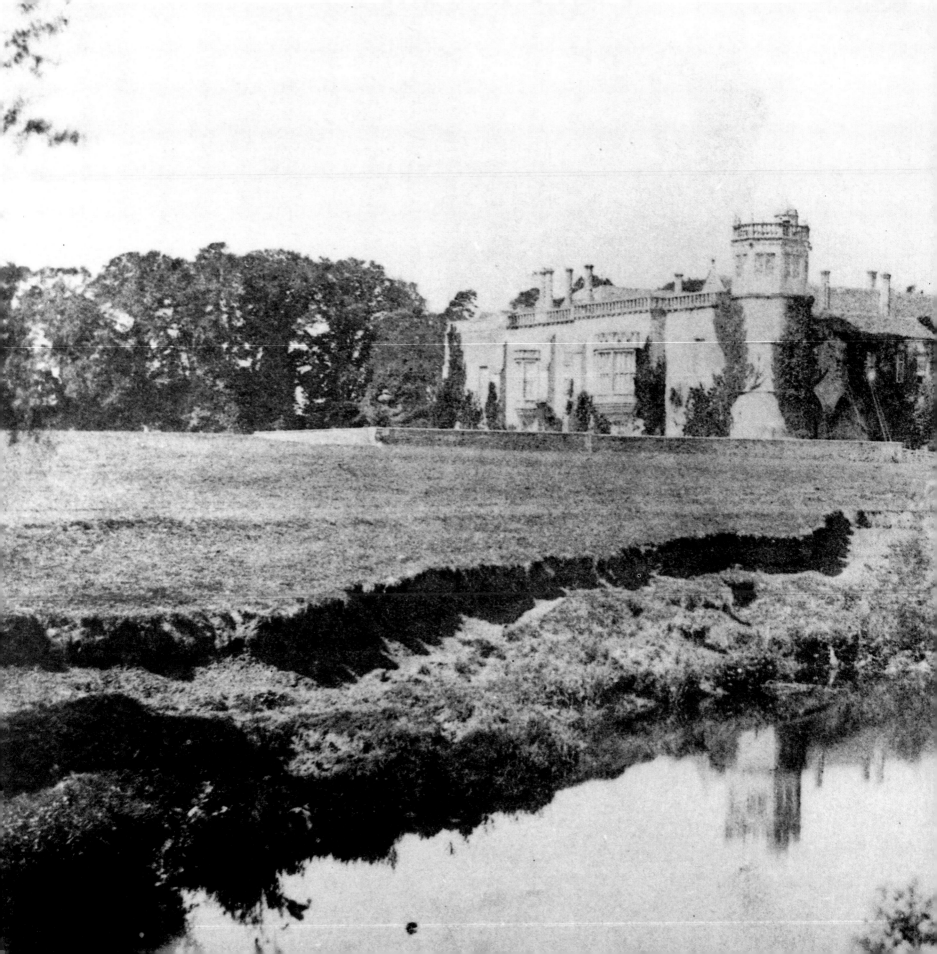

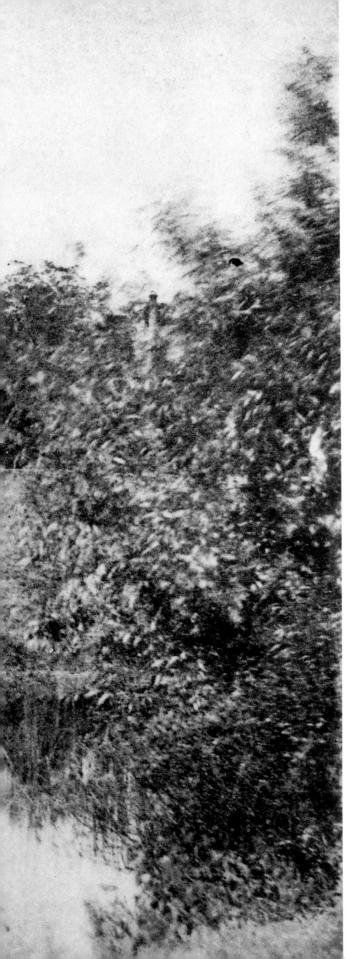

LACOCK ABBEY

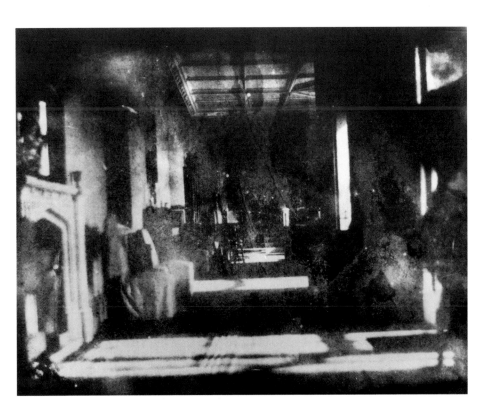

Above: The South Gallery, Lacock. This is one of the earliest known photographs of an interior.

Left: A view of the Abbey across the Avon from the south-east. This early photograph taken by Fox Talbot was published in 1844 in The Pencil of Nature, *the first book illustrated with photographs.*

Lacock Abbey, a charming mixture of medieval, renaissance and eighteenth-century Gothick architecture, is situated in the pretty country to the south of Chippenham through which the river Avon winds. It was originally a convent for Augustinian canonesses, founded in 1232 by Ela, Countess of Salisbury, and as such flourished throughout the Middle Ages until its dissolution in 1539. It then became the property of William Sharington, a powerful Norfolk landowner, who converted it into a private house, his most noticeable addition being the octagonal tower in the south-east corner. It was through his niece, Olive, that Lacock passed into the Talbot family, by a hair's breadth according to John Aubrey. 'Dame Olave, a daughter and coheir of Sir Henry Sharington of Lacock being in love with John Talbot and her father not consenting that she should marry Him: discoursing with Him one night from the Battlements of the Abbey-Church; said shee, "I will leap downe to you": her sweet Heart replied, He would catch Her then: but he did not believe she would have done it: she leap't downe and the wind (which was then high) came under her coates: and did something breake the fall: Mr Talbot caught her in his armes, but she struck him dead; she cried out for help, and he was with great difficulty brought to life again: her father told her that since she had made such a leap she should e'en marry Him.' It was the Talbot family who made the last important additions to the Abbey, John Ivory Talbot calling in Sanderson Miller in 1754 to build the wonderful Gothick Hall, while a century later his great-grandson, William Henry Fox Talbot remodelled the south elevation, creating a gallery lit by a medley of oriel windows.

The earliest known photographic negative is of one of these windows. It was taken in August, 1835, by William Henry Fox Talbot, who had been obsessed by the idea of somehow fixing the images cast by a Camera Obscura ever since he had used one for sketching while making the Grand Tour two years previously. 'This led me to reflect,' he wrote, 'on the inimitable beauty of the pictures of Nature's painting which the glass lens of the Camera throws upon the paper in its focus-fairy pictures, creations of a moment, and destined as rapidly to fade away. It was during these thoughts that the idea occurred to me how charming it would be if it were possible to cause these natural images in imprint themselves durably, and remained fixed upon the paper. "And why should it not be possible?" I asked myself.' On his return to England in 1834, he at once began experiments using paper sensitized with silver chloride. Within a year he had succeeded in producing his first photograph of the diamond-latticed window, using a tiny camera, no more than two inches square, and chemically treated writing paper. Lacock Abbey thus became, in his own words, 'the first building that was ever known to have drawn its own picture.'

Fox Talbot announced his invention to the world in 1839, and two years later patented his new process as 'calotypy'. In 1844 he published *The Pencil of Nature*, an album of actual prints, which was the first book ever to be illustrated with photographs. He died in 1877, after which Lacock passed first to his rather reclusive son, Charles Henry, a keen historian and archaeologist, and thereafter to his great-niece, Matilda Theresa, who presented the house to the National Trust in 1944.

A great oak tree which then stood in the Abbey Meadows on the Lacock estate. Sadly it was blown down a few years ago.

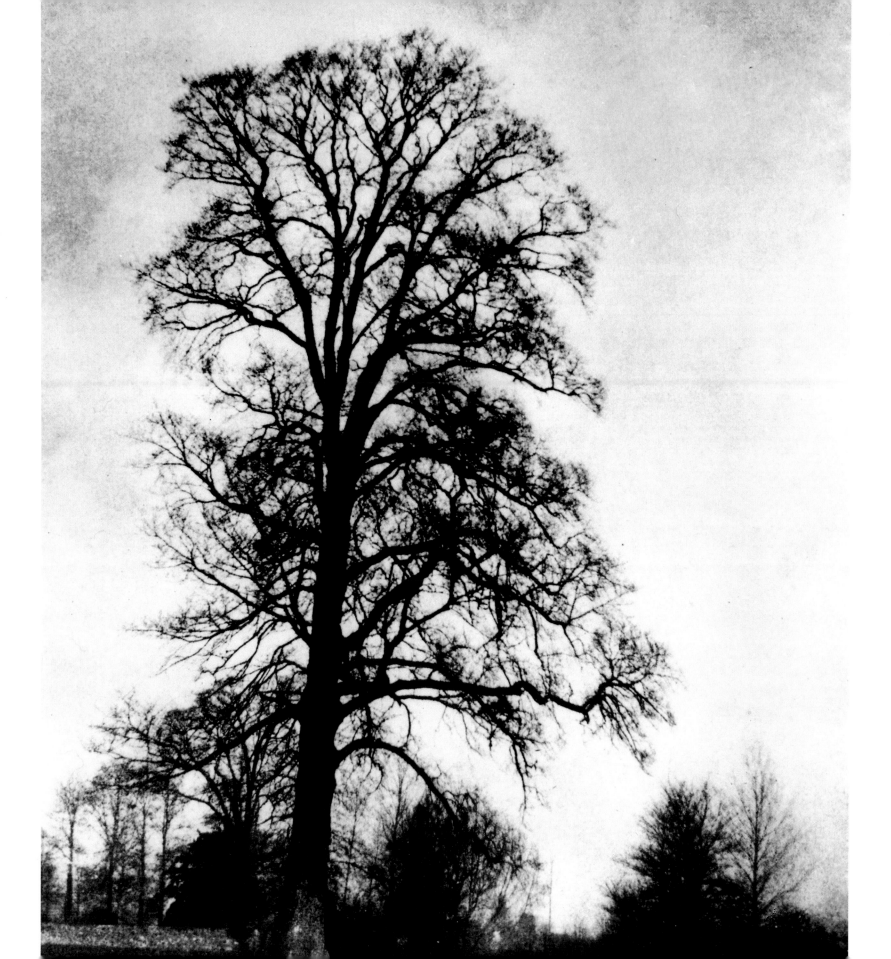

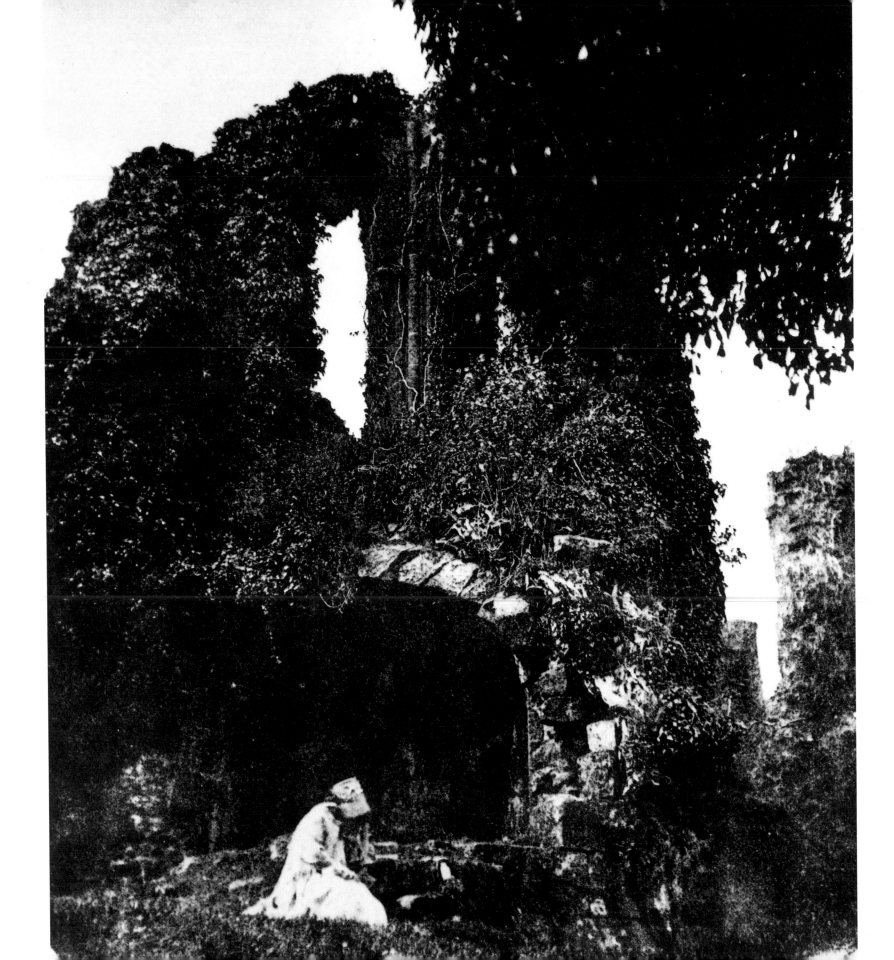

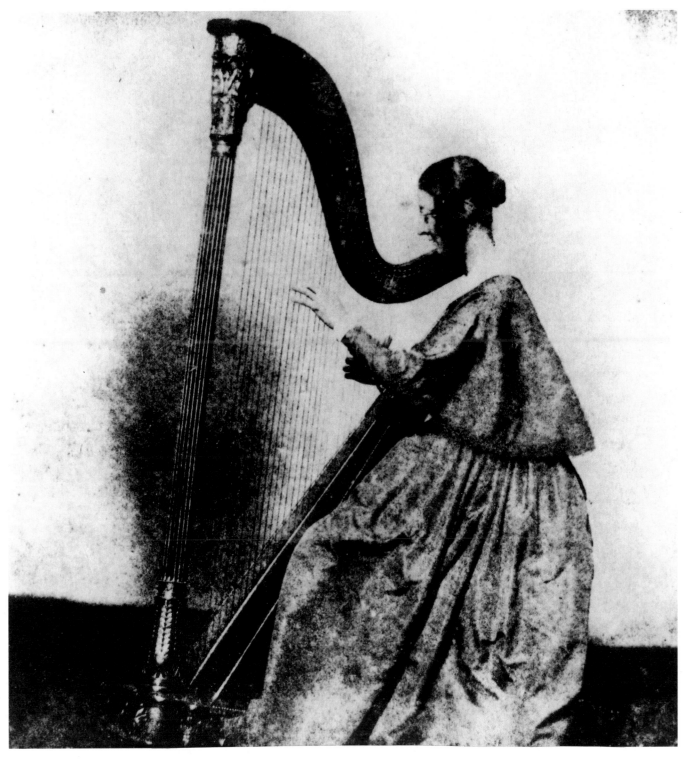

Above: Talbot's half-sister Horatia with her harp, which is still to be seen in the Blue Parlour at Lacock.

Left: A friend of Fox Talbot's photographed in the abbey ruins at Kidderminster.

SCOTNEY CASTLE

LAMBERHURST, KENT

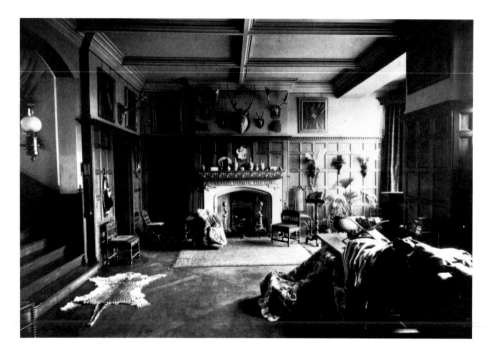

Above: The Hall of the new castle decorated with skins and trophies bagged by Arthur Hussey, a younger brother of Edward III. Mrs Christopher Hussey, who still lives in the house, told me, 'There used also to be a ferocious hyena's head on the stairs which Uncle Arthur had chased on his horse and decapitated with his sword, from the saddle!'

Opposite: A boating party on the Moat.

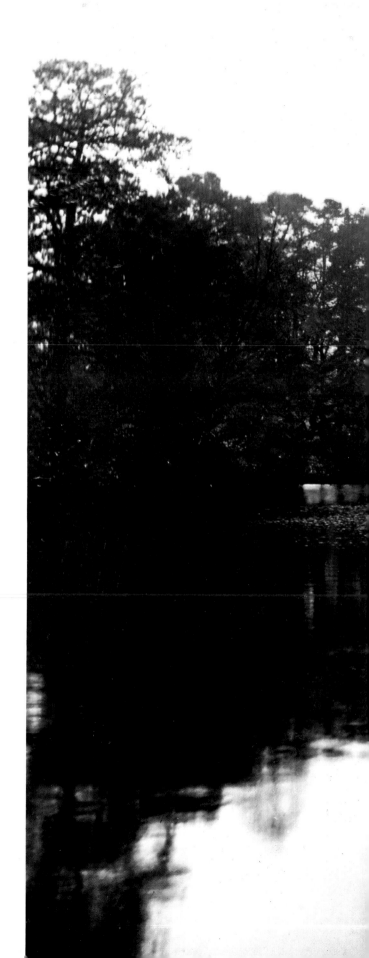

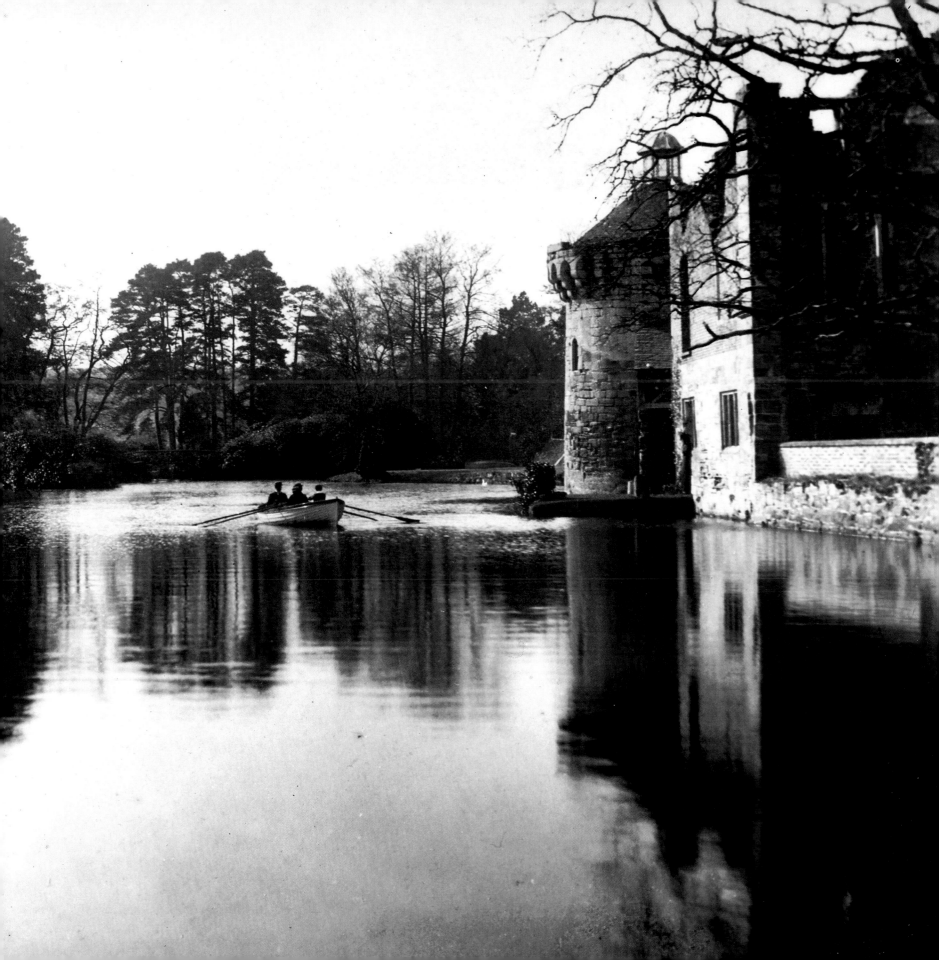

There are few more romantic places than Scotney Castle, whose setting epitomizes the word 'picturesque'. Standing upon the bastion which overlooks the quarry, one looks down a deep ravine to a little castle standing on an island in the middle of a wide moat. A closer look shows that the great round tower which dominates the scene half hides a manor house. This turns out to be the successor to an earlier, medieval building, for Scotney was never intended to be a fortress such as Bodiam Castle, but a fortified house such as Maxstoke Castle, Warwickshire, or Wingfield Castle, Sussex. The tower is all that survives of the original castle which was fortified by its owner, Roger Ashburnham, probably after the sack of Rye and Winchelsea by the French and the burning of Hastings in 1377. Then it would have consisted of four similar towers and a gatehouse, joined by a curtain-wall and enclosing an inner court containing a hall-house. In the Fifteenth Century, Scotney passed into the hands of a local Kentish family called Darell, whose descendants made many alterations in the next two hundred years so that it came to consist, in addition to the tower, of a Tudor wing and a three-storey range of *c.* 1630–40. When the Darells eventually sold Scotney to a local dancing-master, a Mr Richards, in 1774 the sale catalogue described the house as being 'surrounded by a large Moat of running Water, well stocked with Fish; in the Moat an Island, and a Chinese Bridge over a small River; the Ground Floor consists of Front and Back kitchens, etc., Housekeeper's room, a parlour; and 2 Dressing rooms, 5 Bedchambers, a Study and Library; on the second Floor, 8 rooms; Kitchen and Pleasure gardens; without the Gates a Garden, Shrubbery, Warren, Orchard, Coach-house, Brew-house, Stabling for 8 horses and other offices; a cold Bath with an excellent Mineral Well of the same quality as that of Tunbridge Wells.'

In spite of these numerous attractions, Scotney was sold again a few years later to Edward Hussey, who owned an iron-smelting works at Lamberhurst and who was 'a bold and excellent rider and a good cricketer', playing for Kent and Surrey in 1773, frequently for the MCC, and for England against Surrey in 1797. His grandson Edward, no doubt influenced by his mother, who believed the old castle to be unhealthy and subsequently brought up her only son by the sea at St Leonards, decided to build a new house for himself on a site above the original. For this he employed the services of Anthony Salvin, a young architect who was a leading exponent of the revival of Tudor architecture for country houses, and the landscape architect, William Sawrey Gilpin, nephew of the Rev. William Gilpin, whose *Picturesque Tours* had done much to popularize the cult of the romantic landscape. It was Gilpin's brilliant plan to quarry the stone for the new house from immediately below the site, thus creating the dramatic ravine which so beautifully links the two houses and provides such a magnificent setting for the gardens. These were replanted and enlarged in the 1950s and '60s by the late Christopher Hussey who passed Scotney on to the National Trust on his death in 1970.

The builder of the new castle, Edward Hussey III, with his eldest son, Edward Windsor, standing on the steps of the front porch in 1857.

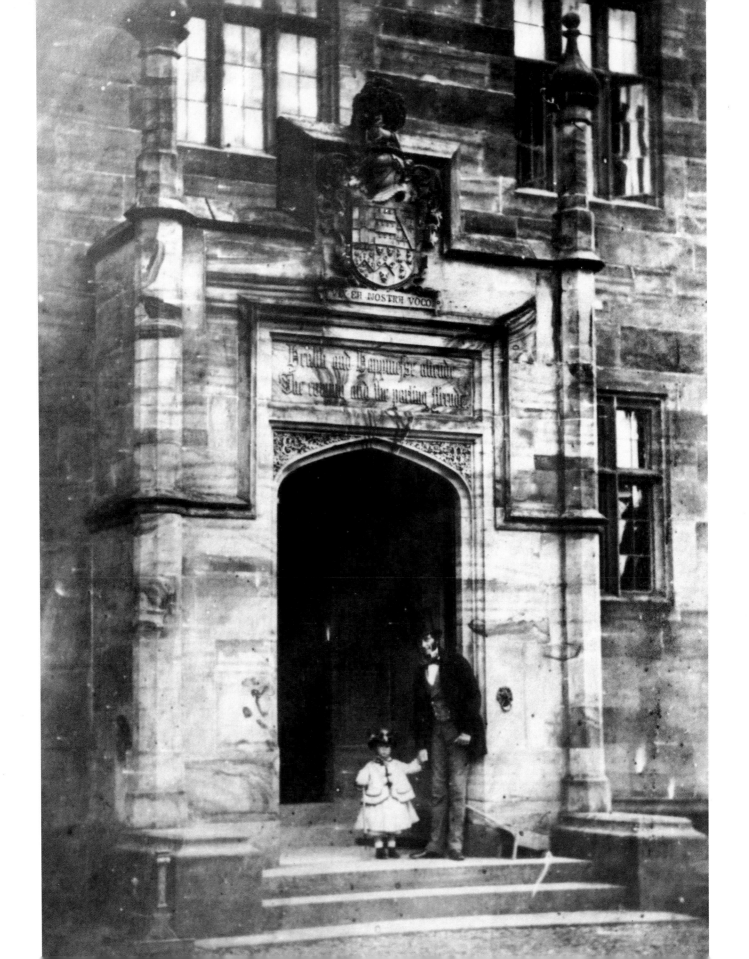

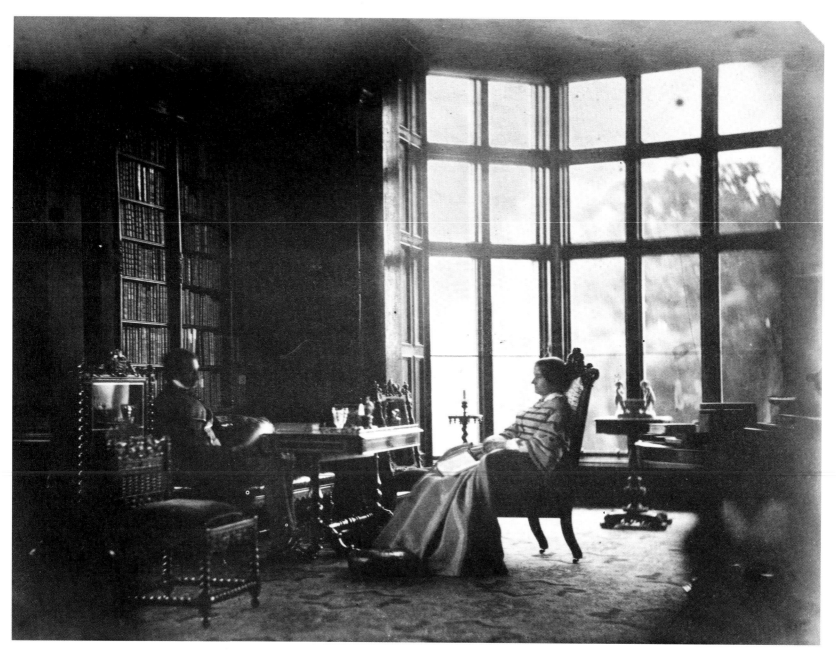

Above: A remarkable early interior of Edward and Henrietta Hussey in the Drawing Room at Scotney, taken soon after their marriage in 1853 by a pioneer woman photographer, Lady Lucy Bridgeman.

Opposite: Mrs Edward Hussey (née the Hon. Henrietta Clive) with two of her sons, Edward and William.

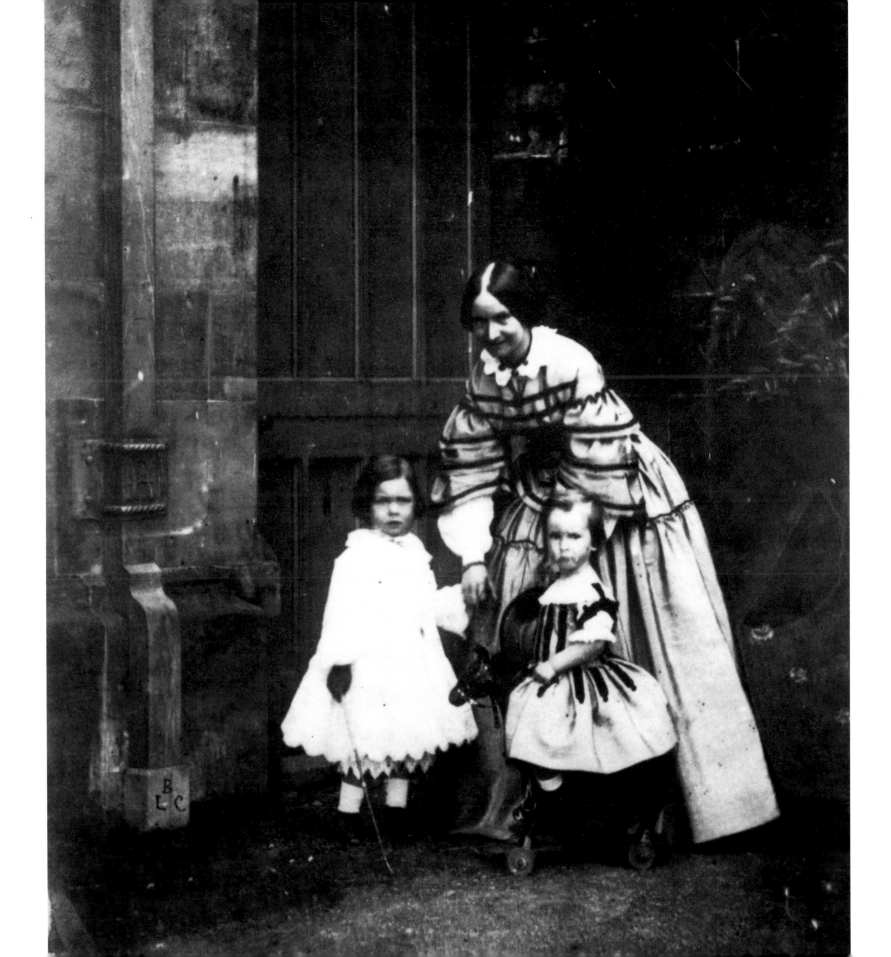

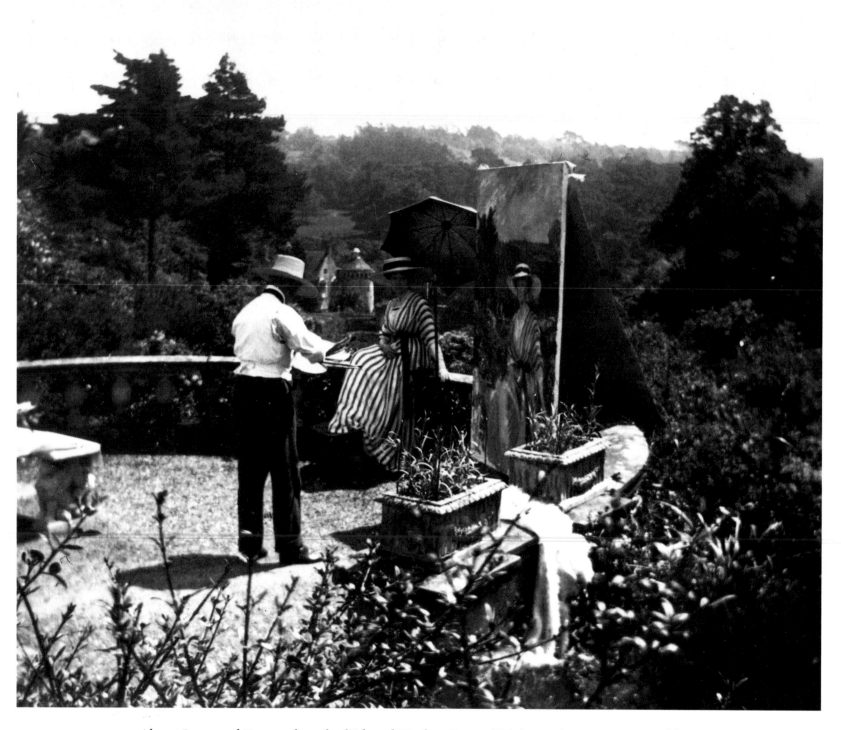

Above: Rosamund Hussey, the wife of Edward Windsor Hussey (IV), having her portrait painted by Shannon on the bastion above the quarry.

Opposite: Gertrude Hussey, the elder daughter of Edward Hussey, posing for a romantic picture on the moat.

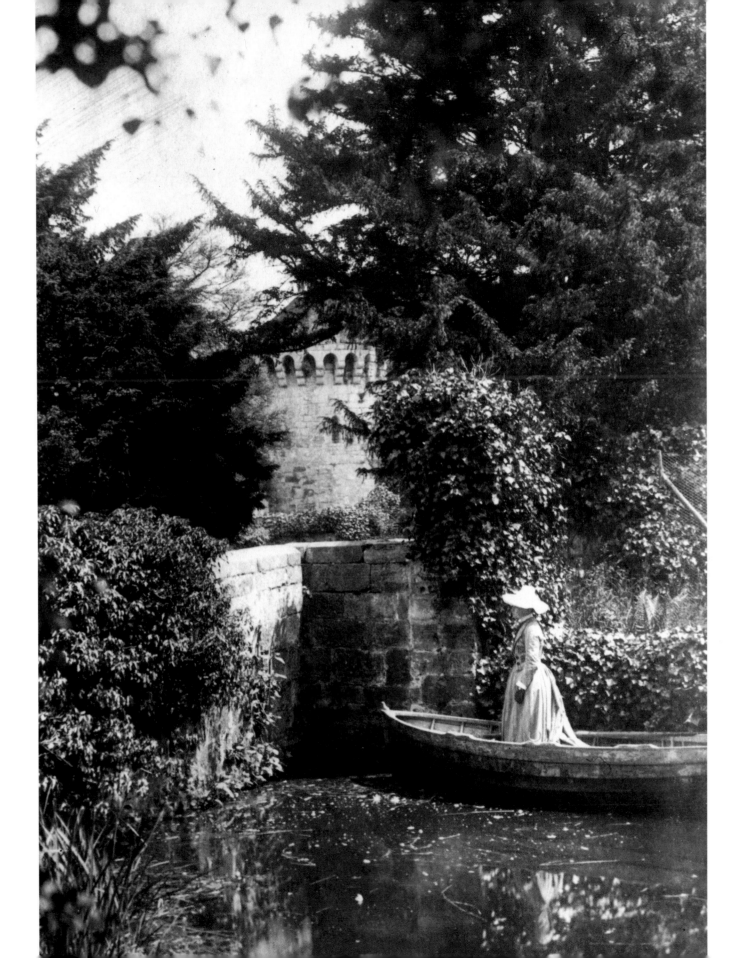

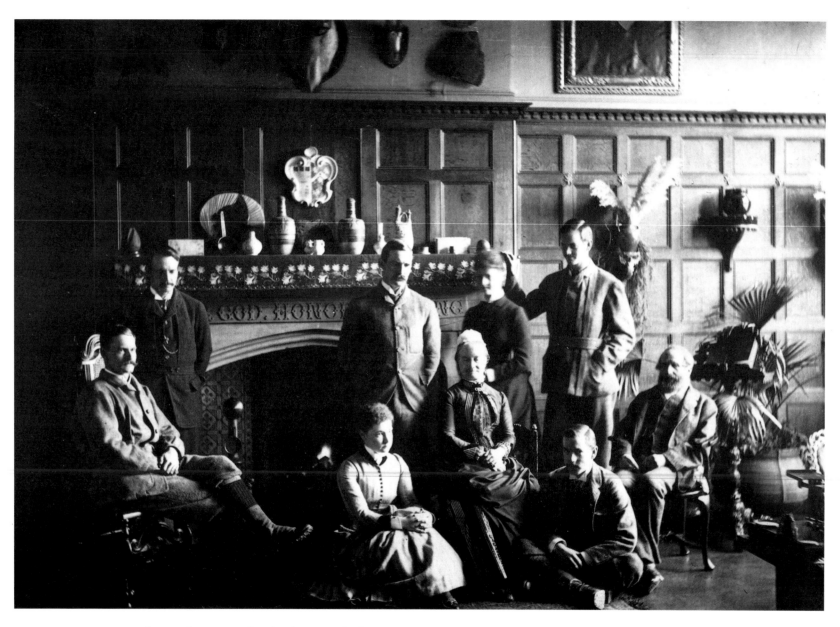

Above: The Hussey family photographed in the 1880s. Left to right: William Clive, father of the late Christopher Hussey; Edward Windsor; Gertrude; Ralph Anstruther, husband of Mildred; Mrs Edward Hussey (III); Mildred; Henry Percy; Arthur Herbert; Edward Hussey III.

Opposite: Gertrude Hussey and her dogs. She was the spinster of the family.

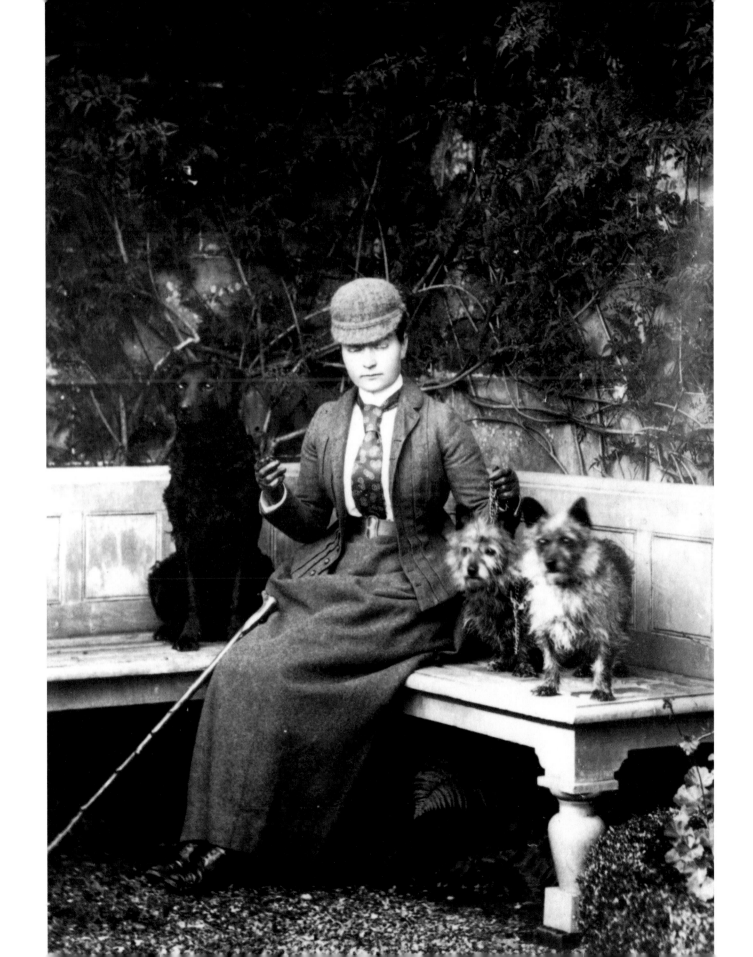

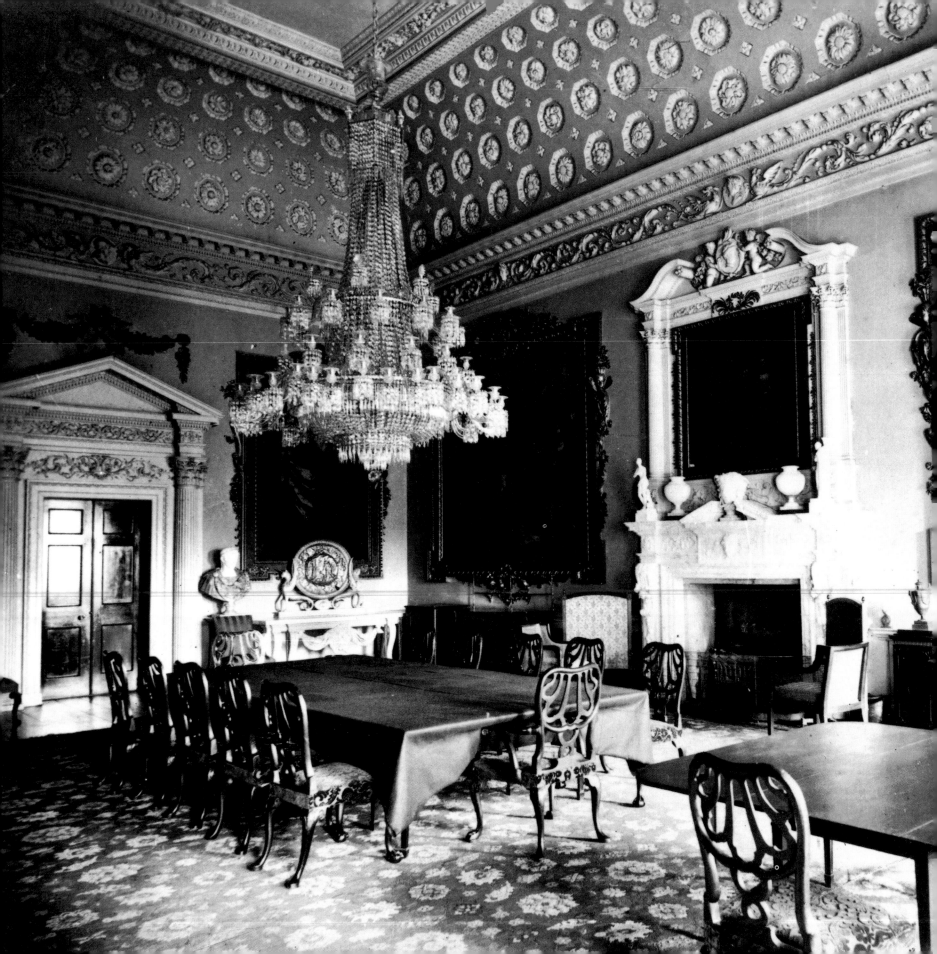

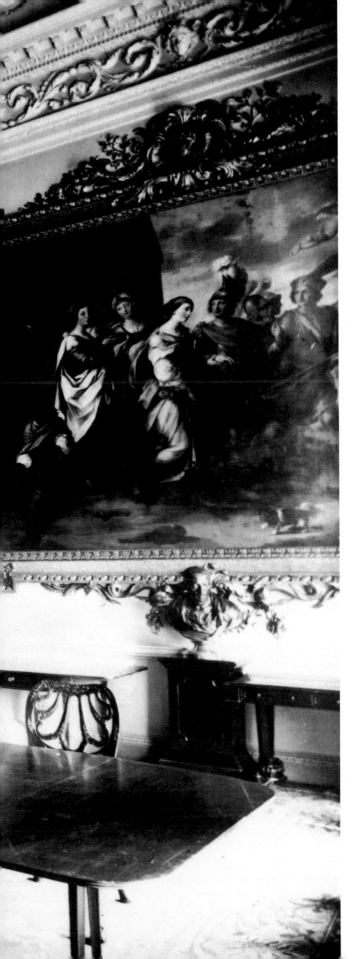

CLAYDON

MIDDLE CLAYDON, BUCKINGHAMSHIRE

*The Saloon in the Nineteenth Century, photographed by Sir Harry's son, Edmund,
who also took the shot of the North Hall which follows.*

The Claydon we see today, with its charming classical west front overlooking the lake, is only a fraction of the original house as conceived and built in 1768 by Ralph, 2nd Earl Verney, a Whig aristocrat with ambition and modern ideas. Having come into a considerable fortune through both inheritance and marriage, he decided to enlarge and remodel the Jacobean manor house in which his family had lived since 1620 in order that it should rival the glories of nearby Stowe. He did this with the help of two extraordinary characters: a previously unknown carpenter-contractor and carver of genius with the unlikely name of Luke Lightfoot, and the eccentric Sir Thomas Robinson, who after Lord Burlington must be considered the finest 'gentleman architect' of the century. The existing house, which formed the west wing of the new building, was the first part to be completed, and the exuberant nature of Lightfoot's work can be seen throughout the interior and no more so than in the wildly elaborate carving of the North Hall, formerly the Great Eating Room. Unfortunately Lightfoot's activities were curbed at this stage with the arrival of Robinson in 1768, who considered the decoration to have gone too far. 'Mr Lightfoot's design for finishing the great Eating Room,' he wrote to Lord Verney, 'shock'd me so much & is so much the ridicule of all who have seen or heard of it – & which when done yr Ldp will undo – that it would be want of that friendship I profess to yr Ldp not to acquaint you thereof . . .' Sir Thomas badgered Lord Verney on this subject until he agreed to dismiss Lightfoot, and the Library and Saloon were duly completed in a more restrained style by Joseph Rose, one of the leading stuccoists of the day.

The additions which Robinson made to Lightfoot's west wing consisted of a central block containing a great marble hall, with a vast rotunda above it, and an east wing entirely given over to a ballroom, the whole building, when completed, stretching to a length of 256 feet. Magnificent though it was, its cost was Verney's downfall. He was an unsuccessful businessman and had lost much of his fortune through poor investments and the East India Company's crash in 1769. The result was that in 1784 he was forced to flee to France to avoid imprisonment for debt. There is a sad family legend that shortly before the Earl's death in 1791, a stable boy on the Claydon estate happened one day to look through one of the cobwebbed windows of the vast abandoned and unfinished pile, only to see the old man wandering disconsolately around the empty rooms, to which he had been brought for one last look. Lord Verney was succeeded by his niece, Mary, who almost immediately set about the demolition of two-thirds of her uncle's house. On her death Claydon passed to her half sister, and thence to a distant cousin, Sir Harry Calvert. It was his son, also Sir Harry, who took the name of Verney and married, as his second wife, Frances Parthenope, the sister of Florence Nightingale, who was to become a regular visitor to Claydon, where she always slept in a bedroom now preserved for posterity as Mrs Nightingale's Room. The house was given to the National Trust by the present Baronet, Sir Ralph Verney.

The North Hall, the rococo masterpiece of Luke Lightfoot, who himself described it as 'such a Work as the World never saw'.

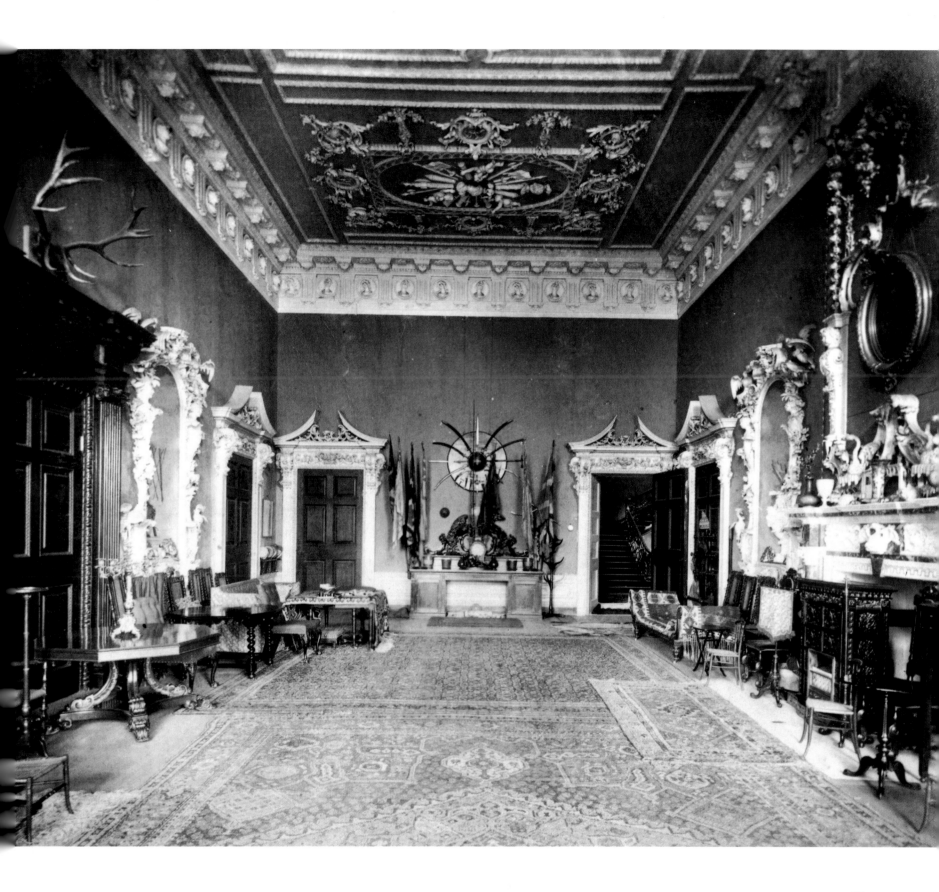

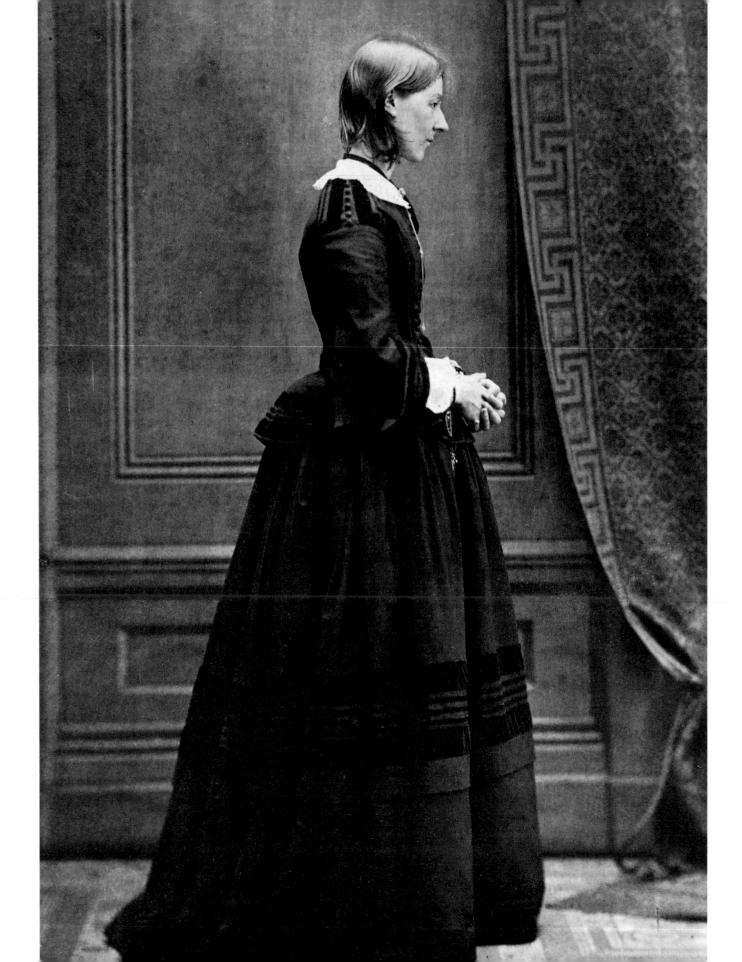

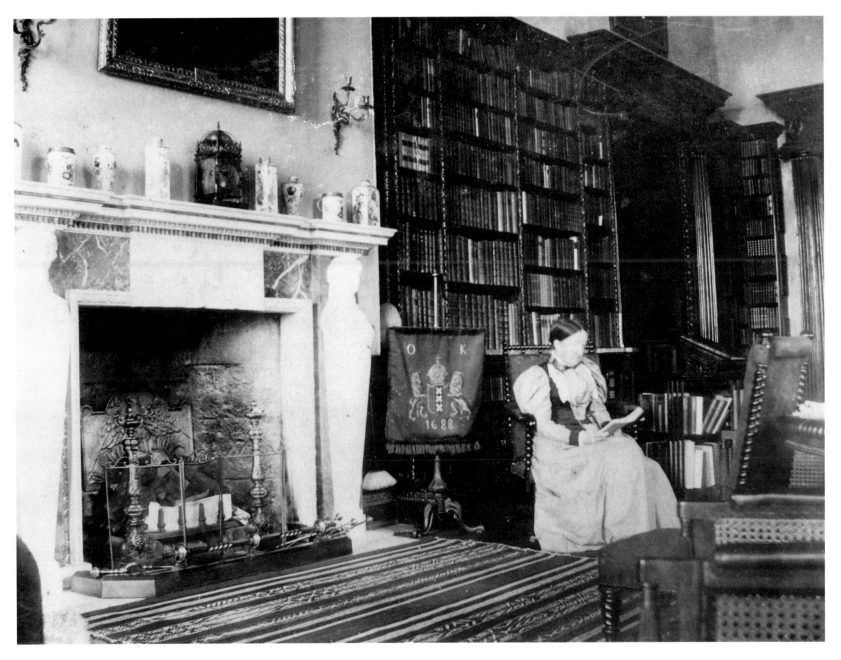

Above: Margaret, Lady Verney in the Library, 1898

Left: Florence Nightingale, the sister-in-law of Sir Harry Verney, 2nd Baronet.

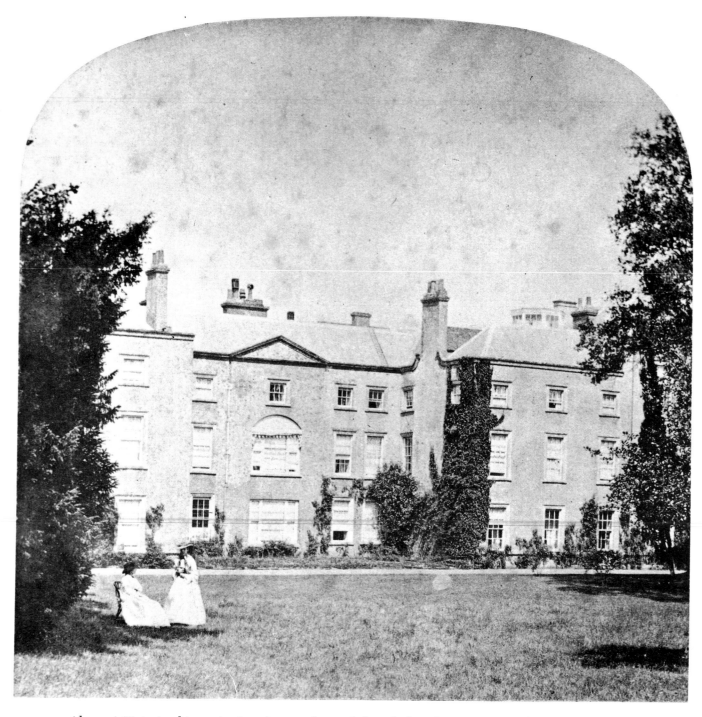

Above: A Victorian bioscopic view showing the south front before the pseudo-Jacobean alterations of 1860.

Opposite: The excavation of a lake in the park in September 1881.

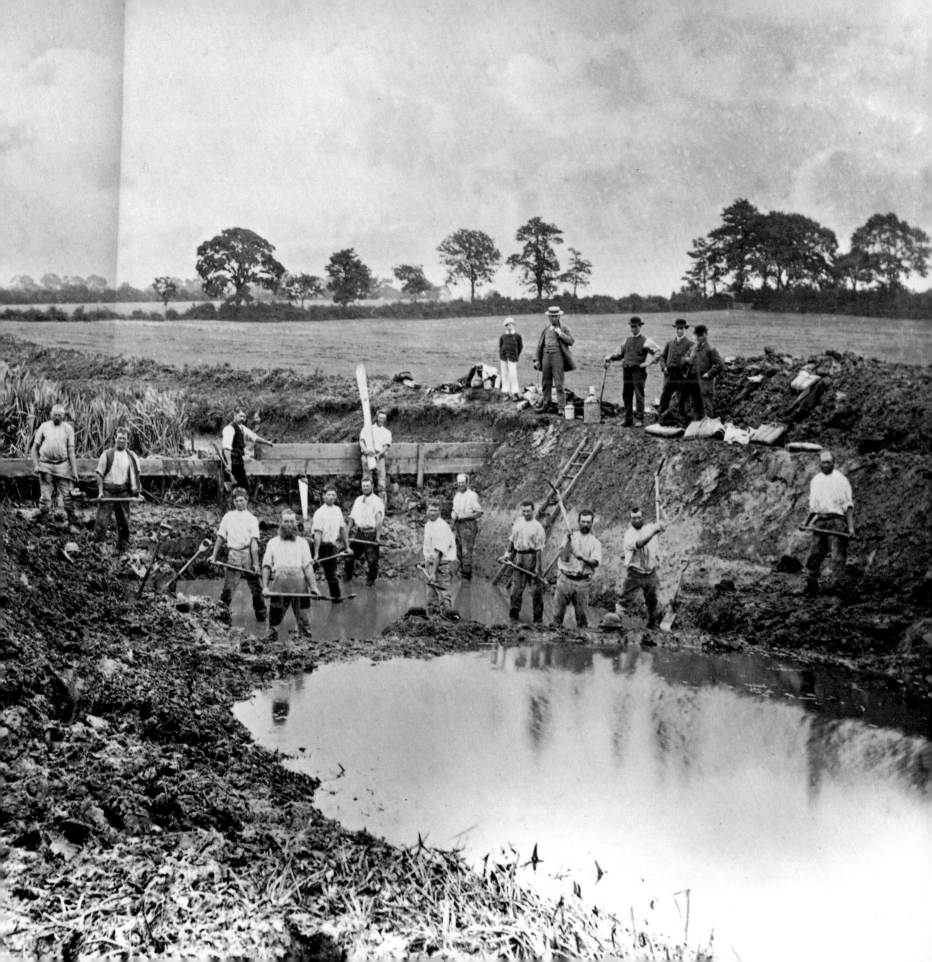

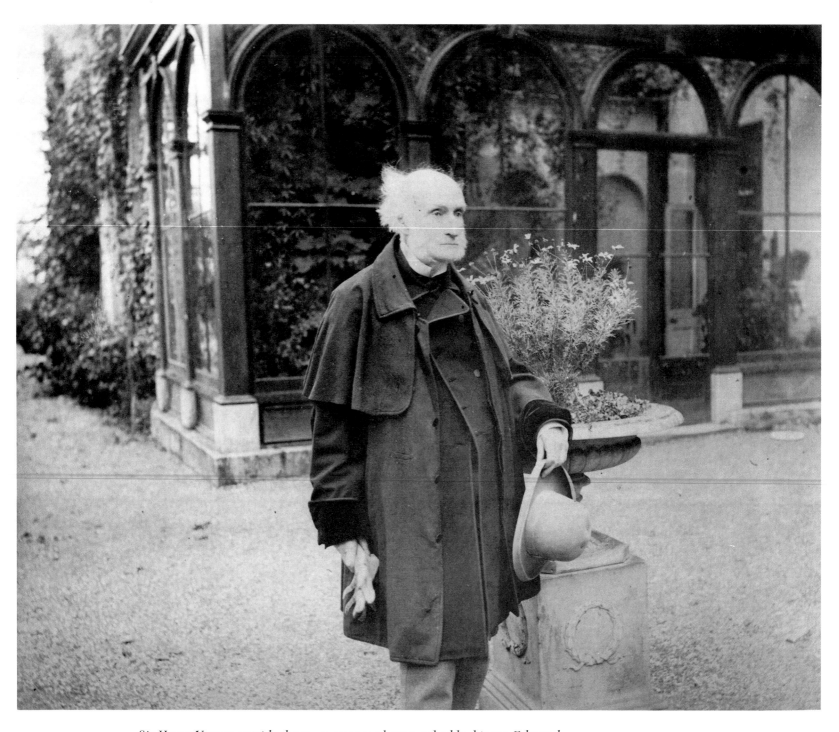

Sir Harry Verney outside the conservatory photographed by his son Edmund.

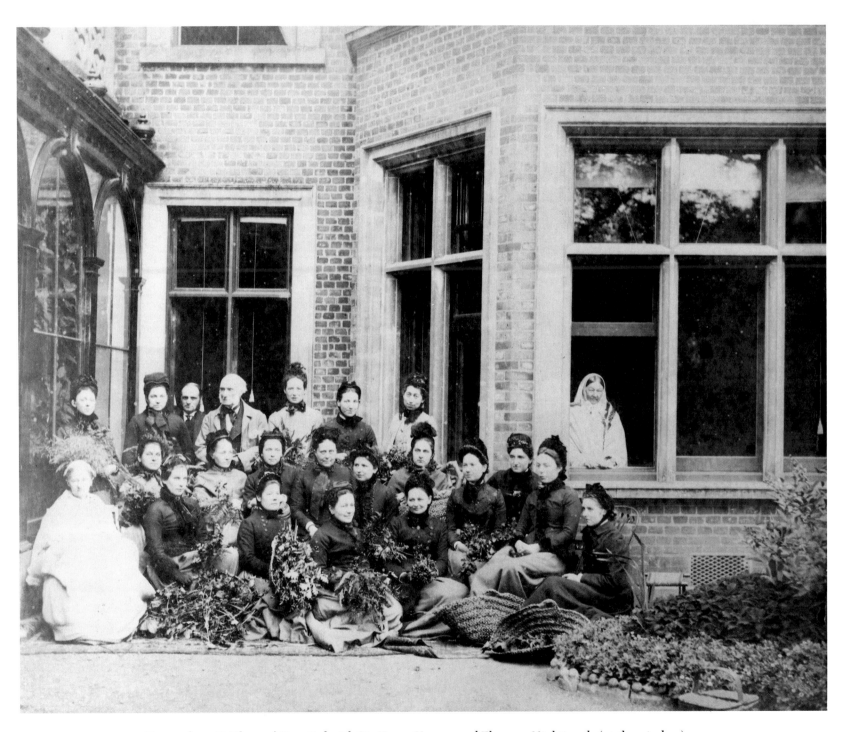

Nurses from St Thomas' Hospital with Sir Harry Verney and Florence Nightingale (at the window).

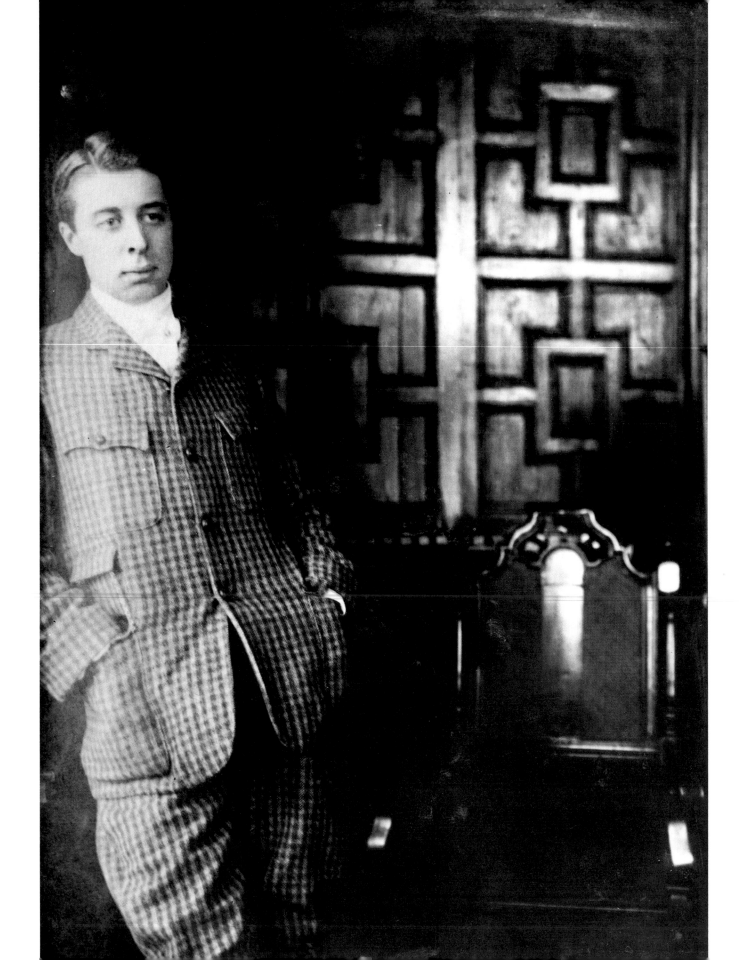

MONTACUTE

YEOVIL, SOMERSET

On Saturday 14 November 1942 James Lees-Milne, appointed in 1937 as Historic Buildings Secretary for the National Trust, wrote in his diary, 'A cold white frost, and a most beautiful Autumn morning. I am very content to be here. To warm myself I walk up the "Mons Acutus", which is slippery with greasy mud. It is an ancient British earthwork with spiral terraces up it, and a 1760 tower at the top. The village below is wreathed in silver mist, and blue smoke from the chimneys is twirled in the crisp air... The house is lovely, with the low sunlight on the orange Ham-stone walls and crinkly glass windows. It is in very fair condition thanks to Shoemark, the village mason, whose family have tended it for generations.' The house to which he referred was Montacute, in Somerset, named after the conical hill up which he had climbed, and acquired by the Trust some years previously after an uninterrupted reign of three hundred and fifty years by the Phelips family.

Montacute was built in the late 1590s by Sir Edward Phelips. He was a man of great riches and importance, the summit of his career being the Mastership of the Rolls. Judging from similar detail by him to be found at Dunster Castle, also in Somerset, and at Cranborne Manor in Dorset, the architect was almost certainly a Somerset mason called William Arnold, who completed the project in 1601. Built out of honey-coloured Ham Hill stone, the house, with its perfect symmetry, its great height and mass of windows, and its wealth of Renaissance detail, is a triumph of the Eizabethan art of building. It has since been altered only once in its lifetime, in the Eighteenth Century, when Sir Edward's descendant, Edward Phelips, built on a new west front to accommodate corridors to link the wings and provide independent access to each bedroom.

The fortunes of Montacute fluctuated wildly during the Phelips' ownership, but their real decline began in the nineteenth century with William Phelips, who inherited in 1834. In one of his *Somerset Essays*, Llewelyn Powys, whose father was vicar of Montacute from 1886, recalls how he had 'inherited eighteenth-century tastes, and through his love of gaming had so compromised the Phelips estate that it never afterwards recovered... Near Ilchester there are two farms called Sock and Beerly. These farms at one time rounded off the Phelips property to the north. I used to be told by country people this story about them. The gambling squire was staying at Weymouth, and on a wet afternoon, having nothing to do, staked a bet on one of two flies that were crawling up the window-pane. When his friend's fly reached the wooden plinth which marked the winning post of this fantastic circus race, the idle sparks who were watching heard the Master of Montacute mysteriously exclaim, "There go Sock and Beerly."' Unfortunately this loss of Sock and Beerly was just the beginning of a sad process of dismemberment which went on until the sale of the very last farm in 1918, by which time the family could no longer afford to inhabit the house, which was let to Lord Curzon. In 1931 it was donated to the National Trust by Ernest Cook, a rich and eccentric recluse, who was at that time one of the Trust's principal benefactors.

Edward Frederick Phelips in the Library at Montacute, 1902.

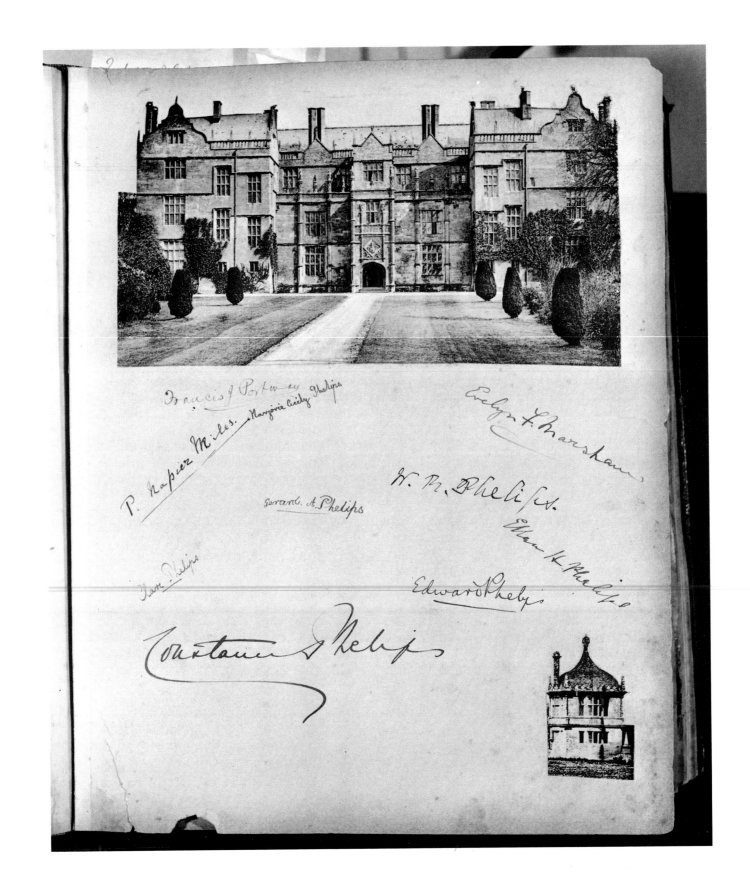

Francis J Portway Phelips

P. Napier Miles   Marjorie Cicely Phelips

Evelyn F. Marsham

W. R. Phelips

Gerard A. Phelips

Ellen K. Phelips

Rose Phelips

Edward Phelips

Constance Phelips

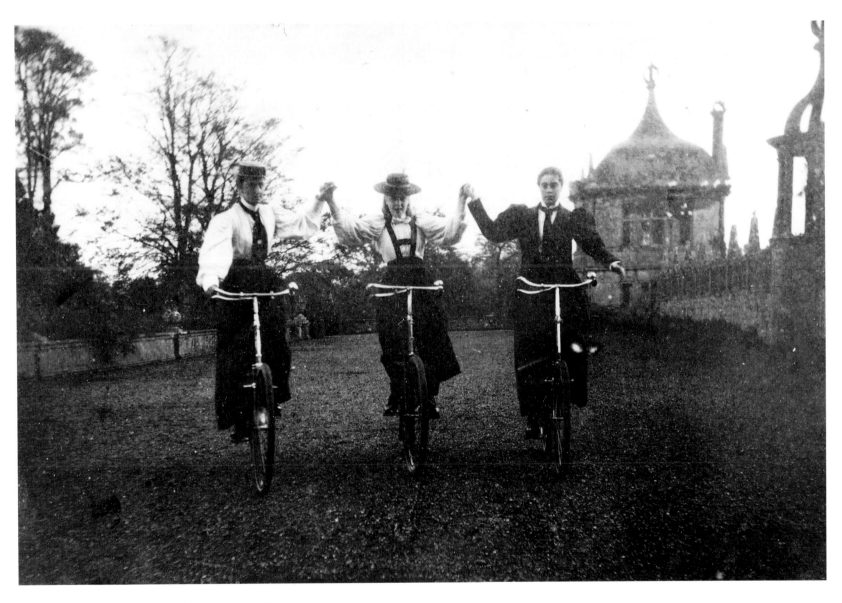

Above: 'Bicycle antics!'

Left: A page from a visitors' book showing the guests who stayed at Montacute at the end of November 1899.

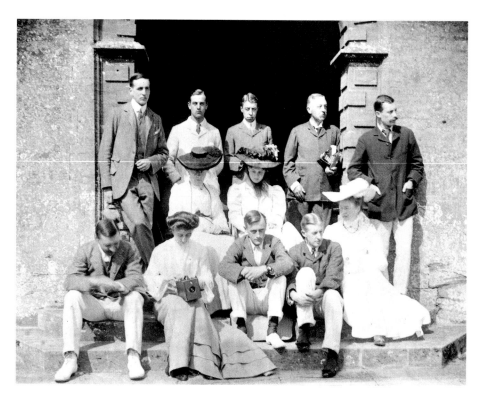

Above: Cricket Week, August 1905.
   Back row, left to right: Mr Foster, Mr G. Headlem, E.F.P., W.R.P.,
      Charles Ponsonby. ·
   Centre, left to right: E.L.P., Miss Lawrence, Constance Phelips.
   Front, left to right: Mr H.B. Medlycott, Molly Ponsonby, John Gore, G.A.P.

Opposite: Gerard Almarus Phelips practising his bowling for Cricket Week.

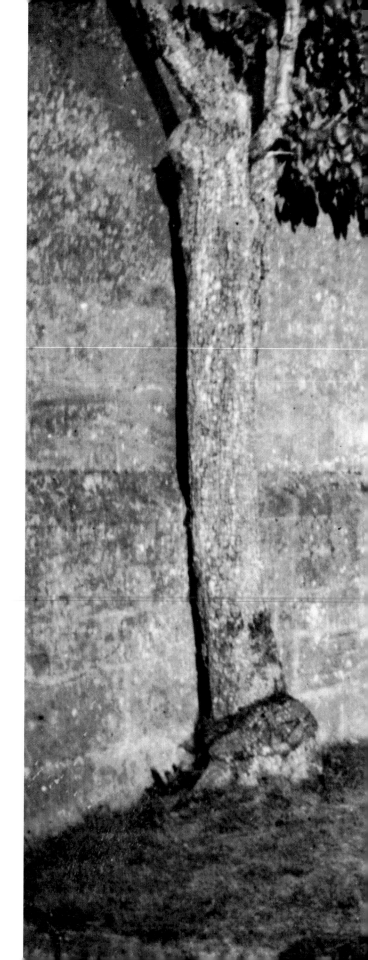

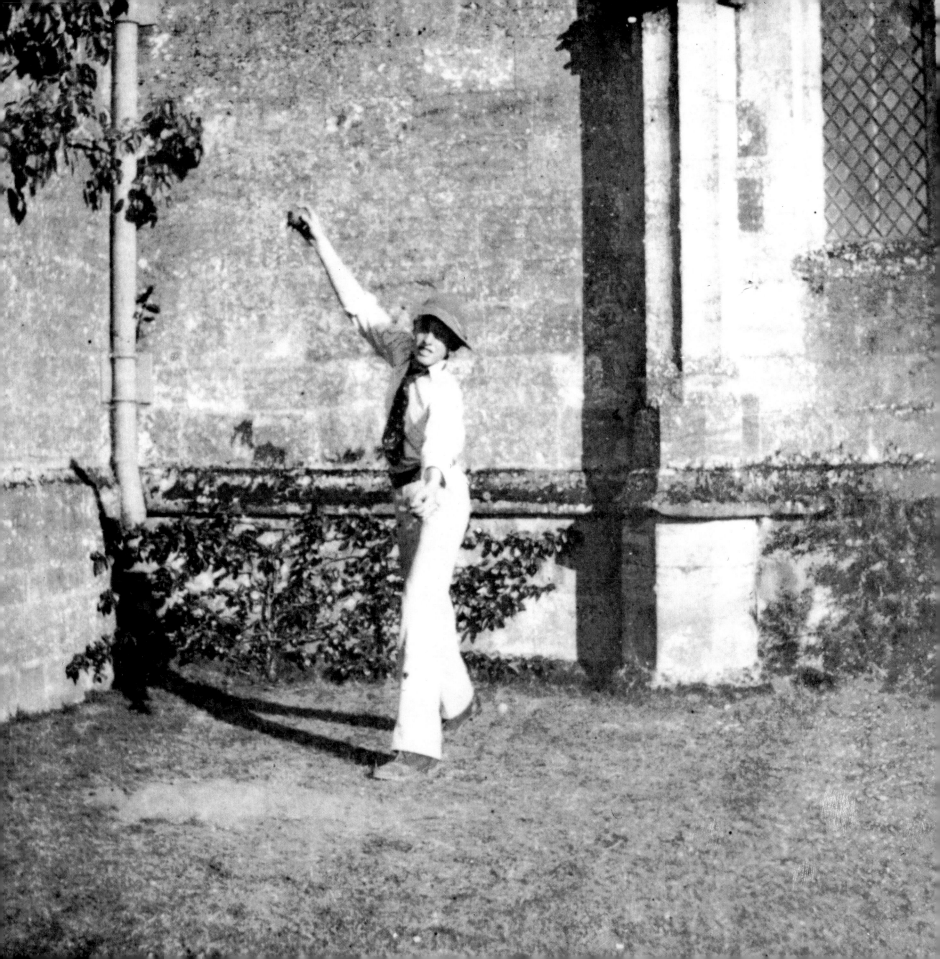

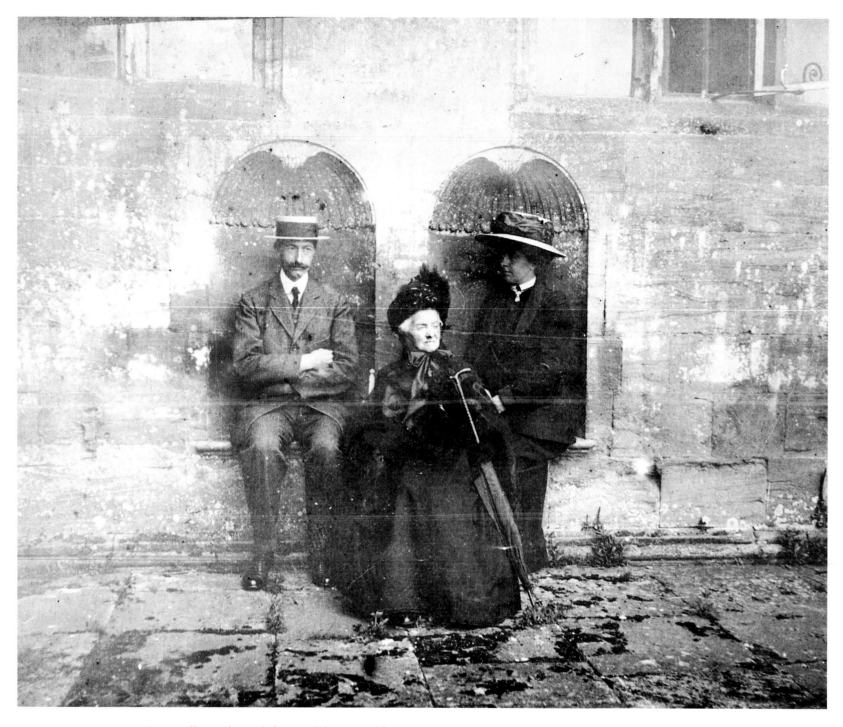

Above: Ellen Helyar Phelips with her granddaughter, Marjorie Ingilby and her husband, John. Llewelyn Powys wrote of Mrs Phelips, 'I do not think I have ever seen an old lady with so delicate a complexion . . . Her head was as ethereal in appearance as was Shelley's head, and she was . . . the daughter of Shelley's cousin, and the poet's first love.'

Opposite: William Robert Phelips having his portrait painted in the Library, 1897.

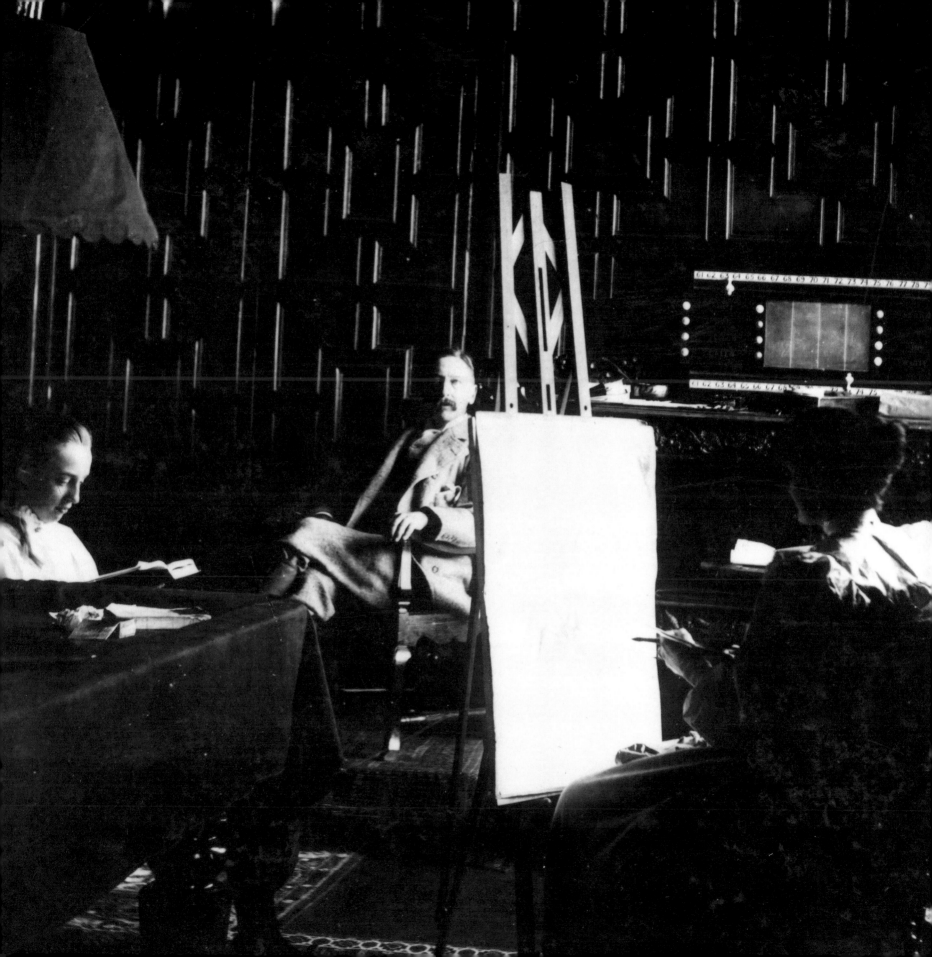

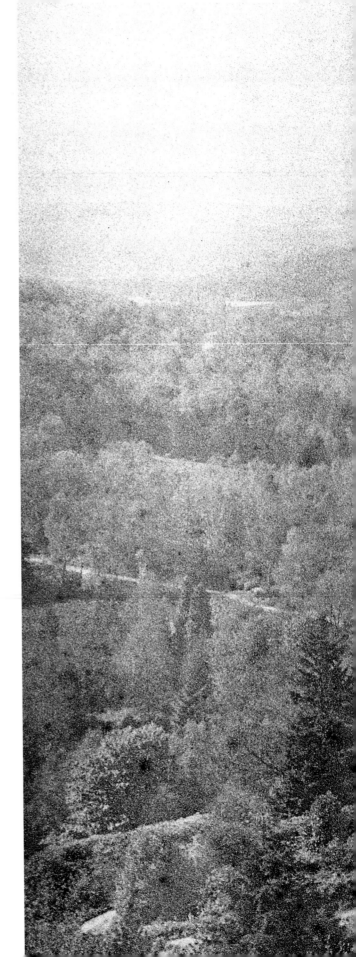

CRAGSIDE

ROTHBURY, NORTHUMBERLAND

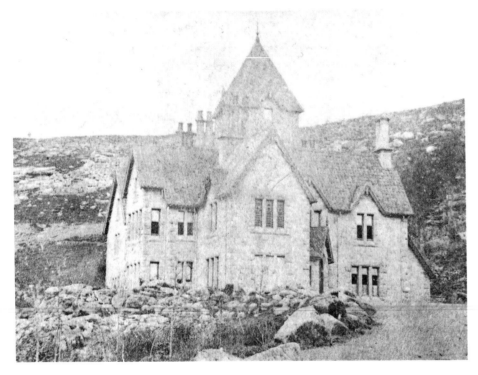

Above: The lodge of 1864–6, before Norman Shaw's additions.

Opposite: A view of Cragside after the alterations and planting, looking west from the top of Cragend Hill.

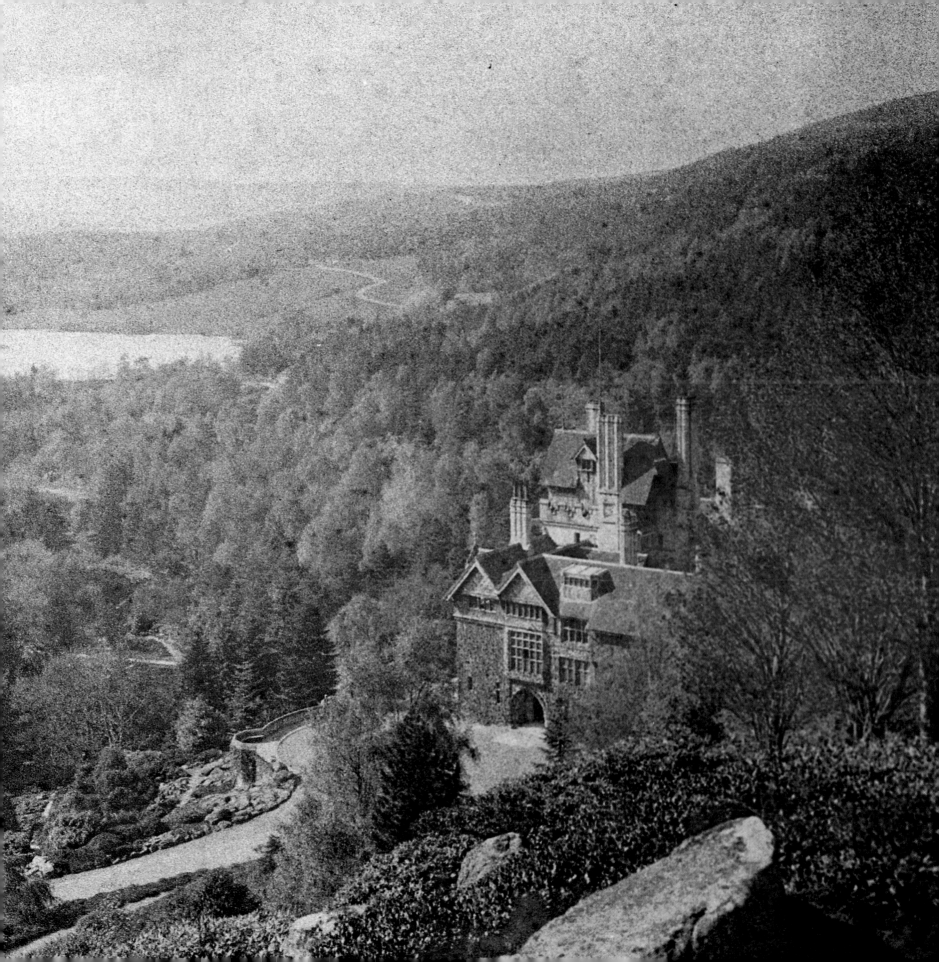

When Sir William Armstrong visited Rothbury in 1863, the trip brought back many happy memories, for it was there that as a child he had come on his annual holiday with his parents, and had discovered the joys of fishing. In the intervening years he had progressed from humble beginnings as a Newcastle solicitor to become an armaments tycoon, the head of his own company, W.G. Armstrong and Co., builder of bridges, cranes and locomotives, and more recently supplier of the Armstrong gun to the British army. having in the process become a very rich man, he decided on impulse to buy as much as possible of the land he had once so loved, and to build 'a small house in the neighbourhood for occasional visits in the summertime'. His first parcel of land, which he bought in November 1863, was only twenty acres, and here he built himself a modest two-storey picturesque fishing lodge in stone. He named it Cragside after Cragend Hill which rose up steeply behind the house, and into whose side he had had to cut in order to build. According to a contemporary account, 'more attention was devoted to covering the bare hillsides with foliage than to building anything great in the shape of a house' which anyway 'appeared almost lost amongst the huge crags by which it was surrounded.' It did not remain lost for long, for in 1869 Armstrong decided to make Cragside his principal home, for which purpose he called in the architect Richard Norman Shaw who, over the next fifteen years, turned the lodge into something which would not have looked out of place among the castles of Bavaria.

The photographs show best the extraordinary transformation of both landscape and house which Armstrong and Shaw effected. The original site was a bare wilderness. Over the years Armstrong systematically bought up all the adjacent land, and by a combination of spectacular planting and the ingenious use of technology, including a massive amount of blasting and excavation both to level the site and to expose the outstanding rocks and features, he created the immensely romantic Alpine setting we see today. In the seventeen hundred acres with which he ended up, he is said to have made thirty-one miles of carriage drives and walks, and planted seven million trees. Most of this work preceded the enlargement of the house which began in 1870. The site was a crazy one on which to build, for what natural ledge there was on the side of the hill was only a very narrow one, and to obtain more space it was necessary to dig out at the back and build up at the front. But Shaw brilliantly turned the difficulties to dramatic uses, for which the medieval style in which he had chosen to build was perfectly suited, and the finished result, with its soaring towers, archways, tall chimneys and roofs and gables all at different levels, is wonderfully dramatic.

Drawing on his great scientific knowledge, Armstrong filled Cragside with all kinds of technical innovation. It was the first house in the world to be lit by electricity driven by water power. Hydraulic machinery operated two lifts, the central heating, a spit in the kitchen and a device in the conservatories to rotate pots. There was an electric sewing-machine, a system of electric gongs, an observatory with a great telescope and telephone communication from room to room. How it all must have impressed the Prince of Wales, who visited in 1884, and the stream of foreign dignitaries, including the King of Siam, the Shah of Persia and the Crown Prince of Afghanistan, who came to conclude arms deals. It was indeed, as a contemporary paper decribed it, 'truly the palace of a modern magician'.

Lord Armstrong died in 1900, since when the house has changed very little. It was bequeathed to the National Trust by his descendants in 1977.

Lord Armstrong and family.

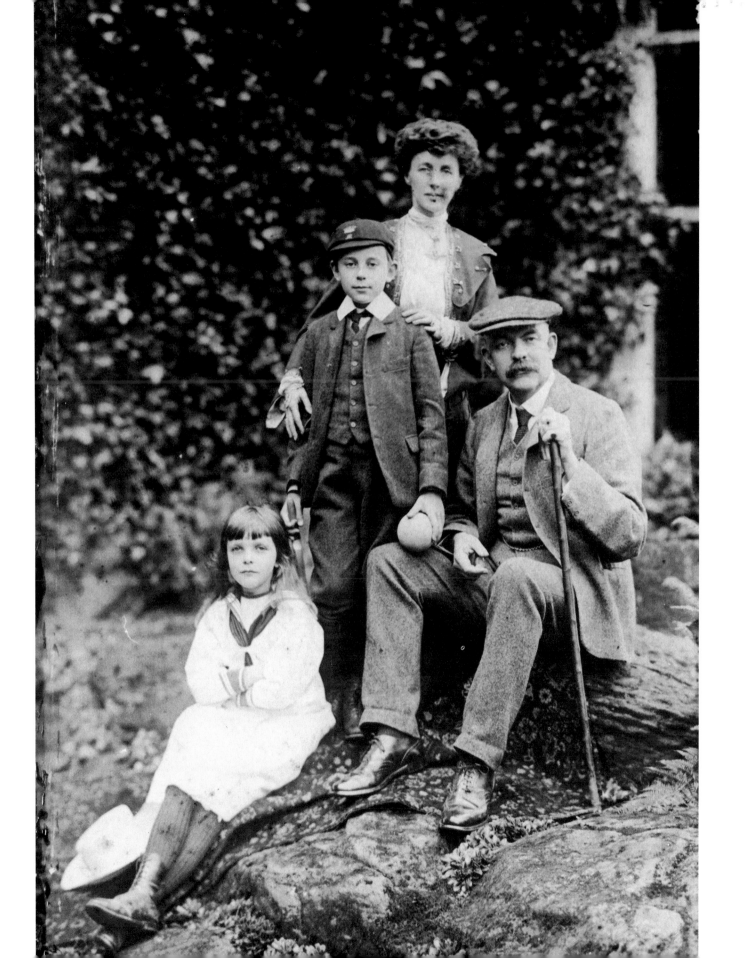

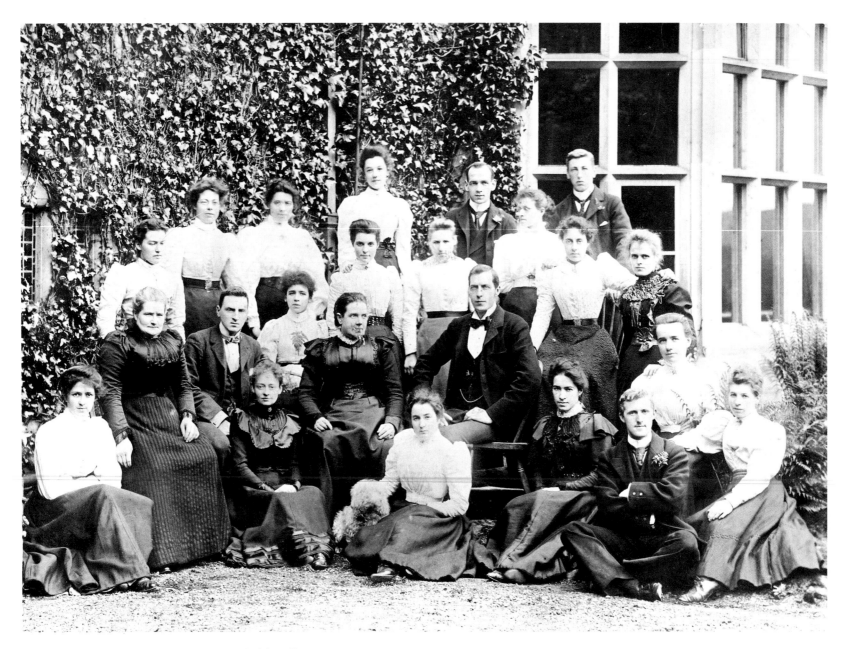

Above: The household staff, 1886.

Opposite: Beatrice, Lady Armstrong, 1929.

Overleaf: The coming of age party of William Watson-Armstrong, the 1st Lord Armstrong's successor, in the Drawing Room, 1884.

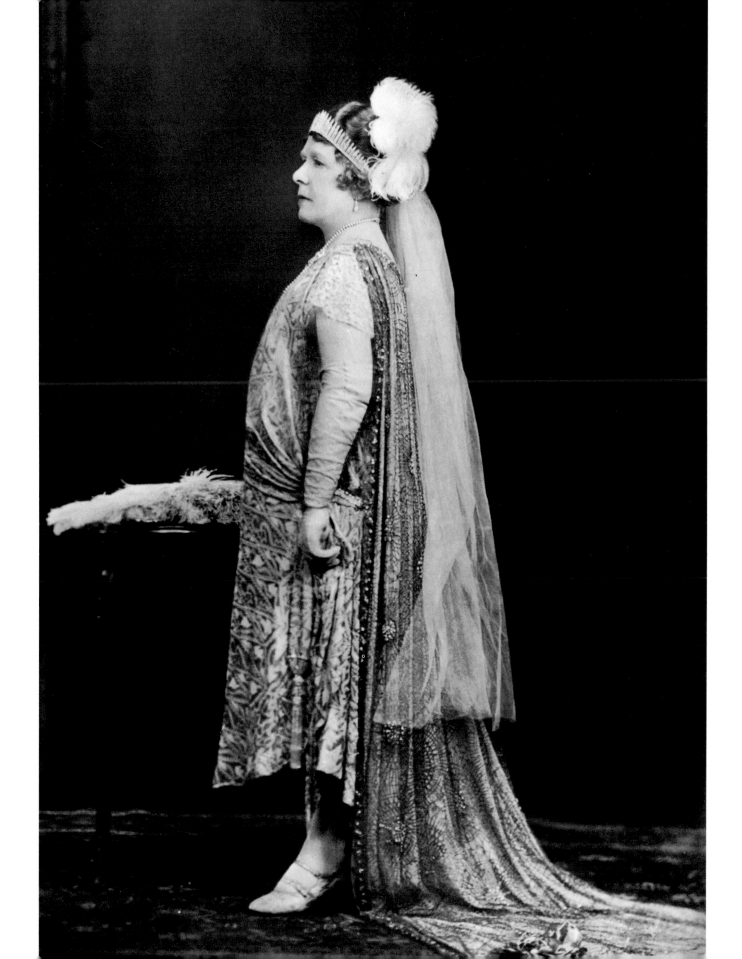

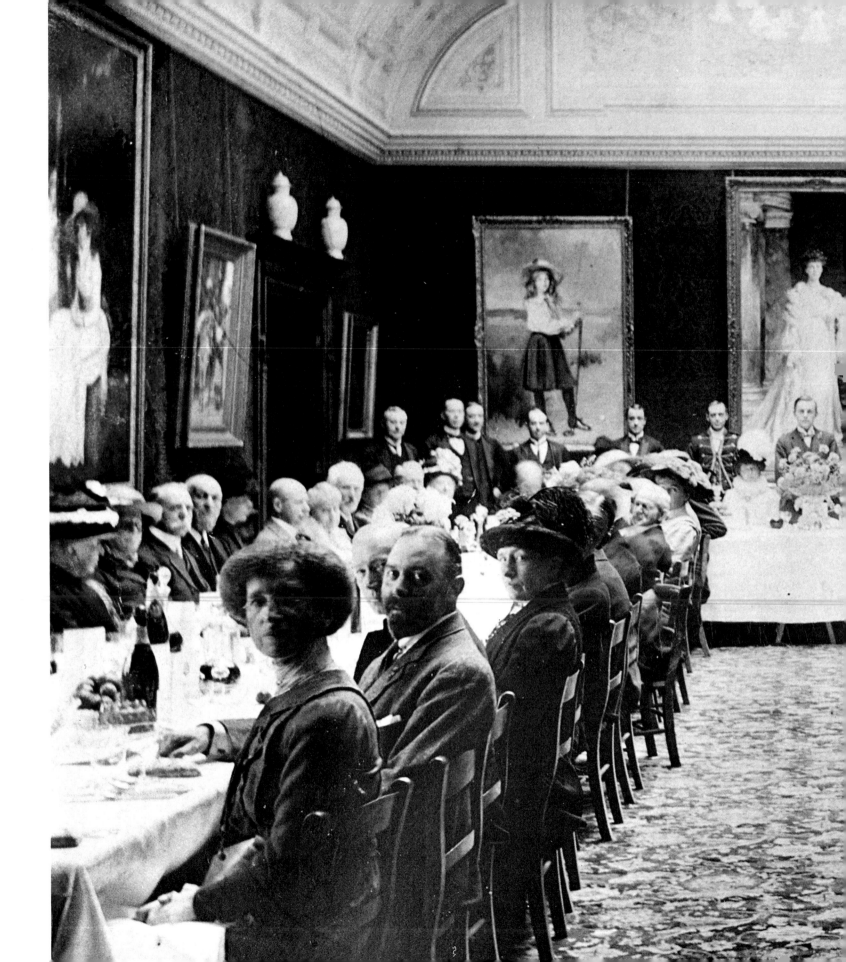

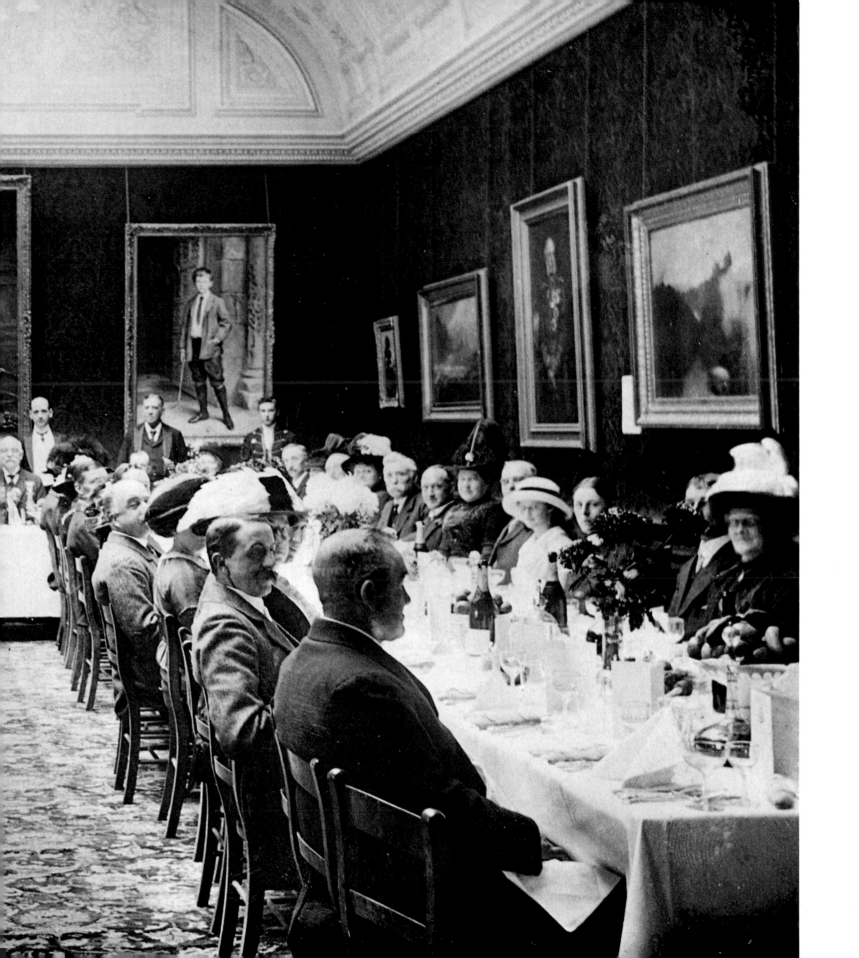

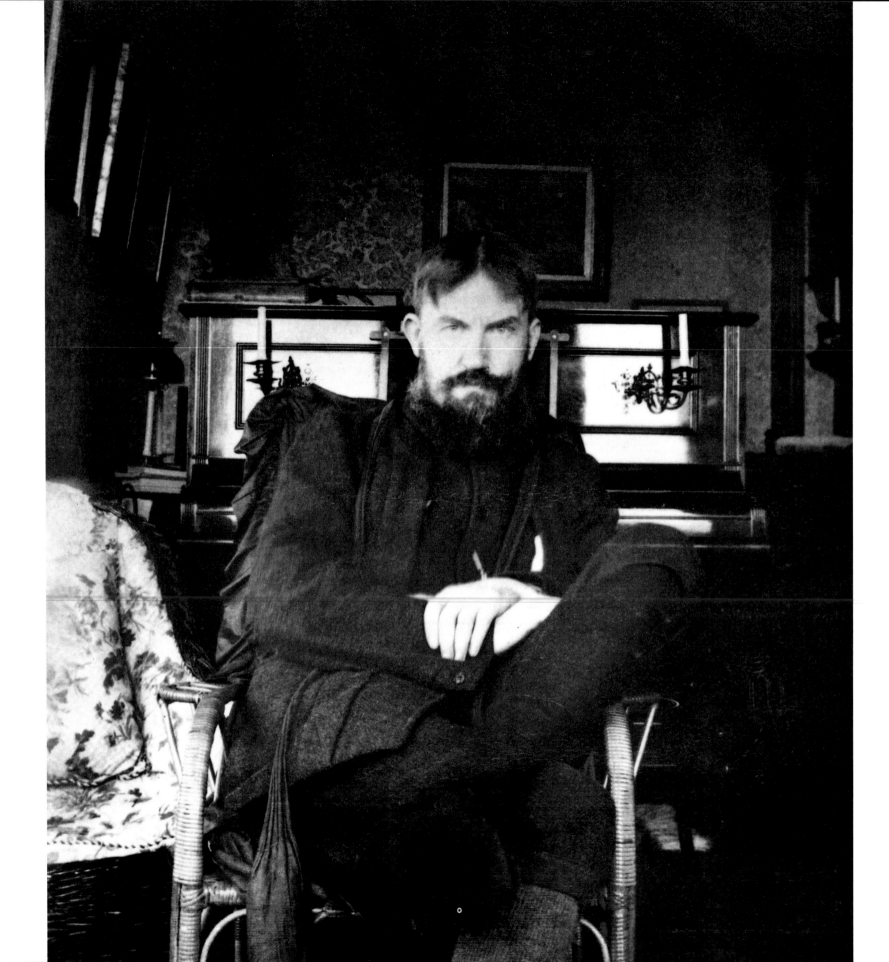

SHAW'S CORNER

AYOT ST LAWRENCE, HERTFORDSHIRE

In 1906, at the age of fifty, George Bernard Shaw and his wife Charlotte moved to the rectory at Ayot St Lawrence. As much in order to avoid misleading people who might otherwise have come to the house in search of the Rector of Ayot as out of conceit, he at once renamed the house Shaw's Corner, and there they both lived for the rest of their lives. The house itself is scarcely worth a mention – 'the National Trust's most hideous property', says Lord Norwich – its importance being solely that of having been the home of the great playwright. There can be no better description neither of it nor of Shaw himself than the account given by James Lees-Milne of his visit there in February 1944.

'Shaw's Corner is a very ugly, dark red-brick villa, built in 1902. I rang the bell and a small maid in uniform led me across the hall to a drawing-room, with open views on to the garden and the country beyond, for the house is at the end of a village. There was a fire burning in the pinched little grate. Walls distempered, the distemper flaking badly in patches. The quality of the contents of the room was on a par with that of the villa. Indifferent watercolours of the Roman Campagna, trout pools, etc. in cheap gilt frames. One rather good veneered Queen Anne bureau (for which G.B.S. said he had given £809) and one fake lacquer bureau. In the window a statuette of himself by Paul Troubetskoy. On the mantlepiece a late Staffordshire figure of Shakespeare (for which he paid 10/-), a china house, the lid of which forms a box. Only a few conventionally bound classics, plus Osbert Sitwell's latest publication prominently displayed on a table. Two stiff armchairs before the fire and brass fender. A shoddy three-ply screen attached to the fireplace to shelter from draughts anyone sitting between the fire and the doorway . . . Presently the door opened and in came the great man. I was instantly struck by the snow-white head and beard, the blue eyes and the blue nose, with a small ripe spot over the left nostril. He was not so tall as I imagined, for he stoops slightly. He was dressed in a pepper-and-salt knickerbocker suit. A loose, yellow tie from a pink collar over a thick woollen vest rather than a shirt. Several waistcoats. Mittens over blue hands . . . G.B.S. said he wished to impose no conditions on the hand-over, but he did not wish the house to become a dead museum. Hoped it would be a living shrine . . . Before I left . . . he talked about his will; said he would not leave any money to his relations for he did not wish them to grow up in idleness and luxury.'

Throughout his life, Shaw was a keen photographer and the results of his work he pasted up in a series of leather-bound albums. Using a variety of cameras, from the quarter-plate mahogany and brass field camera of early days to the more up-to-date Leica, invented in 1925, he recorded the day-to-day life of his family and friends in a series of snapshots which in mood are reminiscent of the work of the great French photographer, Henri Lartigue.

George Bernard Shaw, a self-portrait.

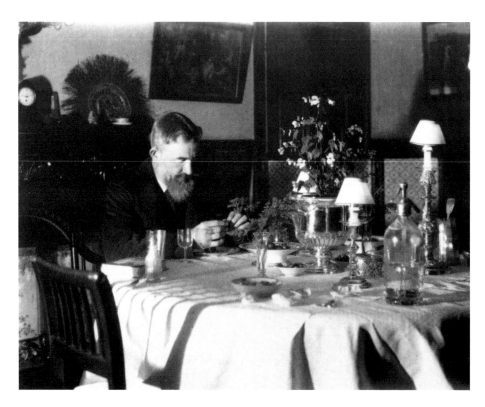

Above: G.B.S. finishing his lunch.

Opposite: G.B.S. sitting in the Drawing Room at Shaw's Corner.

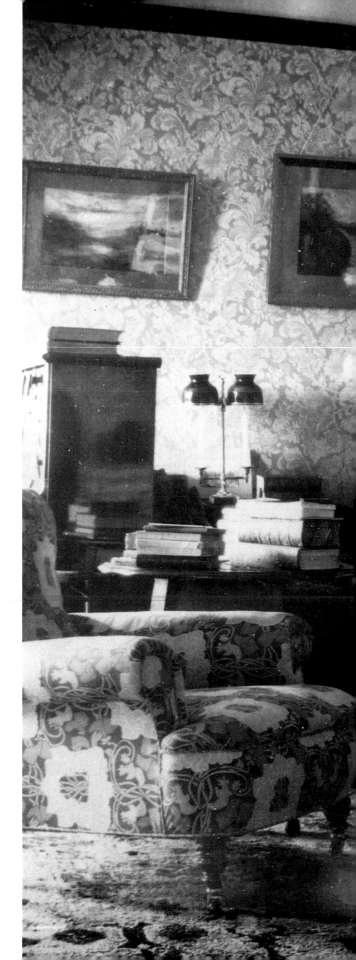

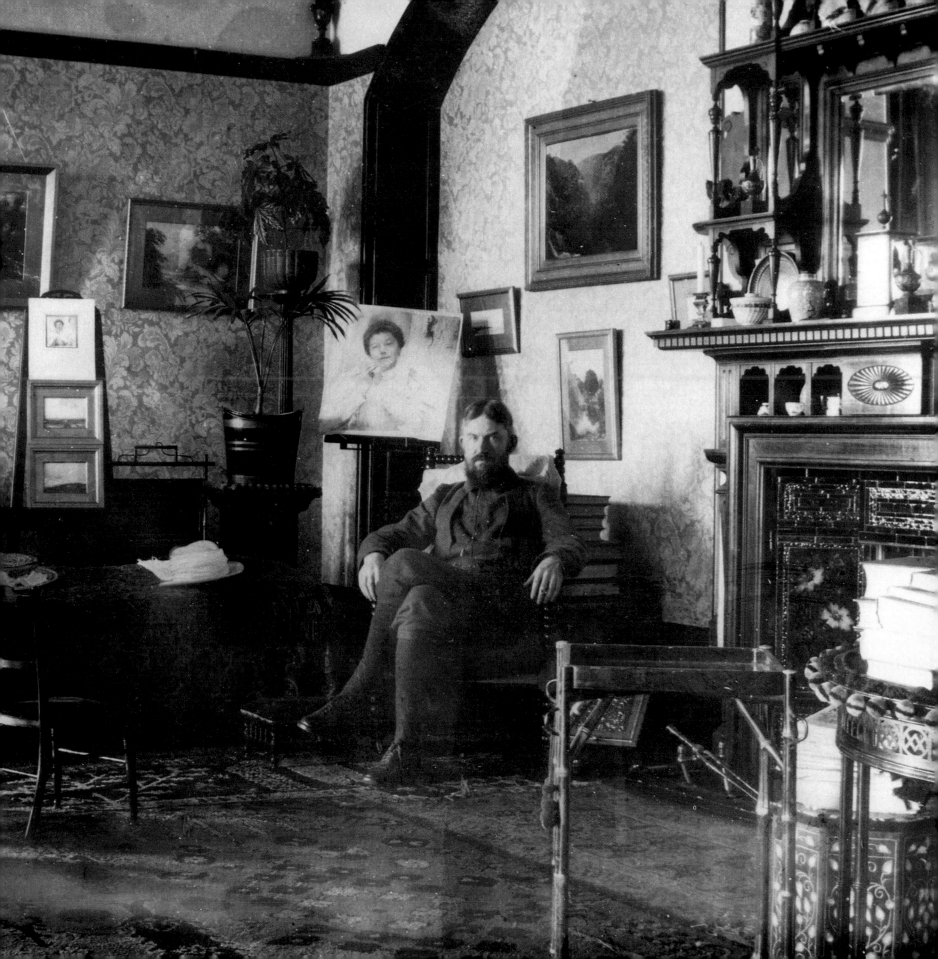

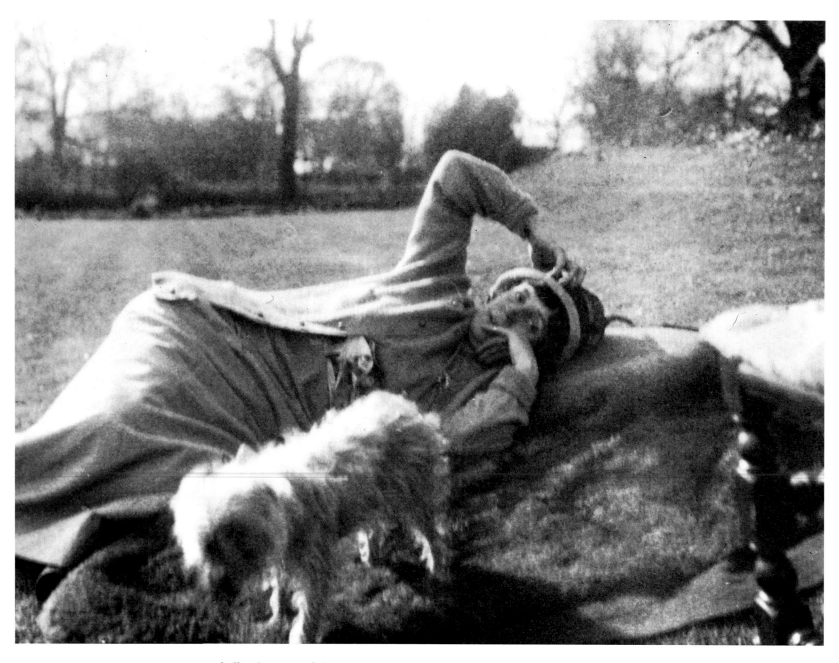

Mrs Pat Campbell, who created the role of Eliza Doolittle on the London stage.

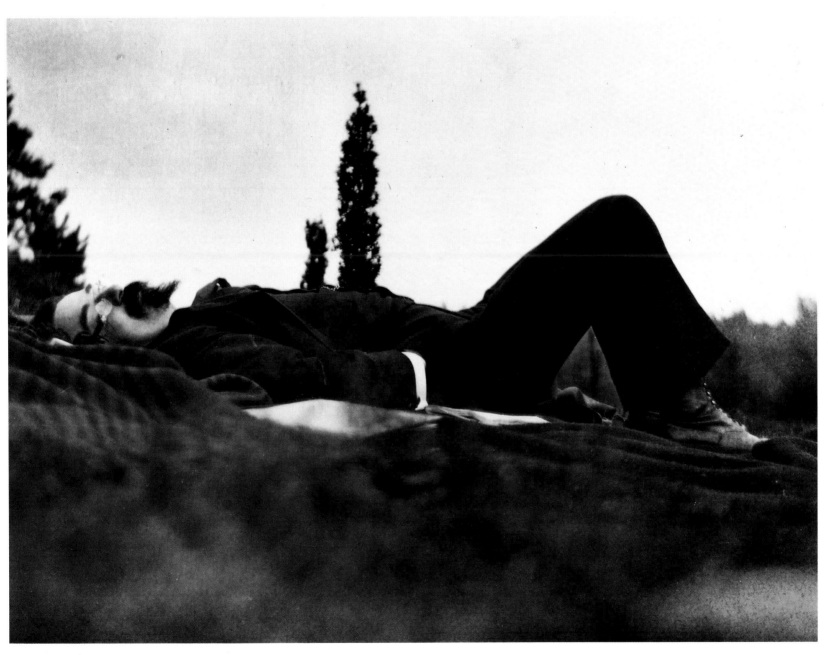

Sidney Webb, a leading member of the Fabian Society and husband of Beatrice Webb.

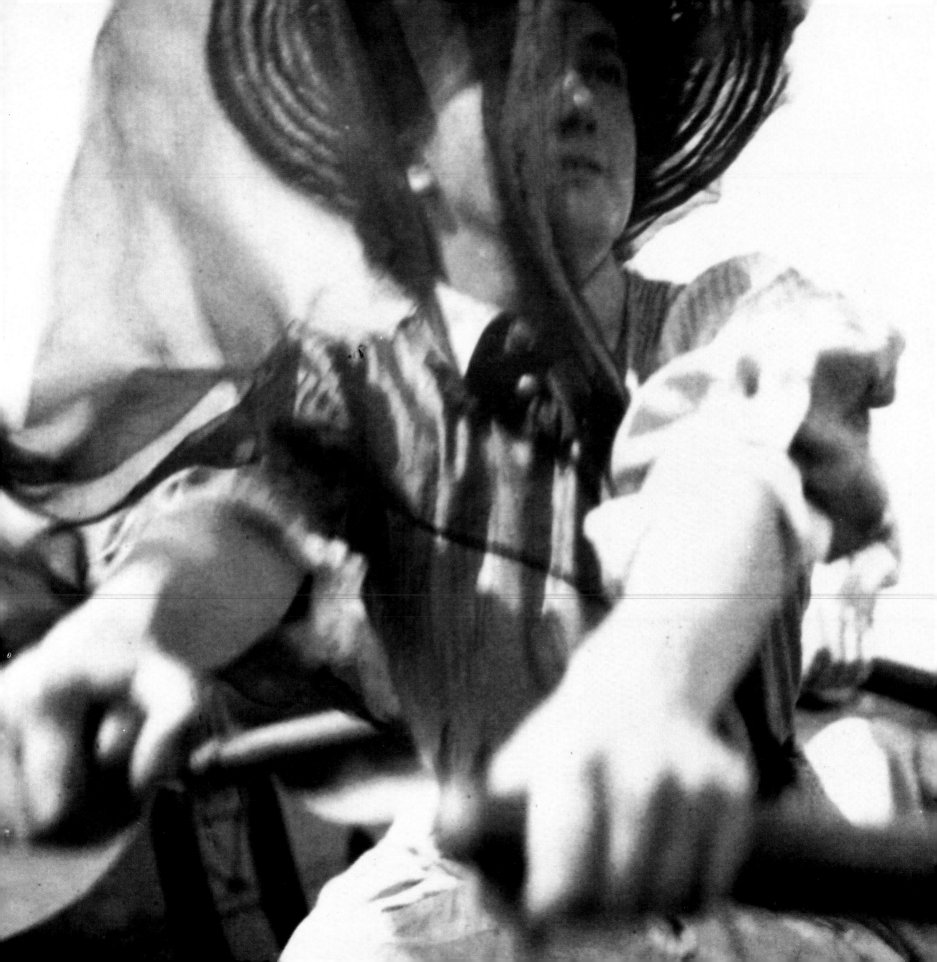

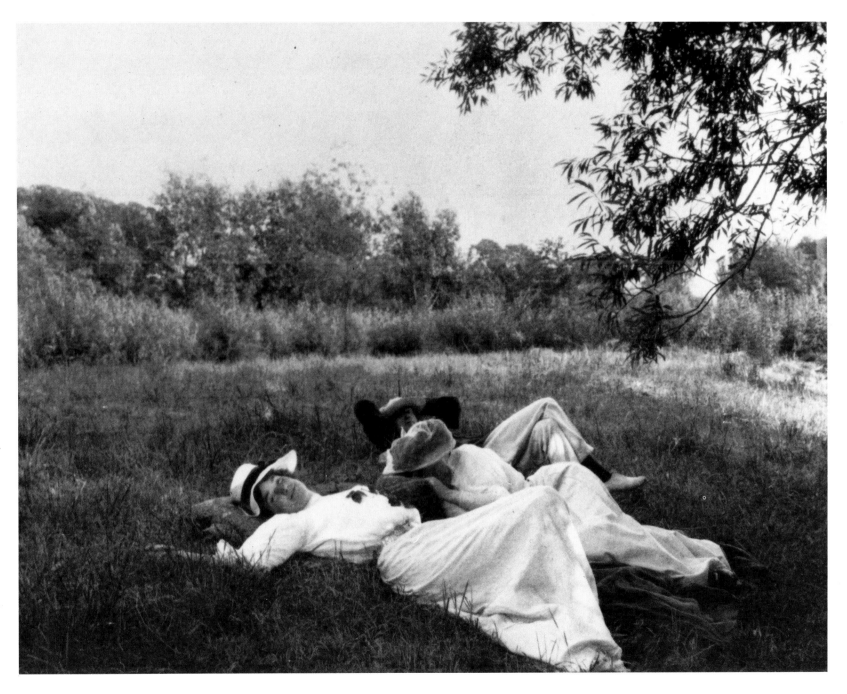

Above: Afternoon siesta.

Left: Mrs Pat Campbell.

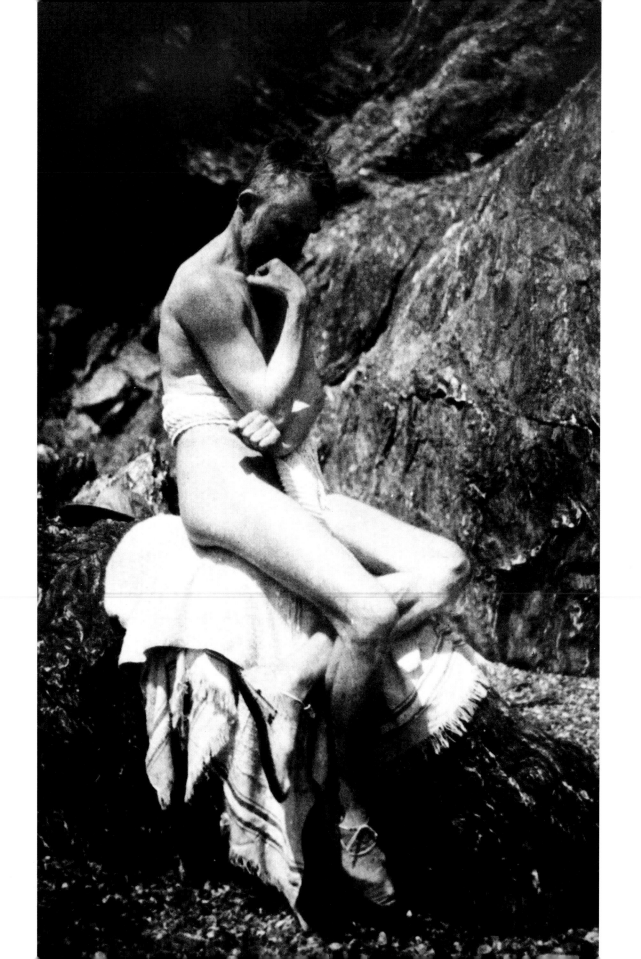

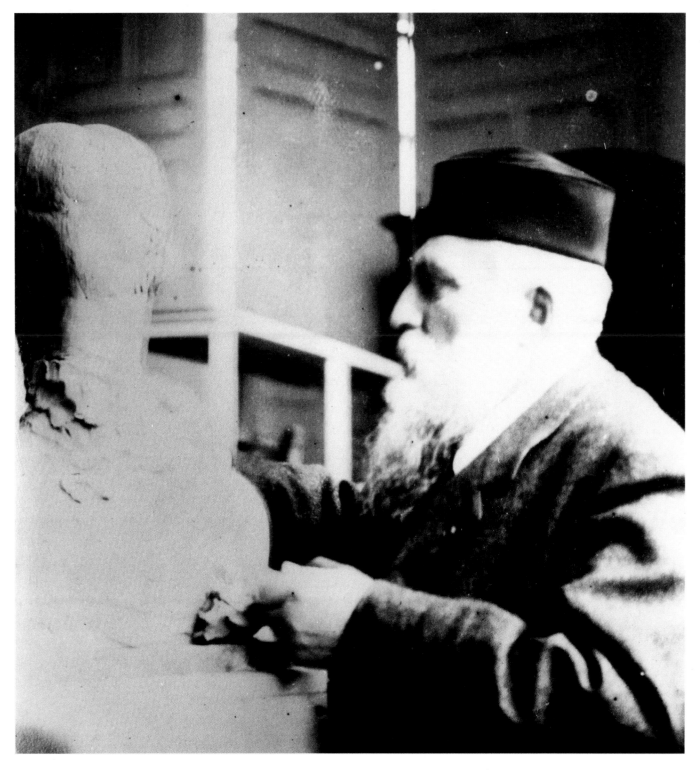

Above: A photograph by G.B.S. of Rodin at work on The Thinker.

Left: G.B.S. adopting the pose of Rodin's The Thinker.

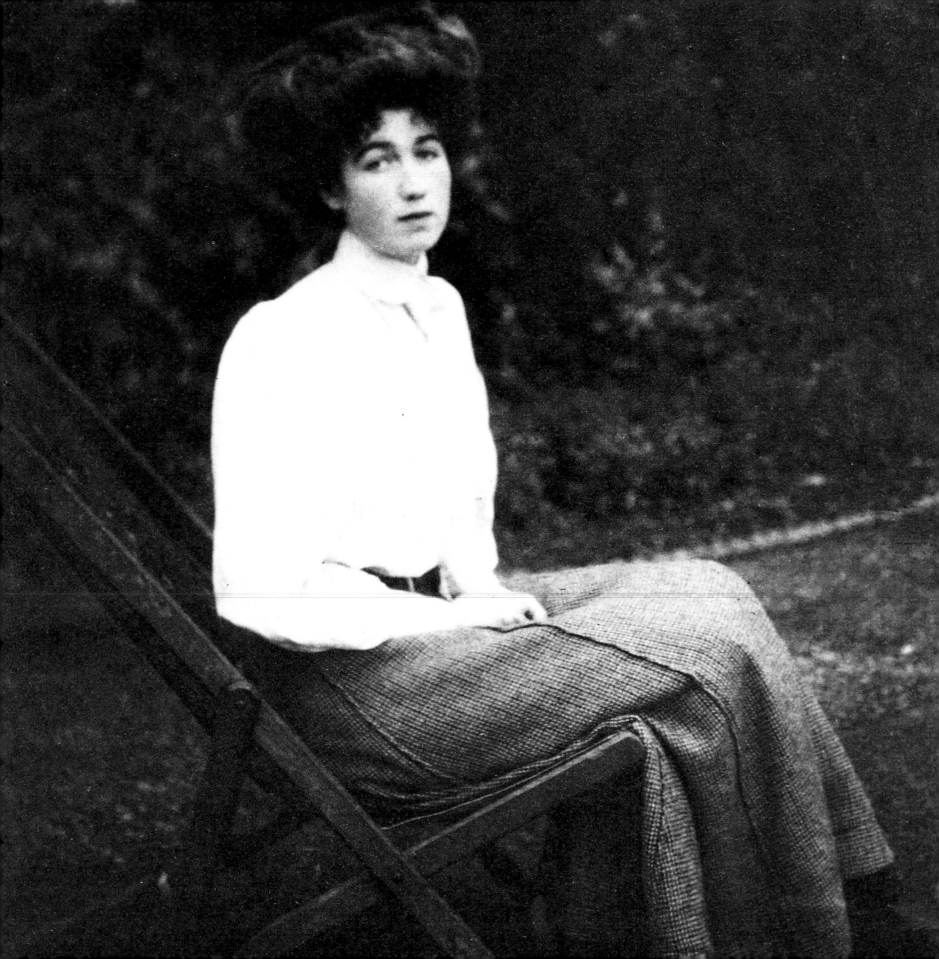

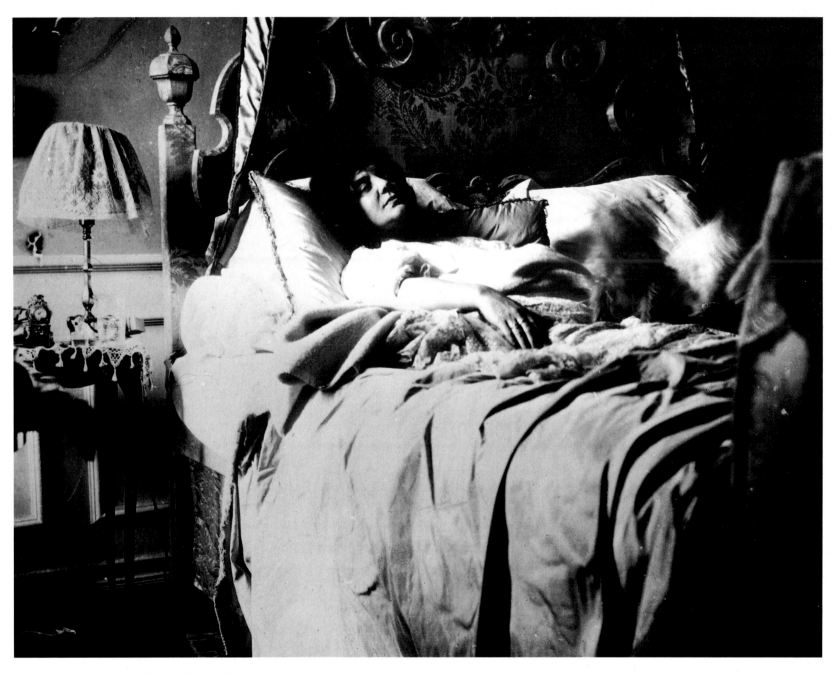

Above: Mrs Pat Campbell.

Left: Lillah McCarthy, wife of the theatrical producer, Harley Granville Barker. She acted in many of Shaw's plays, and created the role of Anne Whitfield in Man and Superman.

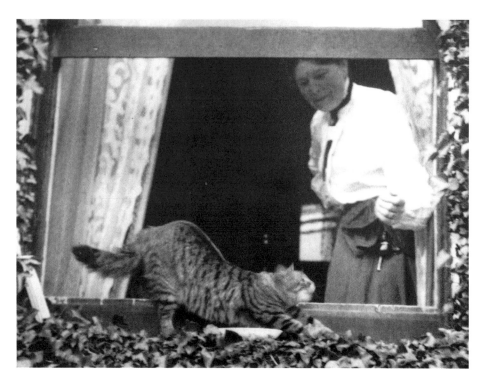

Above: *Charlotte Shaw, wife of G.B.S.*

Opposite: *Self-portrait in a window of Shaw's corner.*

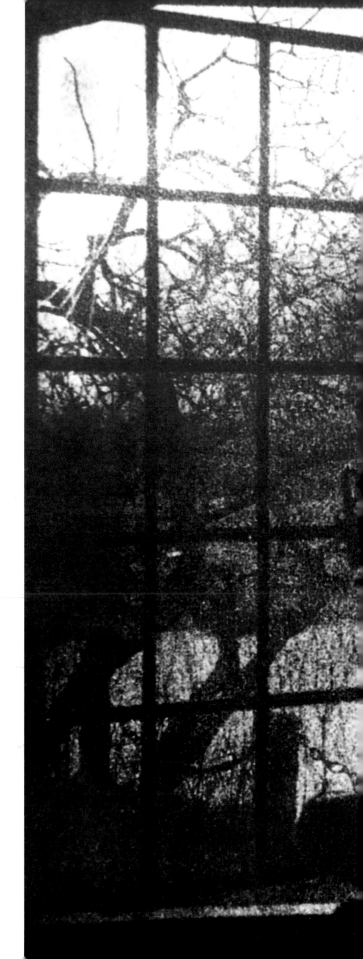

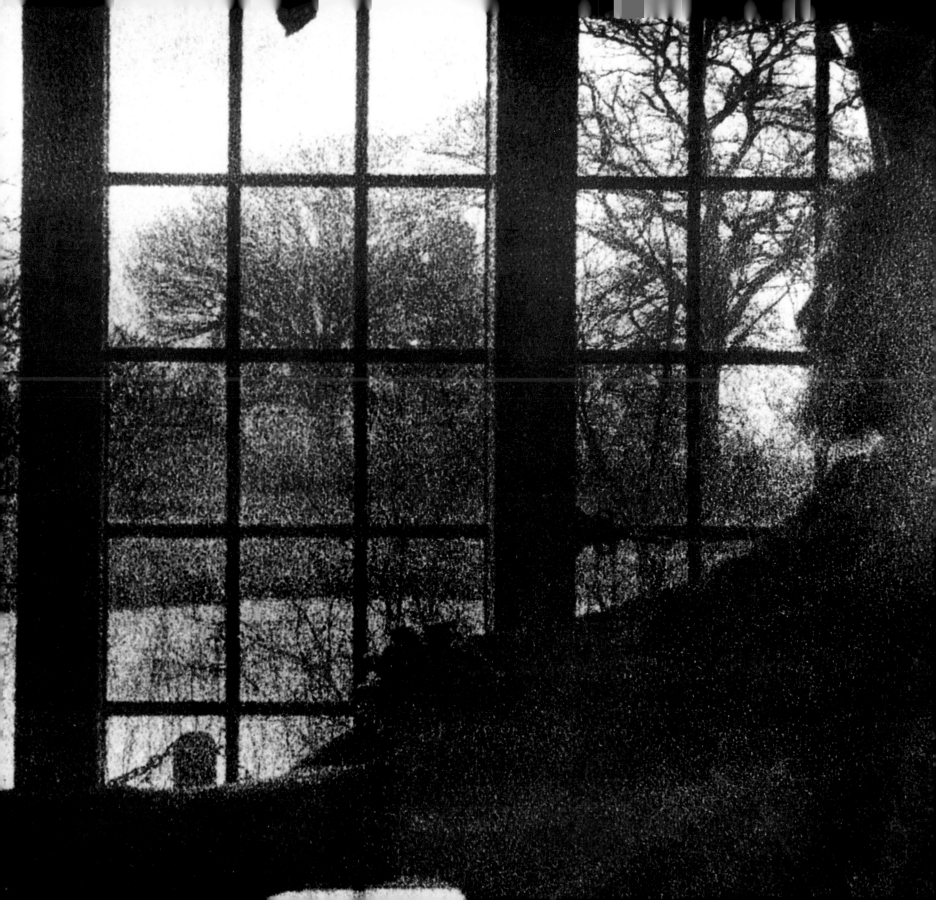

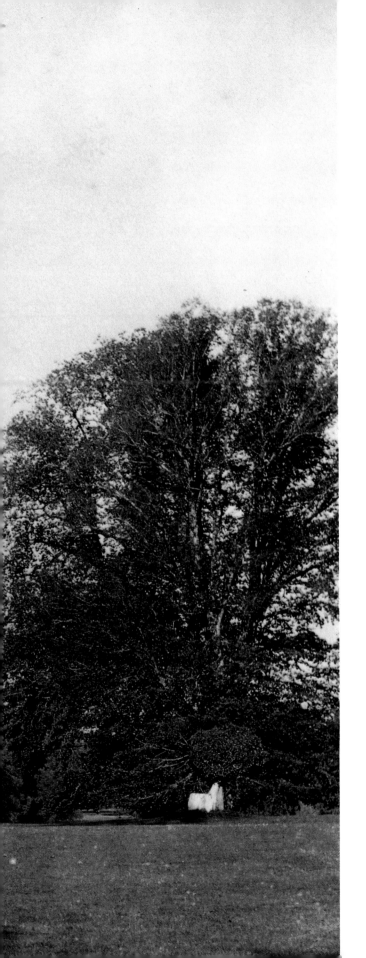

KINGSTON LACY

WIMBORNE MINSTER, DORSET

Kingston Lacy, the south front.

When William Bankes inherited Kingston Lacy from his father, Henry, in 1834, he had already led a fascinating and rather racy life. He had been twice a Member of Parliament, had vied with Byron for the hand of the bluestocking heiress Annabella Milbanke, had made extensive travels through Europe and the Middle East, including a daring expedition to Petra in Bedouin disguise, and had been tried, and acquitted, on a charge of buggery. 'My collegiate pastor, master and patron' who 'rules the Roast – or rather the Roasting – and was father of all mischiefs,'. Byron wrote of his friend at Cambridge, in whose rooms choir boys used to chant round an altar for burning incense. He certainly made an impression on all who came across him. 'Witty as Sidney Smith was,' wrote Samuel Rogers, 'I have seen him at my own house absolutely overpowered by the superior facetiousness of William Bankes.' As for Princess Lieven, she wrote to Lord Castlereagh to tell him how she had not slept a wink the previous night, after attending a dinner at the Duke of Wellington's and listening to the stories of 'a certain Mr Bankes . . . a great traveller who has explored the sources of the Nile and . . . has crossed the most inaccessible parts of Asia.' When he reached the denouement of one of his tales 'there was a burst of laughter; and, from that moment, the poor man could not open his mouth or move his arms without my exploding. I laughed for two hours, and spent nine hours of sleeplessness in bed; I had become almost hysterical with laughing.'

The family home, Kingston Lacy, was built in 1663–5 by Sir Ralph Bankes, second son of Sir John Bankes, Chief Justice to Charles I, to designs by the gentleman architect Sir Roger Pratt. The one surviving drawing shows it to have been a typical red brick Caroline house, with stone quoins, pediment, hipped roof and cupola. It remained virtually unaltered till the latter half of the Eighteenth Century, when Henry Bankes made a number of alterations. By the time William inherited he found 'an altered house that was neither old nor modern in its character but a bad mixture of both'. With the help of Sir Charles Barry, whom he met while on his travels in Egypt, he transformed Kingston Lacy into what we see today, encasing it in stone, raising the attic storey, redesigning the roof and cupola, and adding tall corner chimneys. Inspired by the work of Inigo Jones, whom he believed to have been Sir Ralph's architect, he completely remodelled the inside, adding a Roman staircase of Carrara marble which gave access to a splendid series of state rooms via a loggia. When it was almost complete, in December 1837, William wrote to his brother George in a state of euphoria, '. . . so far as my judgement goes, there is no staircase in England equal to it in effect . . . and not many that surpass it in Italy. I delight in the rich Eastern external Loggia which is finished, but I do nothing but walk up and down the inclined planes of the Staircase.' Unfortunately he was never able fully to enjoy the fruits of his labours on Kingston Lacy, since in 1841 he was threatened with a second trial for buggery and fled to Italy, from where he continued to supervise the completion of building work, and to commission and send home works of art to furnish the house until his death in 1855. When the National Trust took it over in 1981, it had scarcely changed since that date.

Various members of the Bankes family in the Drawing Room, c. 1860.

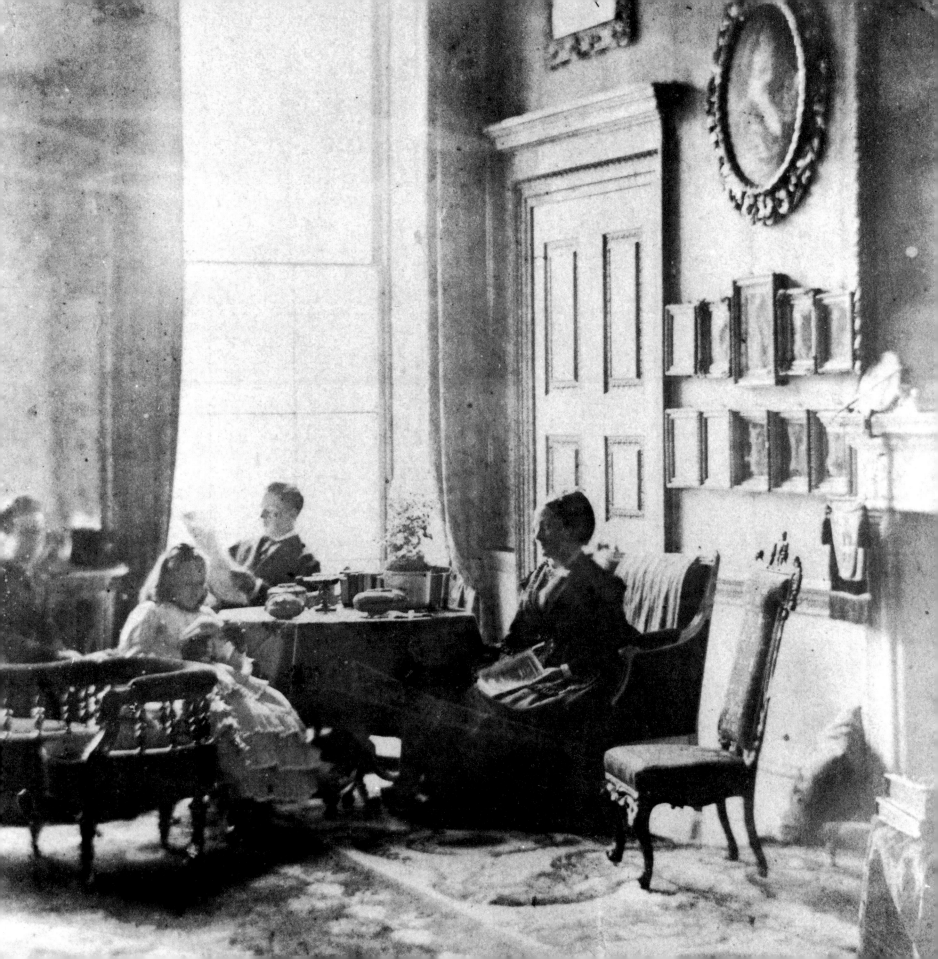

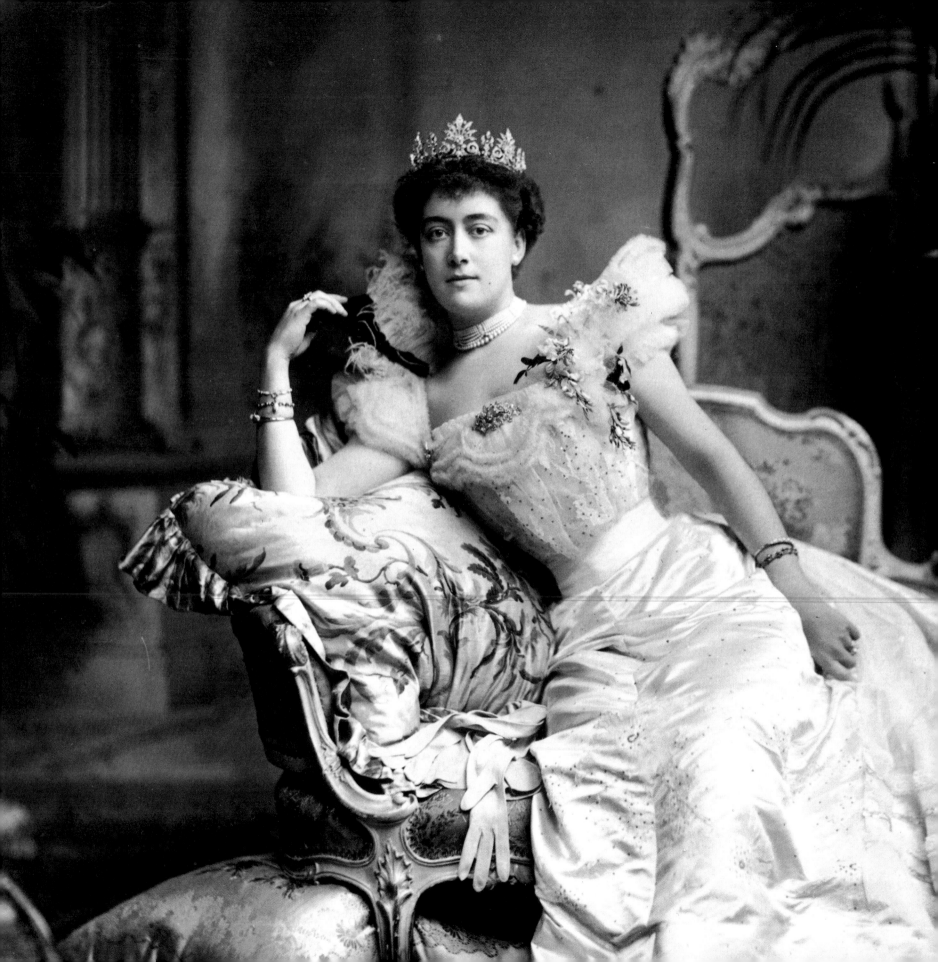

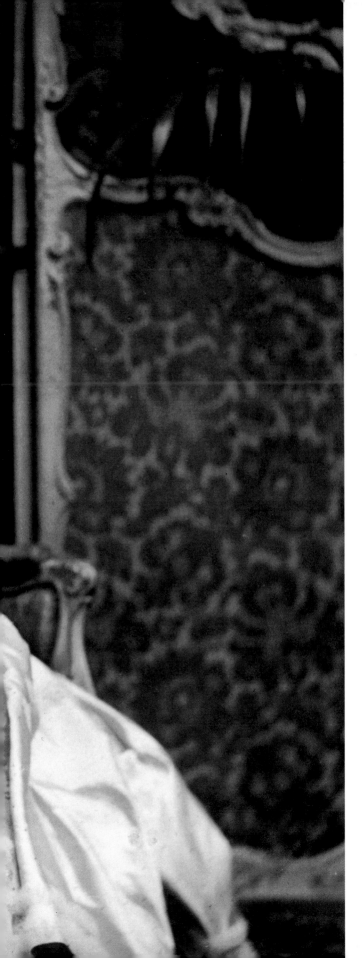

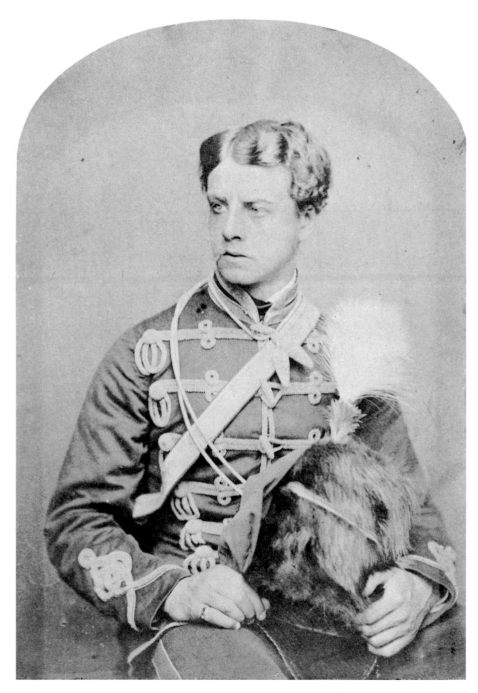

Above: Lt William George Hawtry Bankes of the 7th Hussars. He won a posthumous VC at the siege of Lucknow.

Left: Henrietta Bankes, wife of Walter Ralph Bankes, father of the last owner.

73

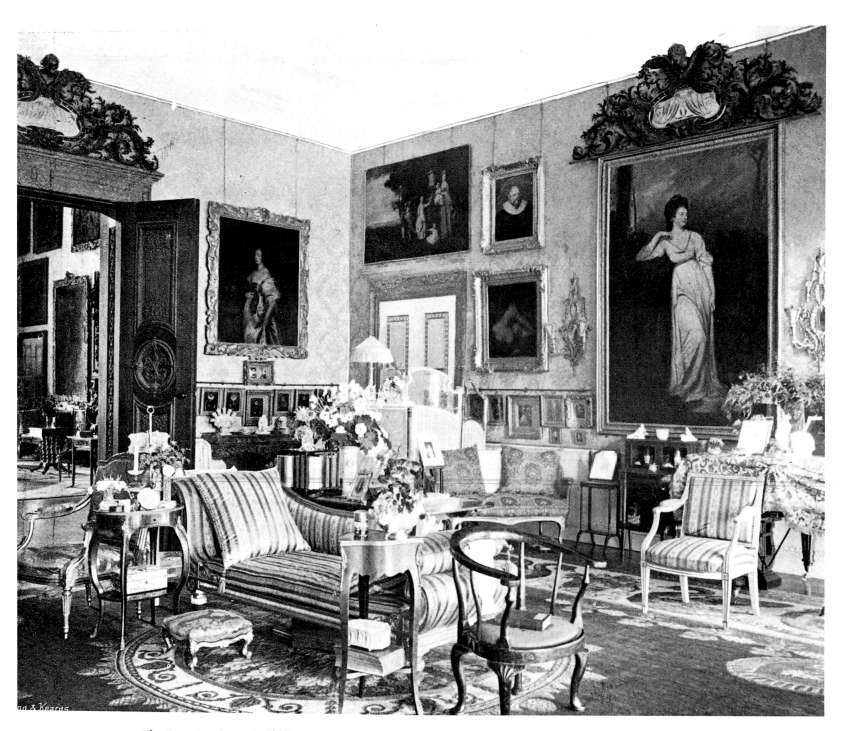

The Drawing Room in 1900.

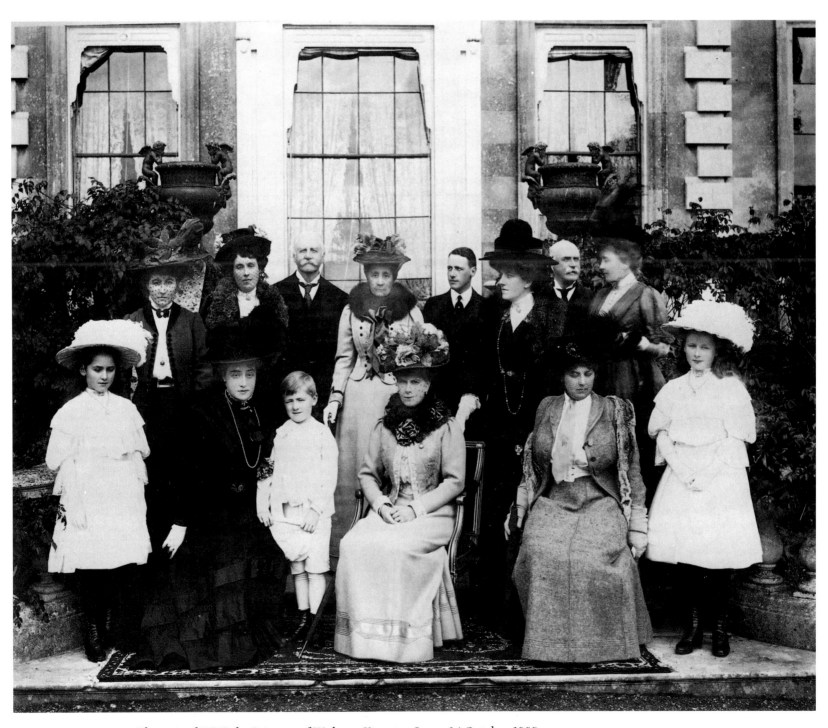

The visit of HRH the Princess of Wales to Kingston Lacy, 14 October 1908.

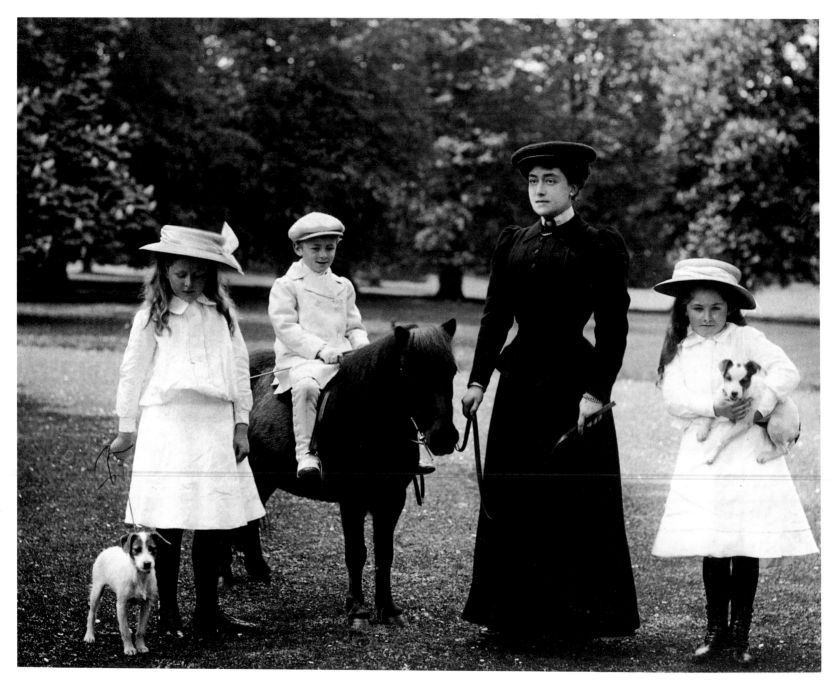

Above: left to right: Daphne, Ralph, Henrietta and Viola Bankes. Kingston Lacy, May 1908.

Opposite: Ralph Bankes with his camera at Bournemouth, 1913.

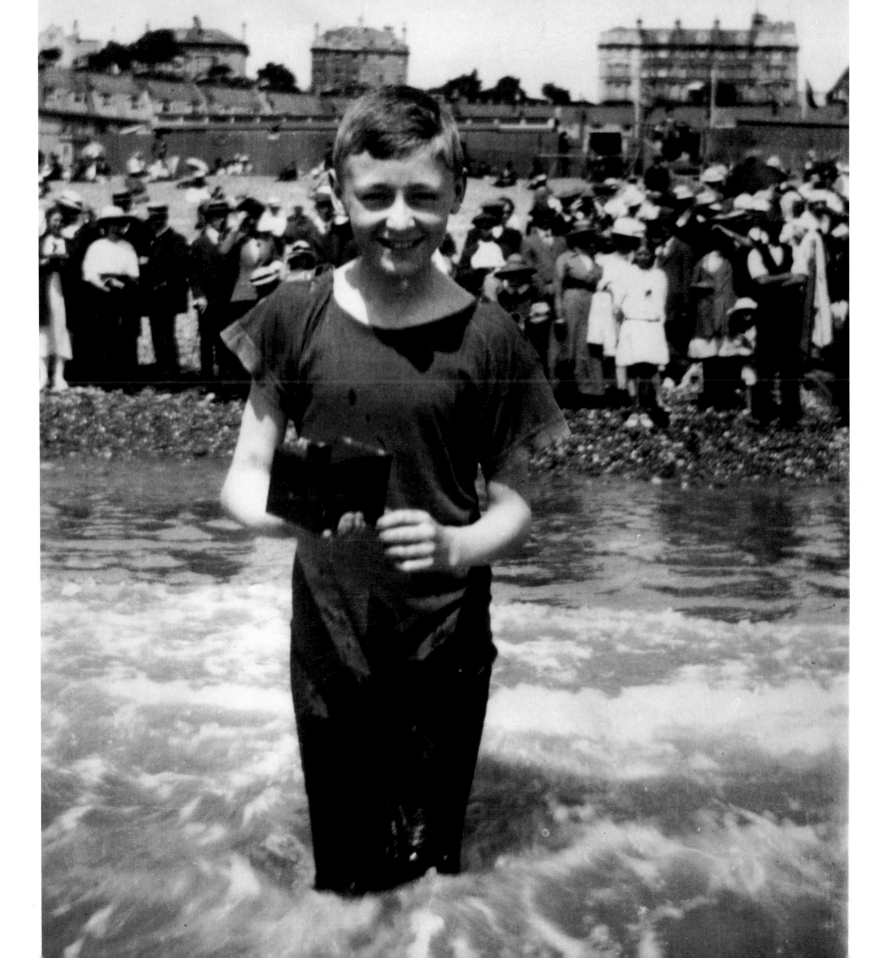

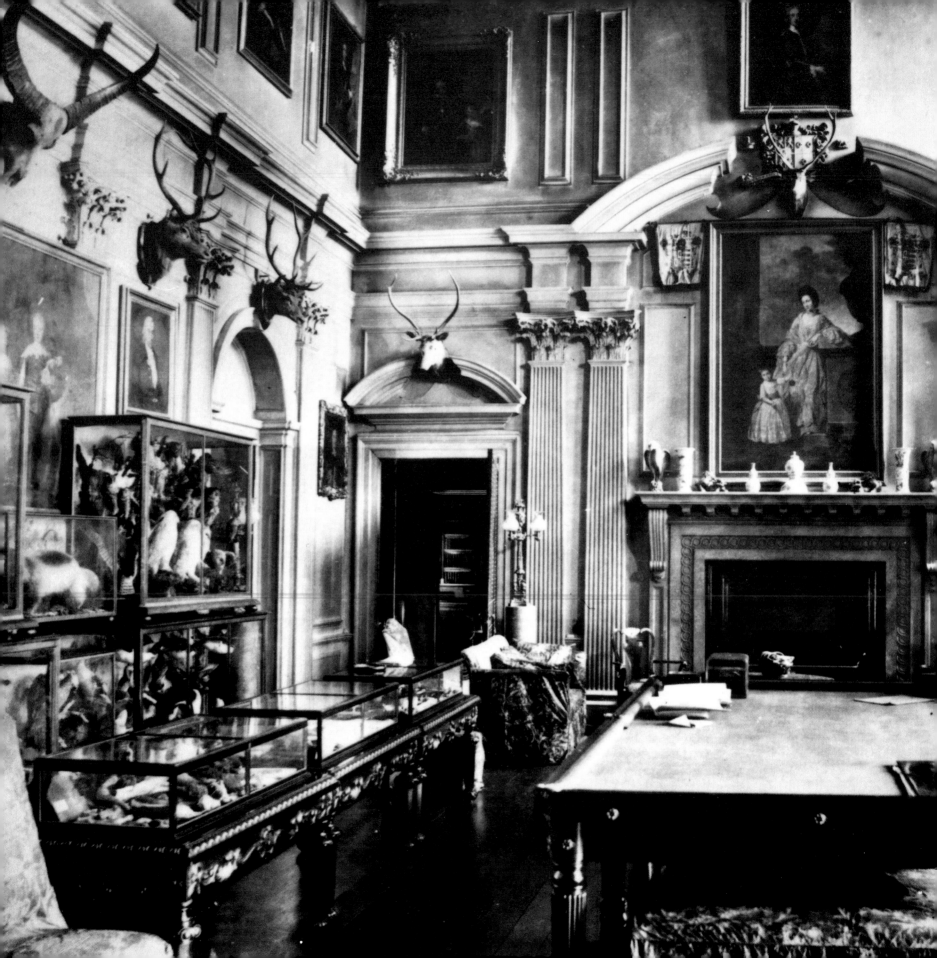

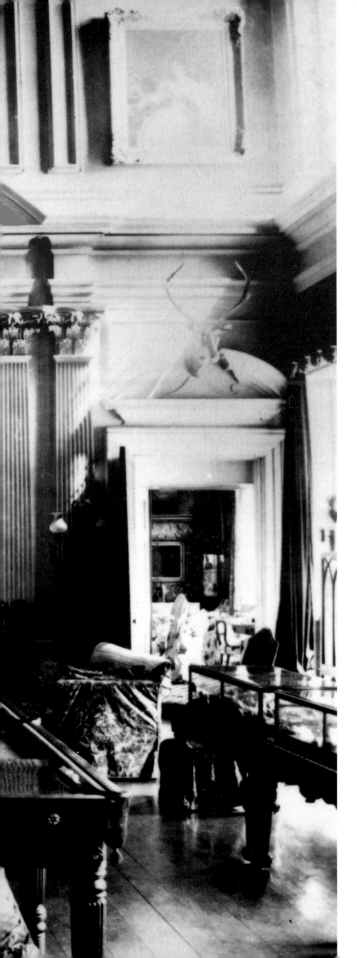

CALKE ABBEY

TICKNALL, DERBYSHIRE

The Saloon photographed in 1886.

When Calke Abbey was handed over to the National Trust in February, 1985, it had been inhabited by the Harpur family since it was built at the turn of the Eighteenth Century. Then Sir John Harpur, who had come of age in 1701 to find himself one of the richest men in the county of Derbyshire, had decided to remodel the existing house which he had inherited into something much grander, which would be an expression of the greater power and influence of the family. With the help of a 'Surveyor' from Nottingham called William Johnson, he designed himself a large and handsome square stone house of three storeys, with projecting corner pavilions, which in size would have been, along with Bretby (the neighbouring seat of the Stanhopes), one of the few serious rivals to Chatsworth in south Derbyshire. He completed the project in 1716, with a magnificent quadrangle of stables, built by William Gilks, a local builder from Burton-on-Trent. Whether his wife Catherine shared her husband's enthusiasm for his new home is doubtful, for she once confided to her friends that 'one had better to be buried alive than married to one that gives disgust.' She still dutifully bore him six children.

It was Sir John's grandson, Sir Harry Harpur, who began the laying-out of the park, and his son, Sir Henry, completed the transformation of the old formal gardens into the picturesque landscape that was so fashionable at the time. The latter, who was known as 'the Isolated Baronet', was an eccentric and introverted character who married a maid and withdrew completely from society. His singular behaviour was reported to Joseph Farington by some Leicestershire gentlemen who had paid him a visit. 'At dinner,' they said, 'he sits down alone at a table covered for several persons, and after dinner glasses are placed as if for company and he takes his wine in that form, but does not allow any servant to wait in the room . . . He keeps a pack of hounds, but does not himself hunt, yet . . . he has pleasure in listening to his Huntsman while he gives an account of each chase . . . He is shy of communication to such an excess that he sometimes delivers orders to his servants by letter.' It was Sir Henry who gave the name 'Abbey' to Calke, it having been previously known simply as 'Hall' or 'House', and who called in William Wilkins to design a portico for the entrance front, to create a new suite of principal rooms, including Drawing Room, Dining Room and Library, and to design lodges to mark the entrances to the park.

The strong streak of reclusiveness shown by Sir Henry has persisted in many of his descendants. His grandson, Sir John, was rarely seen in public and devoted most of his life to the breeding of Longhorn cattle, hanging the mounted heads of his prize oxen in the entrance hall. Likewise, apart from serving as High Sheriff of Derbyshire in 1900, his son, Sir Vauncey, kept out of the public eye, and instead spent every moment of his spare time watching, shooting and stuffing birds, causing his aunt Isabel to lament in 1904, 'How completely he is losing or rather has lost all position in the County. It vexes me terribly, I can't understand him. He does not seem to know how to behave like a gentleman.' On his death in 1924, the estate passed first to his daughter, Hilda, and then to his great nephew, Charles, who took the name of Harpur Crewe and possessed a similarly retiring nature, and in whose lifetime the doors of Calke remained firmly closed to one and all. The result of this curious family trait is that over the years the house and its contents have remained virtually untouched.

Sir Vauncey Harpur's gamekeepers.

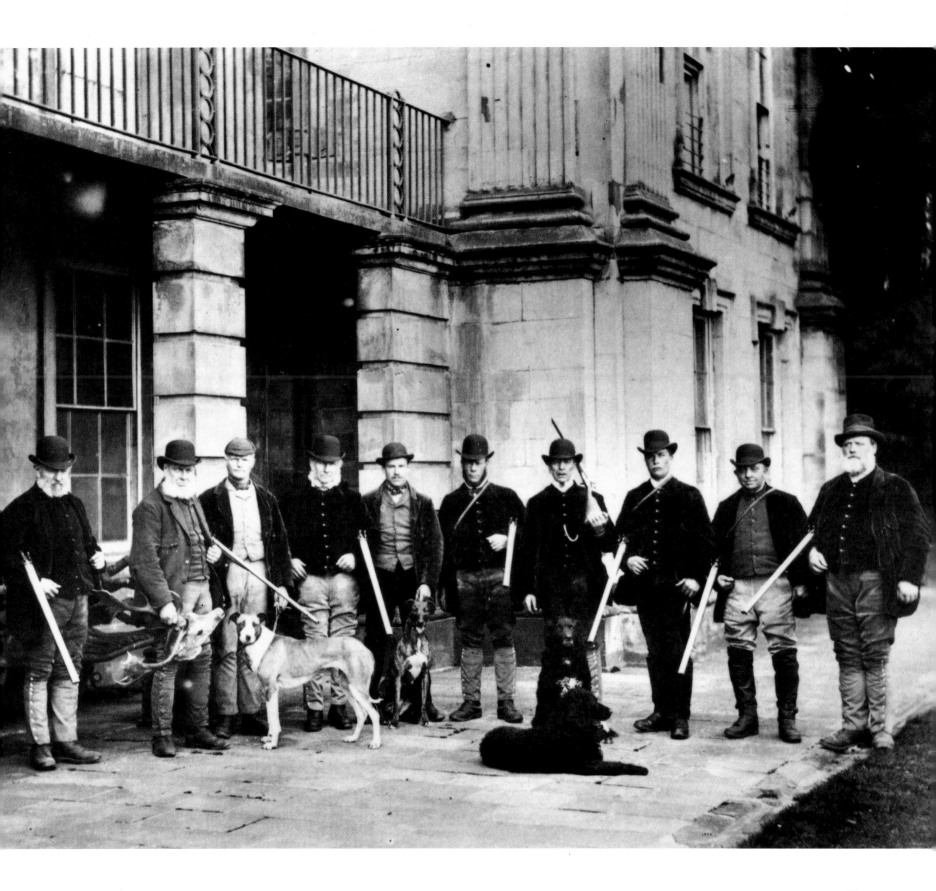

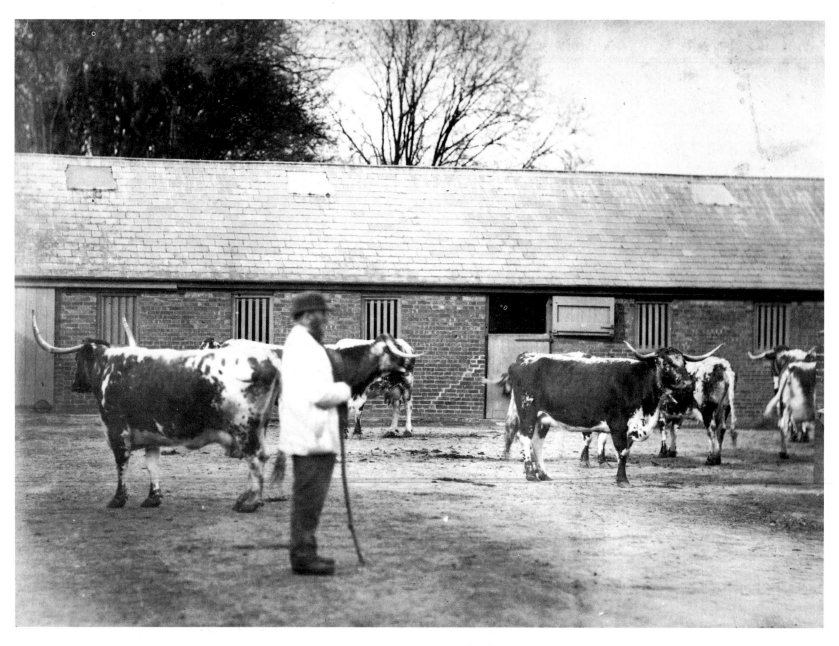

Above: The head cowman with some of Sir John's Longhorn cattle.

Opposite: Various Longhorn cattle.

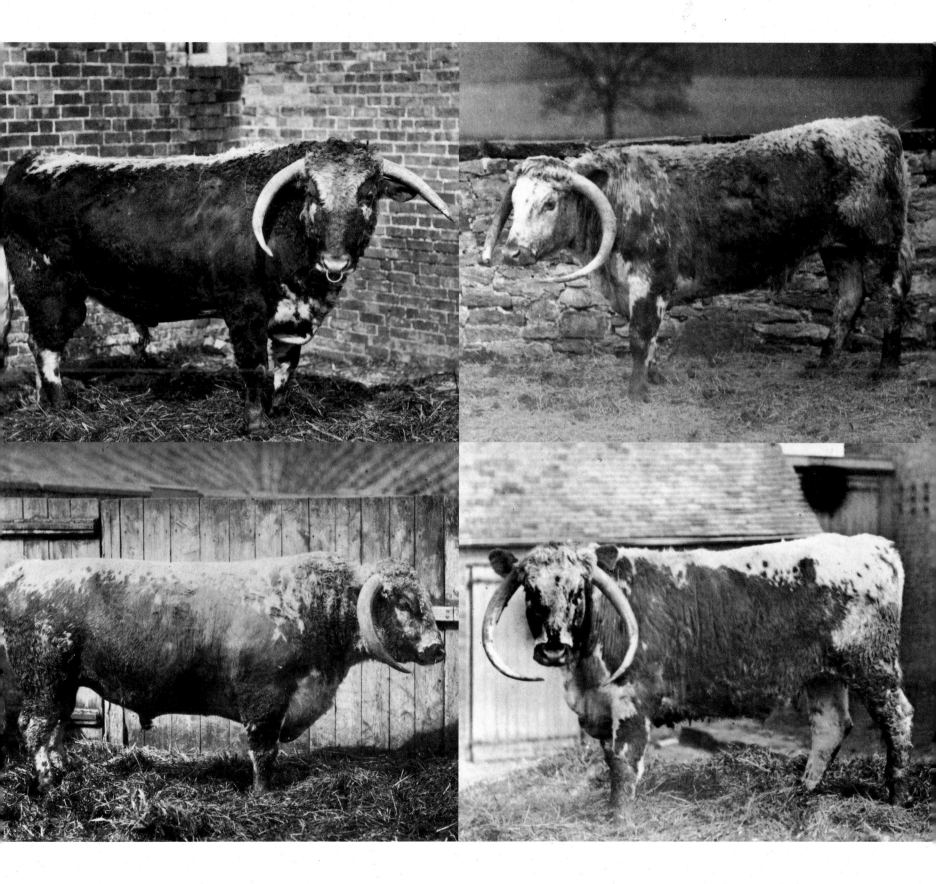

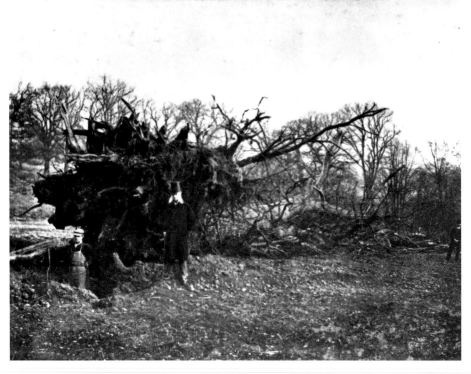

Above: Sir John Harpur in front of a fallen tree in the park.

Opposite: Calke Abbey from the south-west.

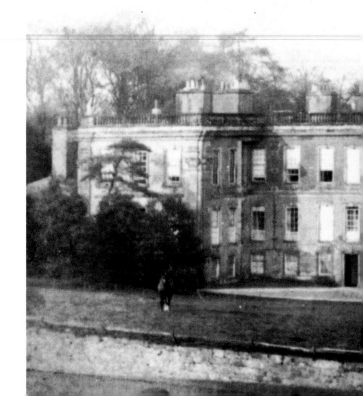

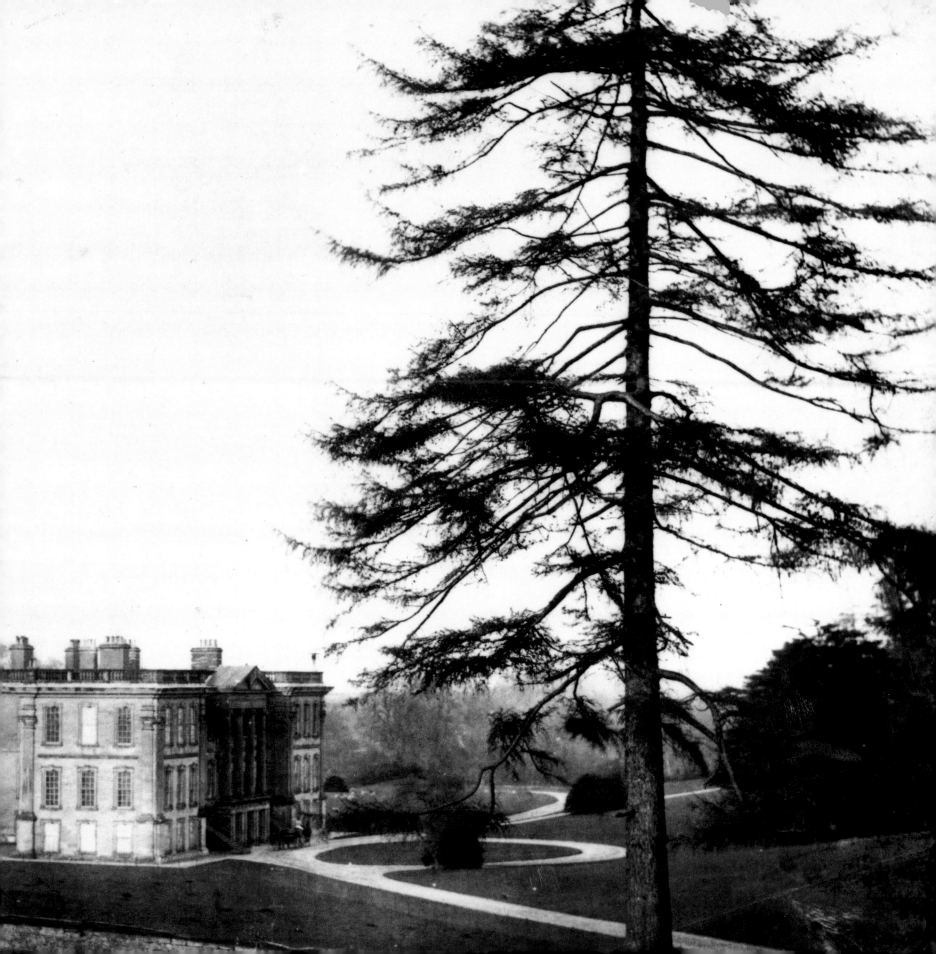

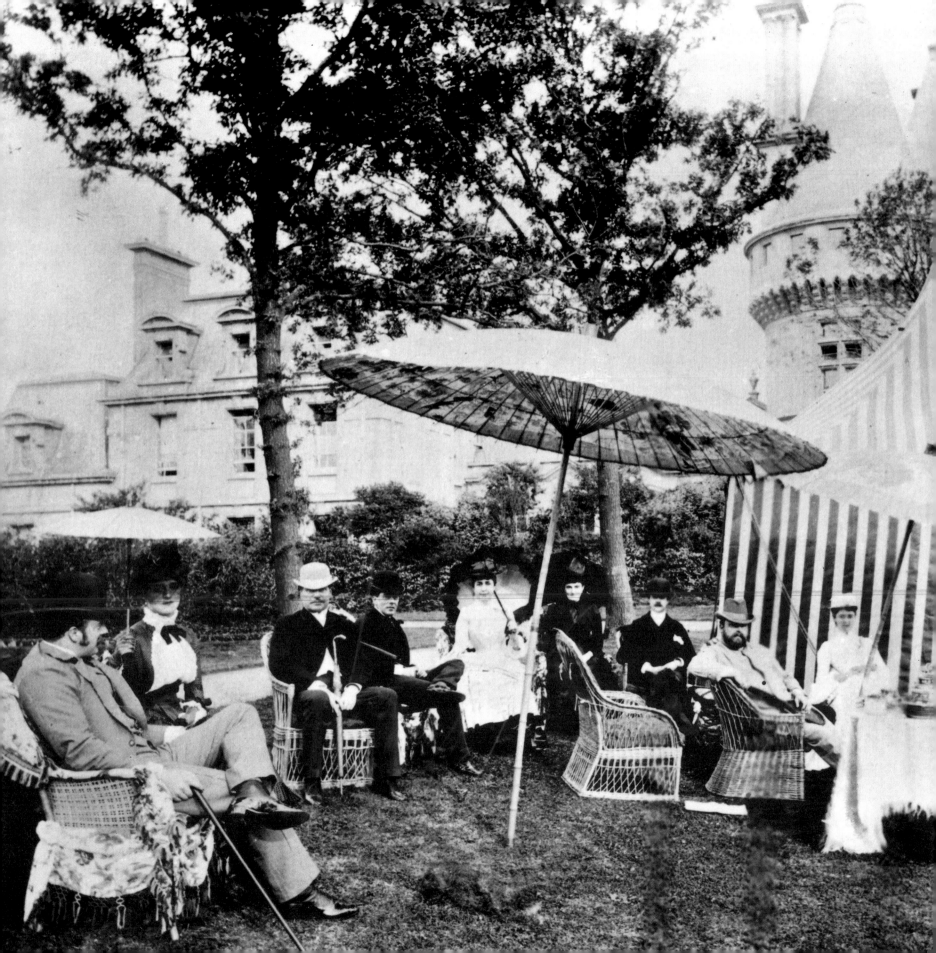

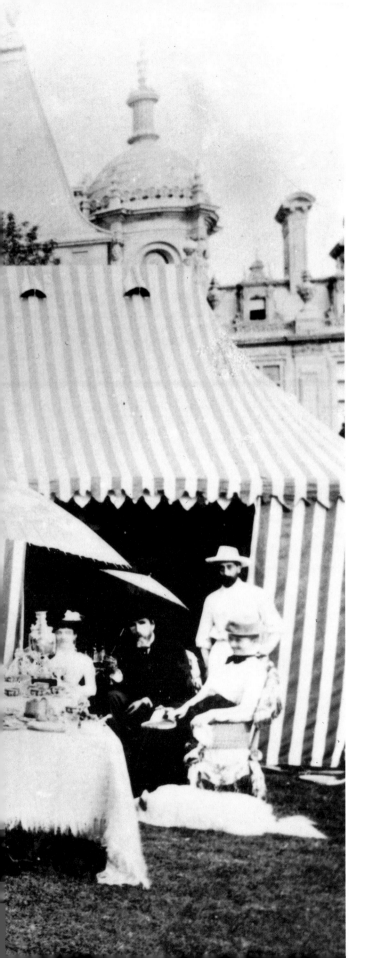

WADDESDON MANOR

AYLESBURY, BUCKINGHAMSHIRE

A picnic at Waddesdon in the 1880s for the Prince and Princess of Wales.

'The difficulty of building a house,' wrote Baron Ferdinand de Rothschild in his *Reminiscences*, 'is insignificant compared with the labour of transforming a bare wilderness into a park.' He spoke from experience, having recently completed both tasks on a scale virtually unheard of since the building of the great Elizabethan 'prodigy' houses. Baron Ferdinand had come to London from Vienna in 1860, and had there fallen in love with and subsequently married his first cousin, Evelina. Together they had planned to build a country house, but sadly she died eighteen months after the wedding, as a result of a railway accident. The plan was abandoned until a few years later when, while out hunting in Buckinghamshire with his sister Alice, he was inspired to revive it by the discovery of a magnificent site on the Waddesdon estate, a property of the Duke of Marlborough, which he bought in the autumn of 1874. '. . . In its favour,' he wrote, 'it had a bracing and salubrious air, pleasant scenery, excellent hunting, and was untainted by factories and villadom.' The disadvantage was that there was neither house nor park.

The Baron decided that the top of a particular cone-shaped hill, Lodge Hill, which commands panoramic views over several counties, was the perfect site for his new house. The transformation of this barren terrain was the first and most formidable task, for the entire summit had to be levelled. Labourers from the neighbourhood, supplemented by gangs of navvies from London, all under the direction of a French landscape gardener, Monsieur Lainé, toiled day and night digging out the steep hill so as to give an easy gradient to the roads and a natural appearance to the banks and slopes. There were many problems. Seven miles of pipes had to be laid to bring water from the Chiltern Hills. There were constant landslips. 'The part of the hill we had selected as the site of the house consists of sand, and the foundations having been proceeded with for some months proved not to have been set deep enough, as they suddenly gave way. The whole of the brickwork had then to be removed and thirty feet of sand excavated until a firm bottom of clay was reached. I now began to realize the importance of the task I had undertaken . . . and I was so disheartened at first by the delay and the worry that during four years I rarely went near the place.'

The site was eventually finished, and the great house began to rise from the rubble. Ever since he had once made a tour through Touraine and been impressed by the ancient châteaux of the Valois, it had been Baron Ferdinand's dream to have a house built in the same style, and this is what his French architect, Gabriel-Hippolyte Destailleur, gave him. When it was completed, in 1889, he wrote 'By the side of the grand châteaux of the Touraine, Waddesdon would appear a pigmy. The castle of Chambord, for example, contains 450 rooms, the smallest of which would dwarf the largest at Waddesdon. But its main features are borrowed from them; its towers from Maintenon . . . and its external staircases from Blois . . . Though far from being the realization of a dream in stone and mortar like Chenonceaux, M. Destailleur's work had fairly fulfilled my expectations.'

Sadly it was others who were to reap the chief benefits of Baron Ferdinand's labour of love, for he died in 1898. In those nine years, however, he filled the house with all the great men and women of the day, and made a collection of works of art which, to quote Mark Girouard, leaves 'an admirer of the Eighteenth Century in a state half drunk and half dazed with the splendour and extent of what he has seen'. Waddesdon was handed over to the National Trust by the Baron's descendant, Mr James de Rothschild, in 1957.

Opposite above: Baron Ferdinand with one of the many exotic birds he kept in his Aviary.

Opposite below: Baron Ferdinand in his sitting room with his dog Poupon.

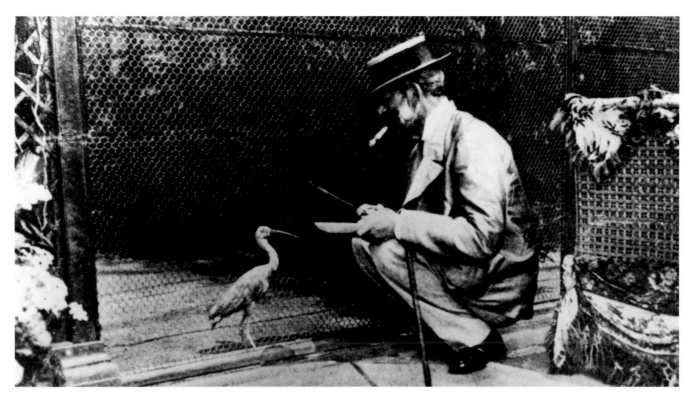

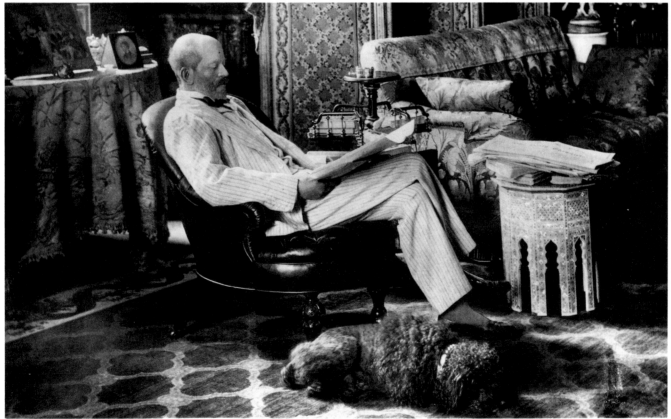

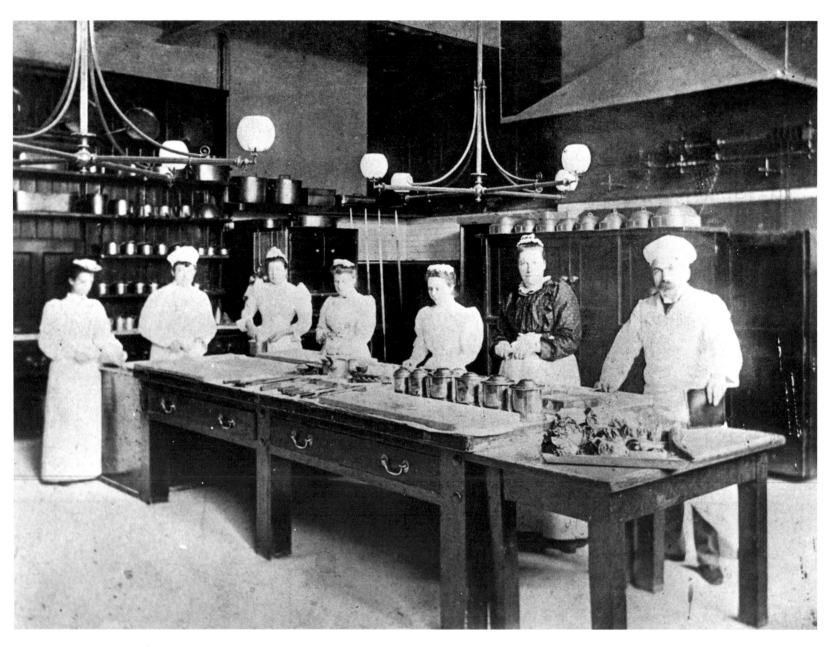

The Kitchen staff, 1910. Waddesdon had a separate kitchen for the Pastry Chef.

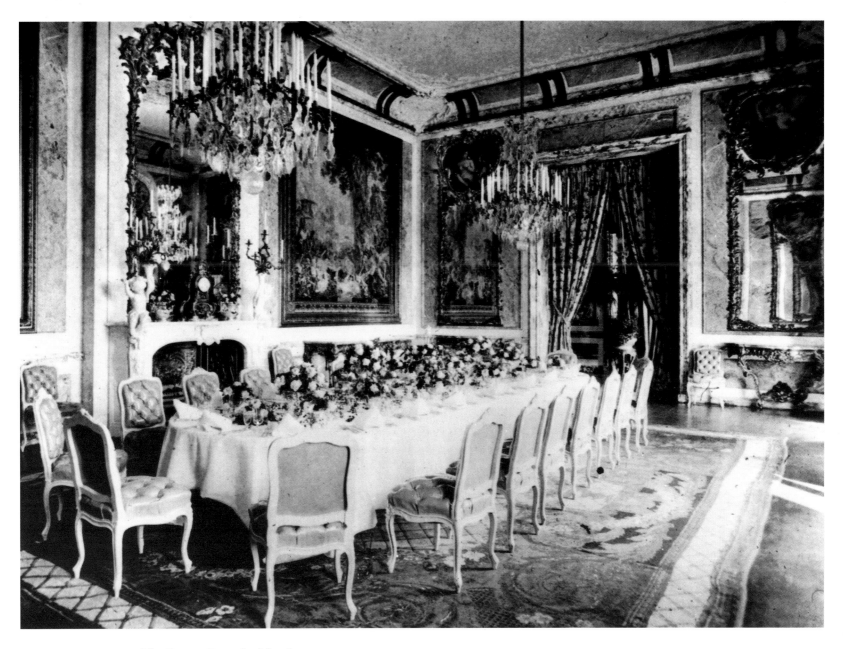

The Dining Room laid for dinner.

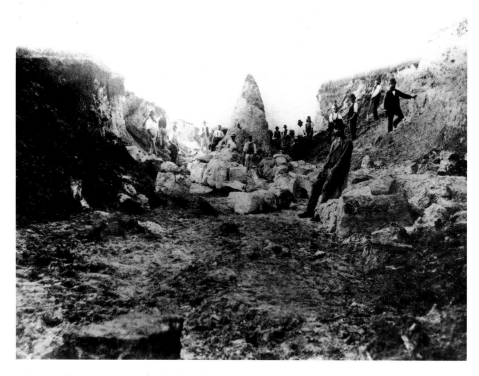

Above: The preparing of the foundations.

Opposite: An early view of Waddesdon Manor.

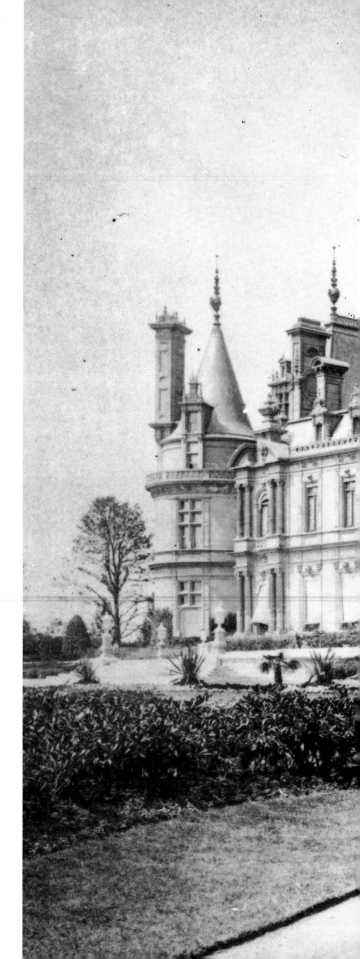

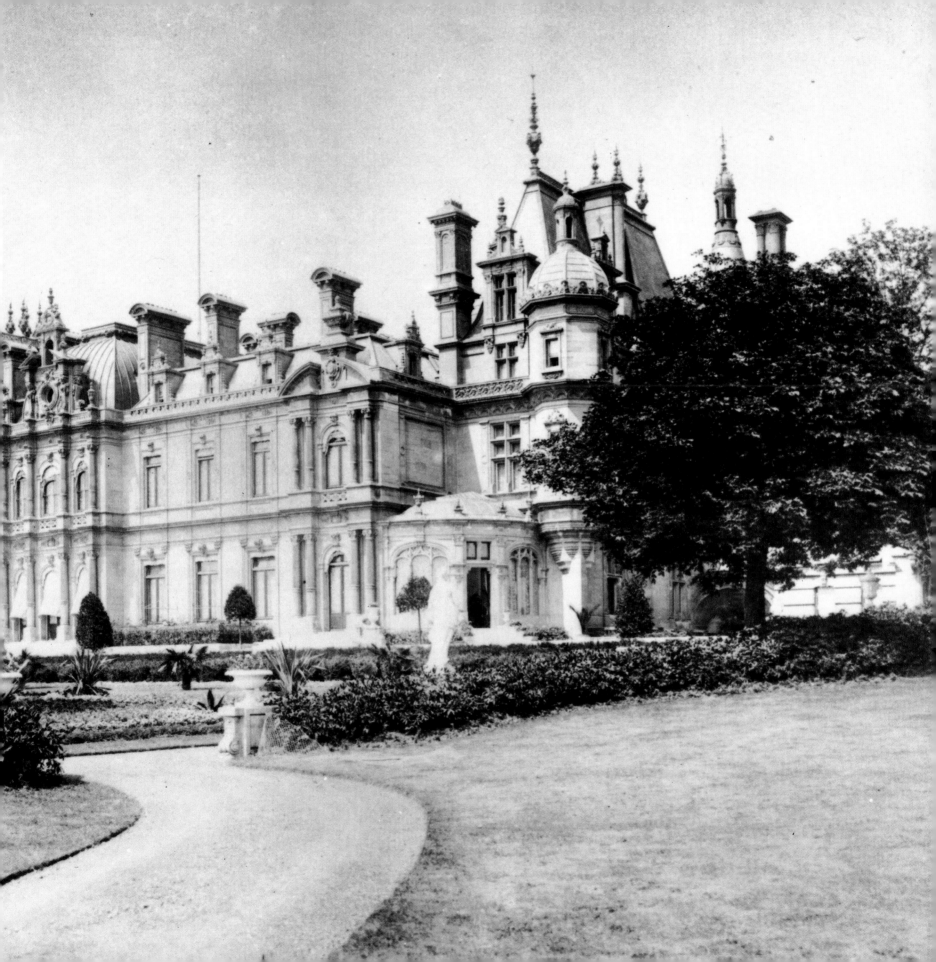

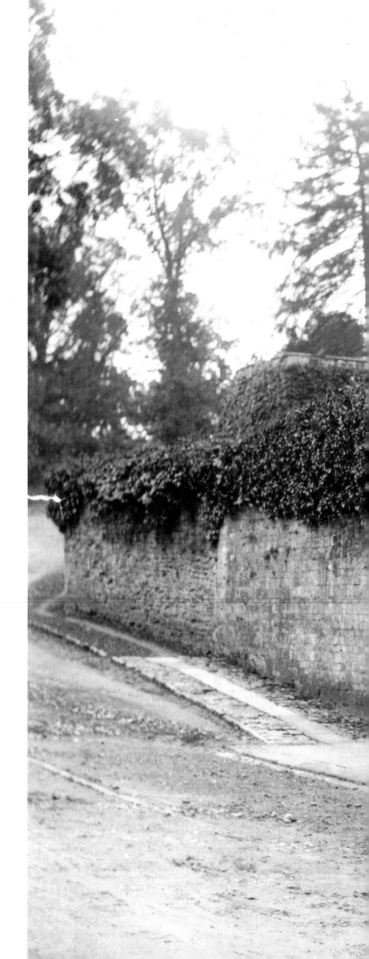

DYRHAM PARK

BATH, AVON

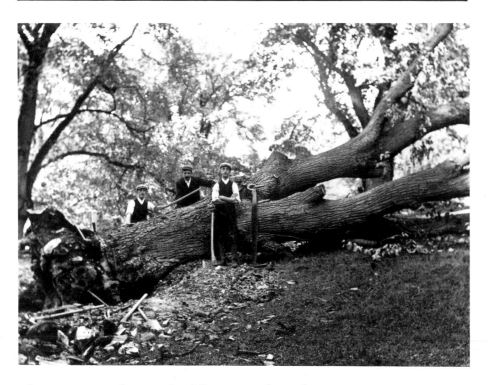

Above: Estate workmen with a fallen tree in the park.

Opposite: A rough shooting party. Left to right: George Blathwayt, Margaret Blathwayt, Mr Vesey, Taudy (keeper), Robert Blathwayt.

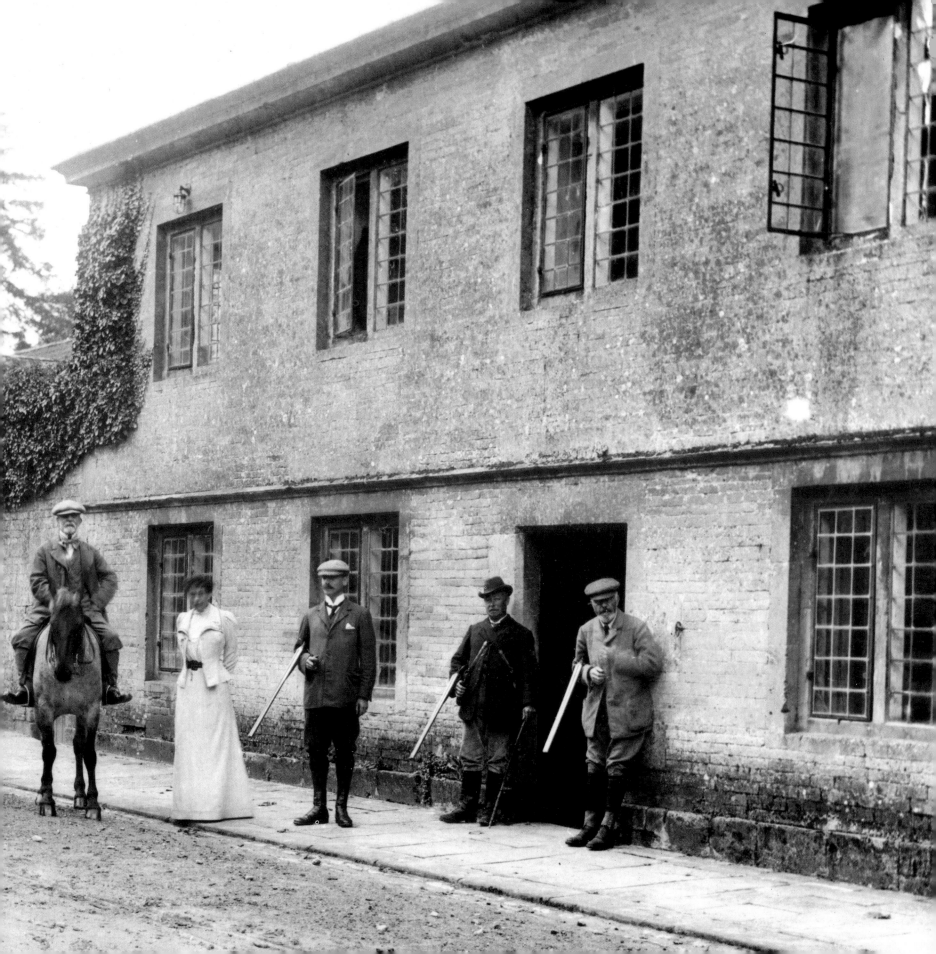

On Friday 1 June 1716, the traveller Dudley Ryder set out from Bath on a picnic accompanied by his friend Mr Powell. 'Mr Powell and I,' he wrote in his diary, 'prepare matters for our journey today to Mr Blathwayt's with the ladies. Hired a chaise and a pair of horses for which we gave 10s and 4s for the chaise. We set out about 11 o'clock. Upon the road I was very uneasy to see Mr Powell so much taken notice of more than myself. Mr Blathwayt's house is a very handsome one very well furnished with pictures and good rich beds, but the gardens are the most pleasant. The situation of them is upon several hills that entertain the eyes with a variety of prospects. The parterre runs along between them with a pretty canal in the middle at the end of which there are several fountains and a cascade from a very steep hill of 224 steps, the finest in England except the Duke of Devonshire's. We saw all the waterworks play which were very agreeable and delightful. At one side of the gardens there is a wilderness of high large trees in which there are a great many agreeable shades. In one of them we made our dinner of some cold things we brought and sat down upon the grass for two or three hours. We gave the gardener 5s and the woman that showed the house the same.'

William Blathwayt, nicknamed 'the Elephant' by one of his friends, on account of his rather ponderous manner, was a high-flying civil servant who had made in 1686, a judicious marriage to an heiress, Mary Wynter, the possessor of a house and estate at Dyrham in Gloucestershire. If it was a marriage of convenience, fate soon played an even more convenient and speedy hand, killing off Blathwayt's father-in-law in 1688, and both his mother-in-law and wife in November 1691, leaving him in sole control of the Wynter estate. He at once began work on a series of enlargements and alterations that were to continue throughout his life and were to raise the status of Dyrham from that of Tudor manor house to something more akin to palace. He first employed an unknown French architect, Samuel Hauduroy, to build a new west front with projecting wings and pavilions, the most northerly of which is joined to the church by a covered walkway. The result is a charming grouping of house and church which is almost the ideal image of the English country house. Blathwayt, being a businessman, no doubt chose Hauduroy because he was cheap. Indeed he complained in one letter that during the winter of 1692–3 he had been expected each day to rise two hours before dawn and draw plans until two o'clock the following morning, for which slavery he had been paid no more than ten pounds, four of which were for his travelling expenses.

Seven years later Blathwayt, by then King's Secretary of State, was richer and grander, and his ambitions had grown accordingly. He thus employed the Comptroller of the Royal Works, William Talman, architect of the south front of Chatsworth, to build him an altogether more monumental east front with stables on one side and a great greenhouse on the other. The result is that Dyrham has the curious appearance of two houses built back to back. Other than the formal gardens being transformed into parkland in the Nineteenth Century, little has subsequently changed at Dyrham which – apart from a short period from 1938 to 1946, when it was let to Lady Islington – remained in the Blathwayt family till 1956, when it was acquired by the National Trust.

Opposite: A corner of the Ante Hall.

Overleaf: The west front, 1875.

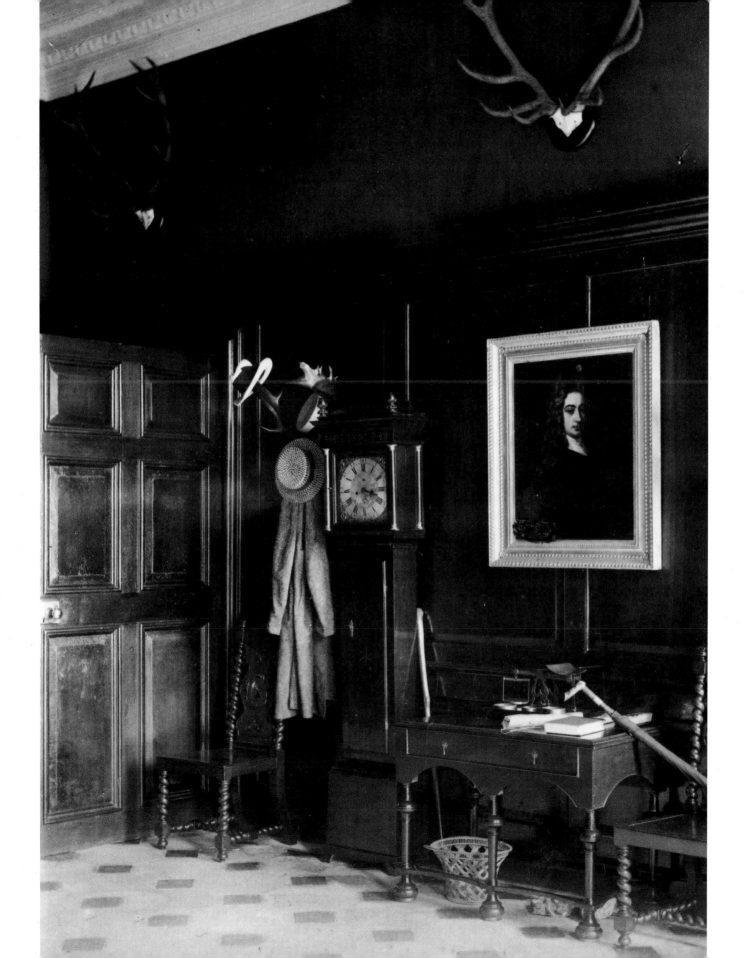

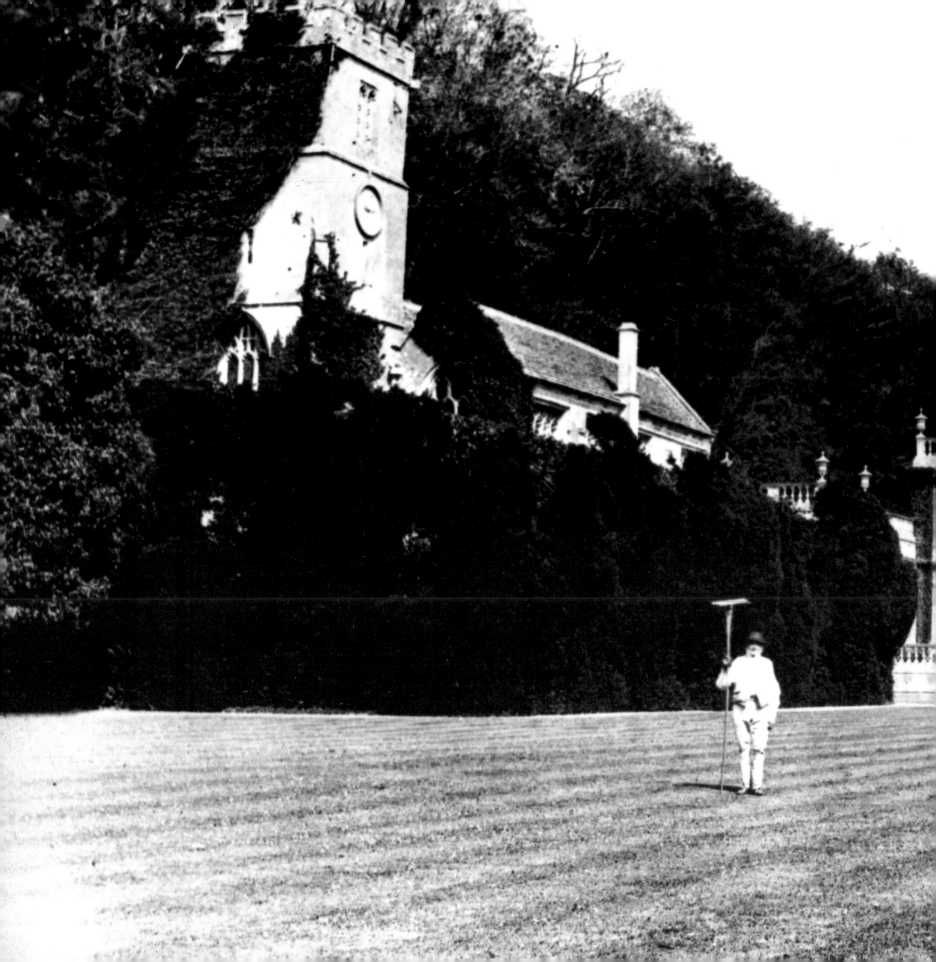

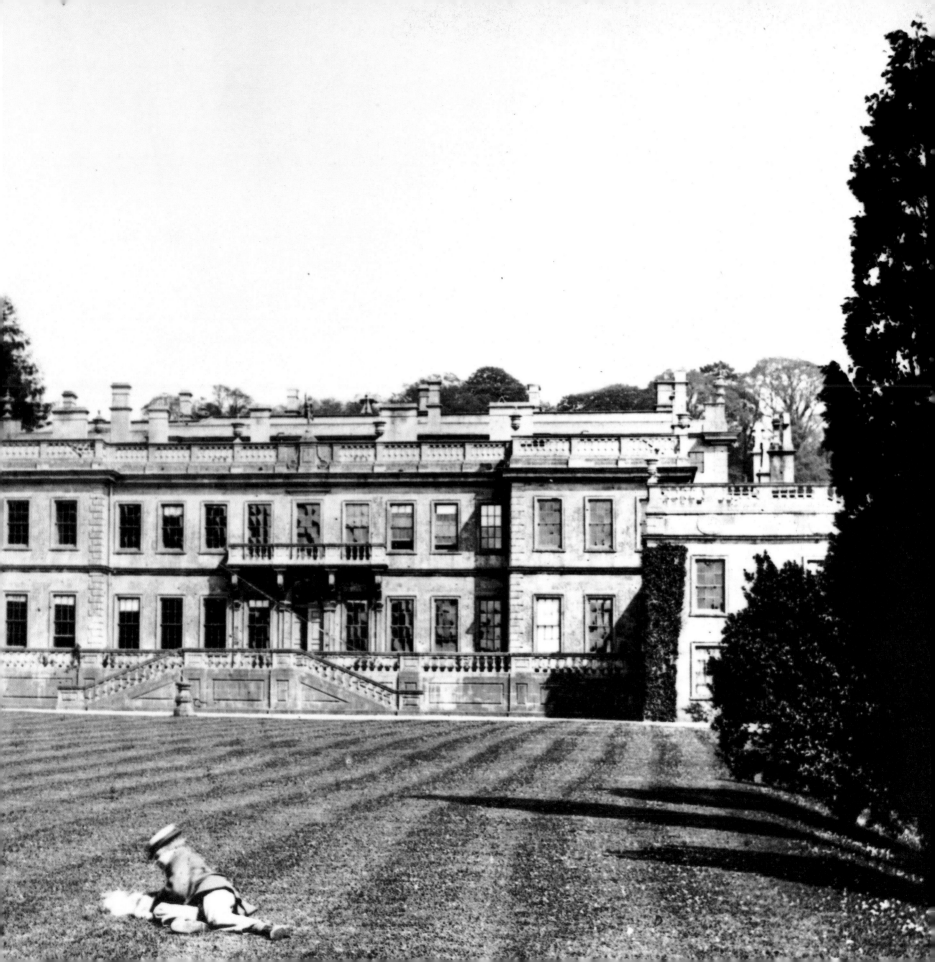

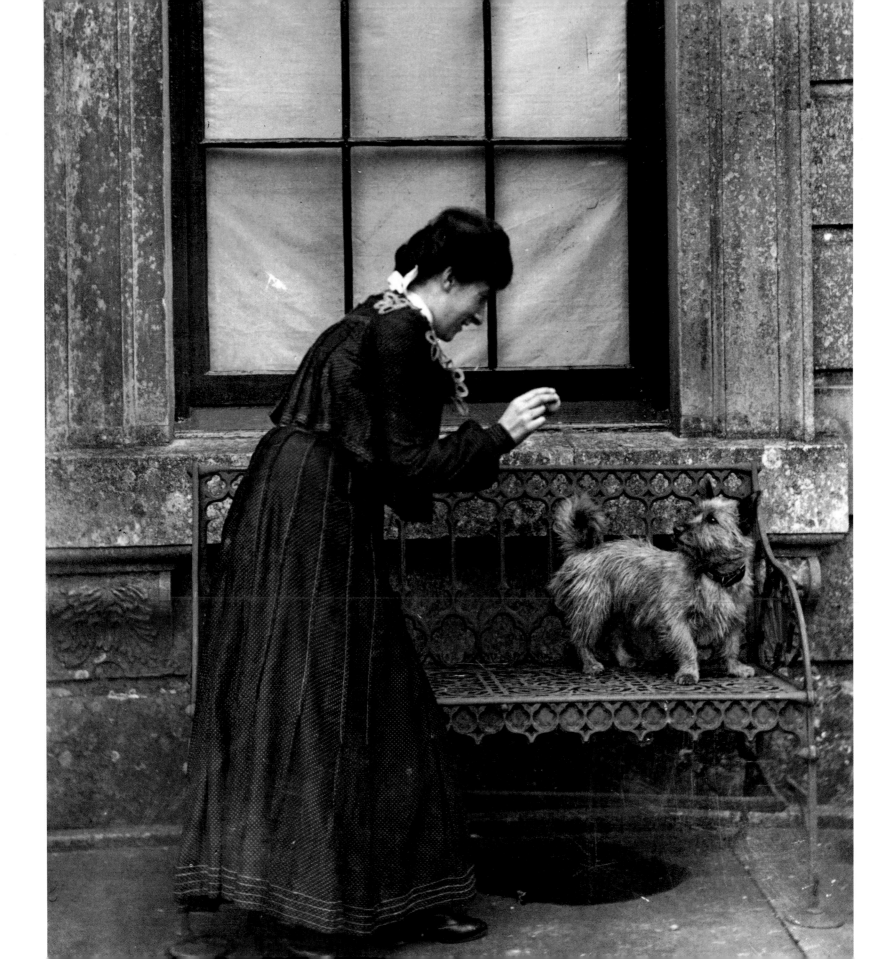

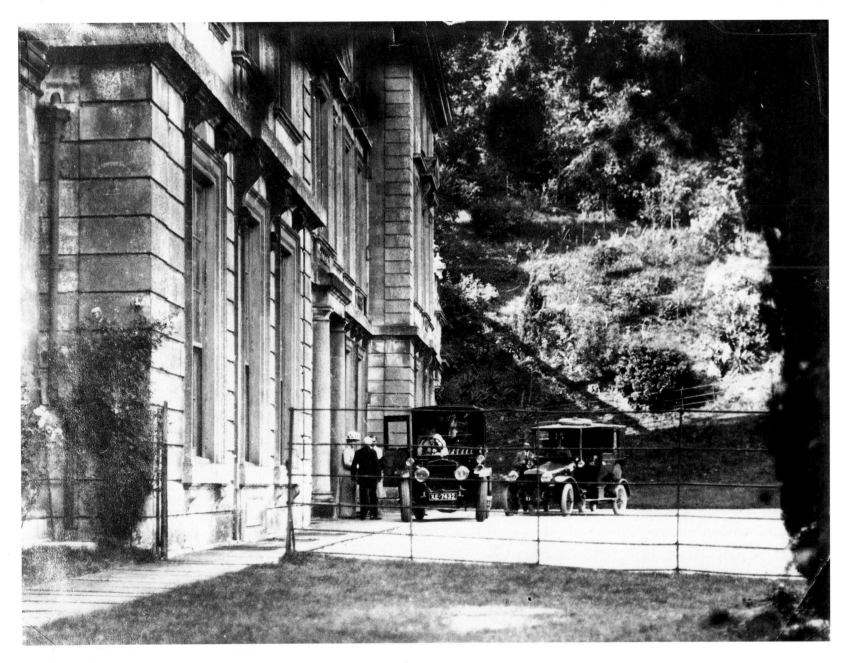

Above: A visit to Dyrham by Queen Mary.

Left: A Blathwayt lady with her terrier.

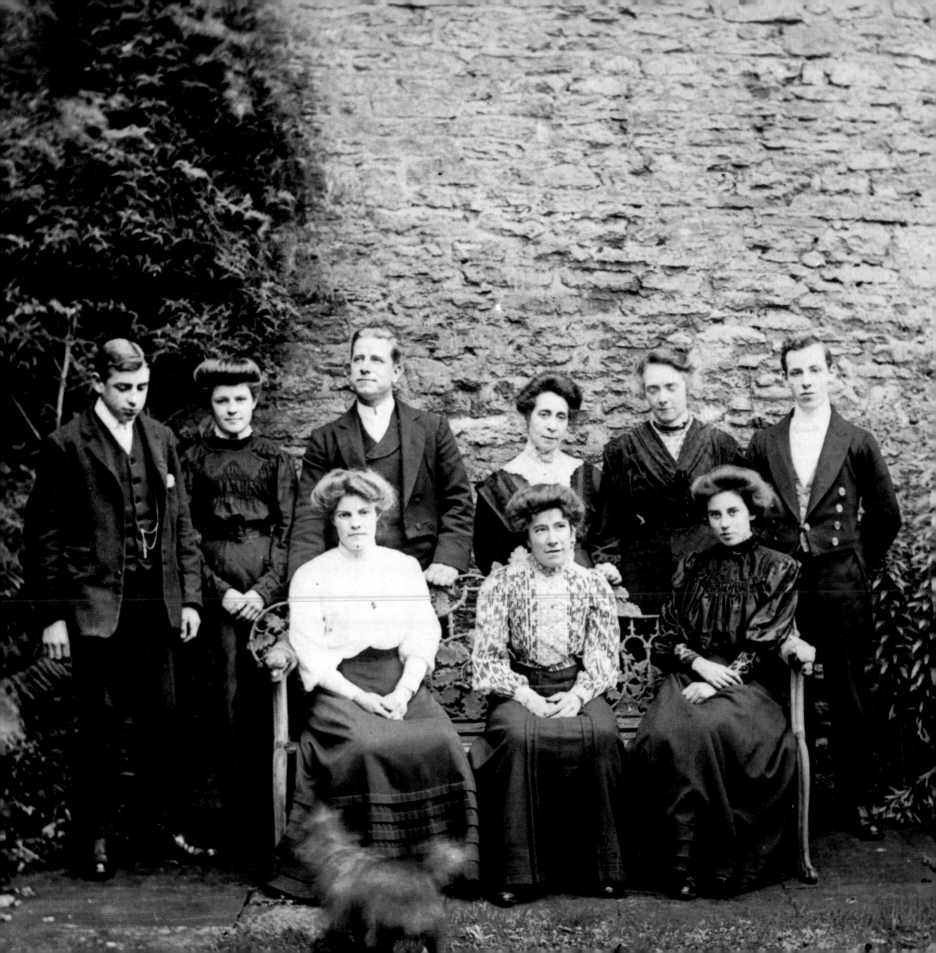

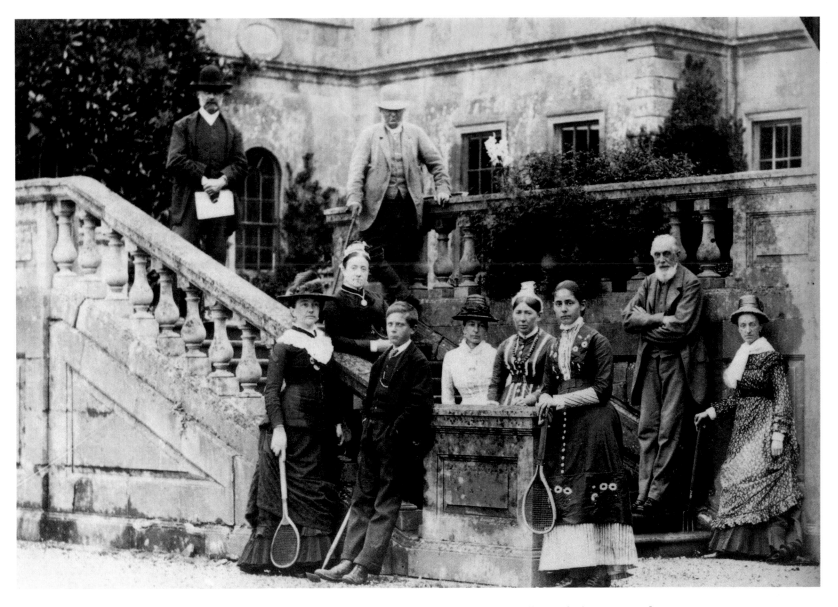

Above: The Blathwayt family c.1880, at the time of Captain George William Blathwayt (standing in light bowler at the back).

Left: A group of household servants.

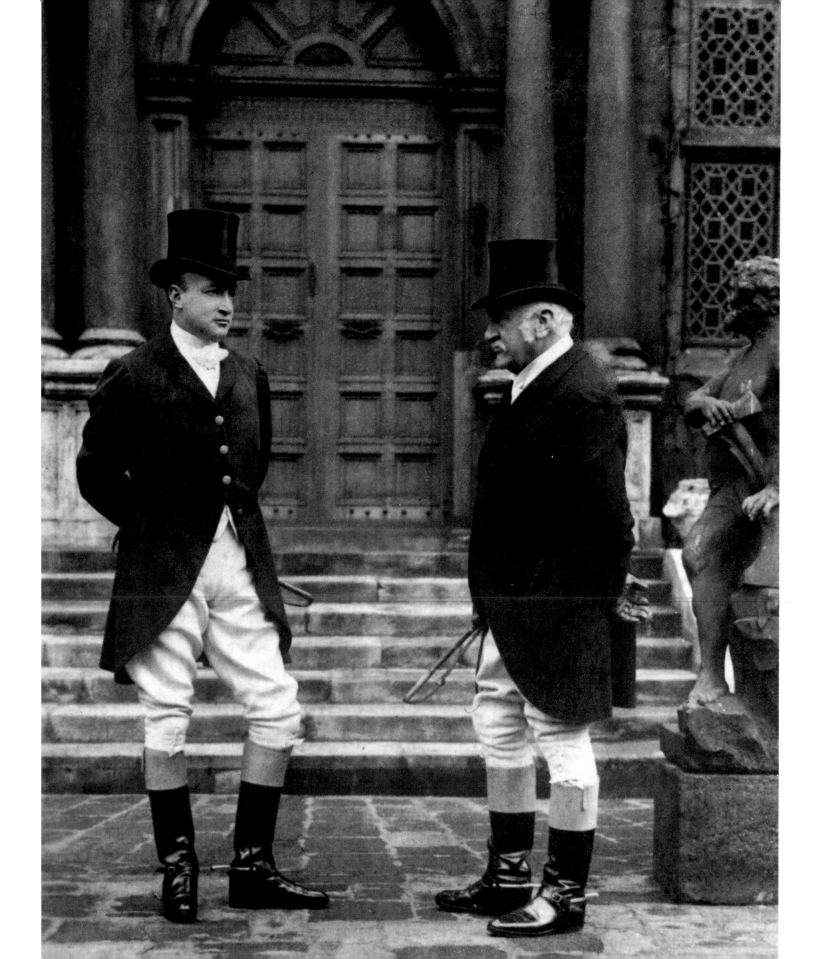

TREASURER'S HOUSE

CHAPTER HOUSE STREET, YORK

It would be easy to have a superficial knowledge of York without ever coming across the Treasurer's House, tucked away as it is in a quiet corner between the Minster and the city walls, overshadowed by the Chapter House and choir. It is a treat to stumble upon it quite by accident, and something of a surprise since it has the air of a country house, built in the Seventeenth and Eighteenth Centuries. Yet its origins go back much further. The first Treasurer's House dated from the end of the Eleventh Century, while the discovery of the remains of a Roman column in the basement shows the site itself to have been built on since the earliest times. Much of what one sees today is a restoration carried out in *c.* 1900 by the architect Temple Moore on behalf of the Yorkshire industrialist Frank Green who bought and rescued it in 1897, when it was divided up into three houses. A wealthy bachelor and dandy, Frank Green employed a large household and was very keen on royal visits that might establish him in higher society. He lived there from 1898 to 1930, when he presented it to the National Trust, along with his fine collection of period furniture and pictures. He never, however, lost his interest and its upkeep, and watched over the new guardians like a hawk, as James Lees-Milne discovered when he visited him in April 1943.

'The old tyrant lay in a large four-poster, wearing a striped dressing-gown and a woollen nightcap with a bobble on the end of a string. The bobble bounced up and down his nose as he spoke. His face is that of a rugged, wicked John Bull ... He dismissed the subject of Culverthorpe, which was the purpose of my visit, and concentrated on the Treasurer's House, York. Was he to understand that someone had dared, had dared to shift the furniture in one of the rooms? Did I not realize that he had put little studs in the floors to mark the precise spot on which every single piece of furniture in the house was to stand? I did. Then no piece of furniture was ever to be shifted therefrom. He looked me full between the eyes in an accusatory manner. I flinched under the awful gaze. "There!" he cried out, "*you* are guilty. I knew it," and the bobble on the string flew around his cheeks and on to his mouth. In a rage he blew it up again. In actual fact I was not guilty. I hadn't been to the house for ages. "Mark my words," he went on, "I am an old man. I may not have very long to live. But I warn you that, if ever you so much as move one chair leg again, I will haunt you till your dying day." And he wagged a skinny finger under my face. I slunk off, chastened, with my tail between my legs. The taxi driver who was waiting for me said "You look as though you had seen a ghost, sir." "I have," I said.'

Frank Green (right) and his brother dressed for hunting.

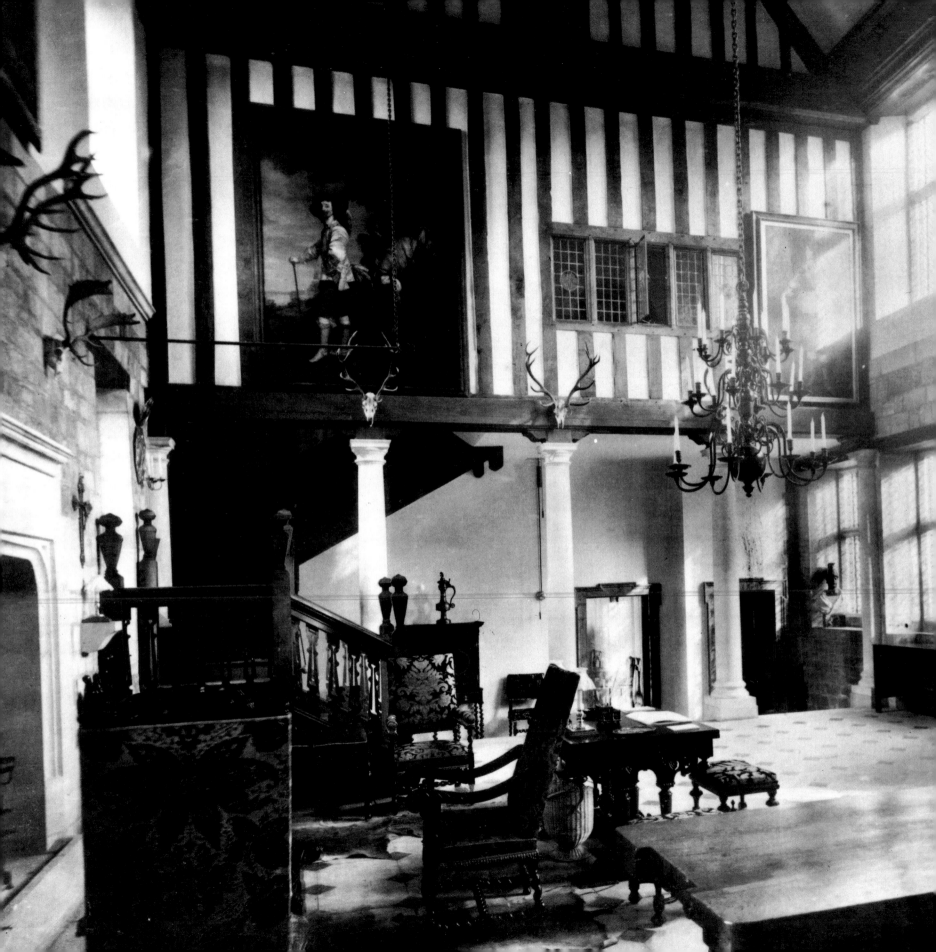

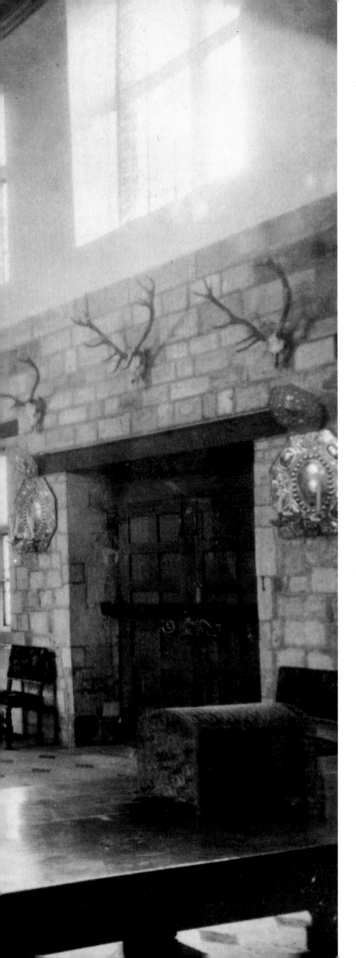

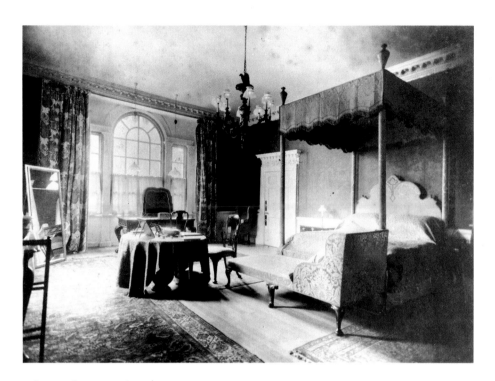

Above: The Queen's Room.

Left: The Hall.

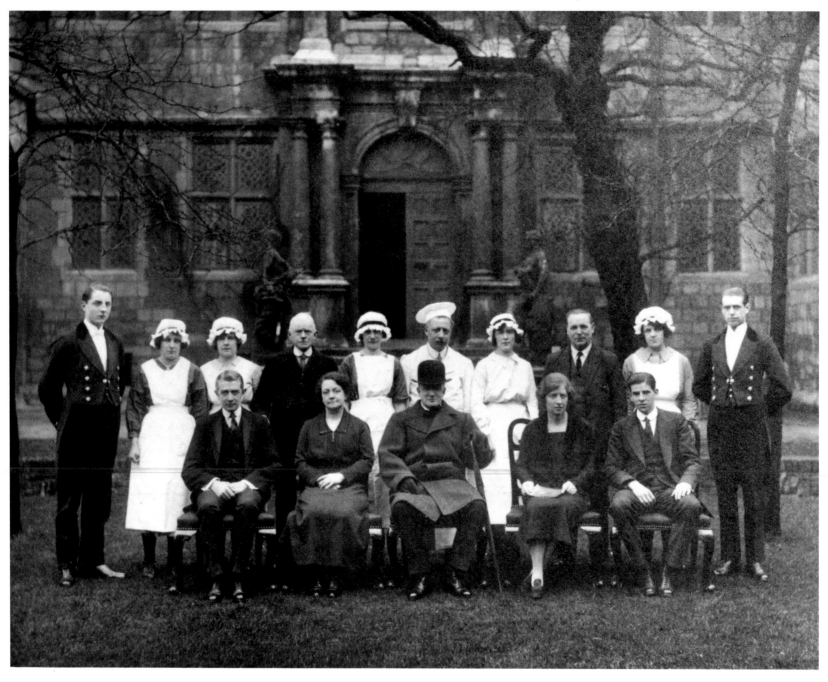

Above: The household staff.

Opposite: The Royal visit of King Edward VII and Queen Alexandra.

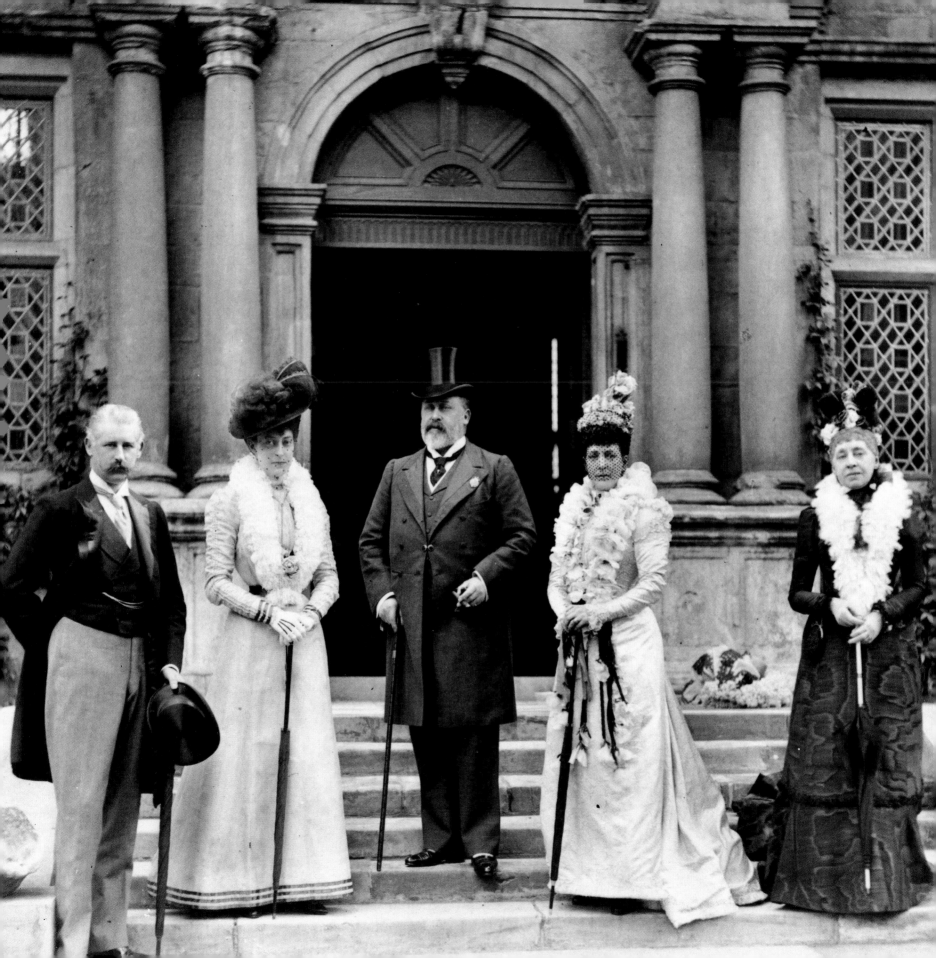

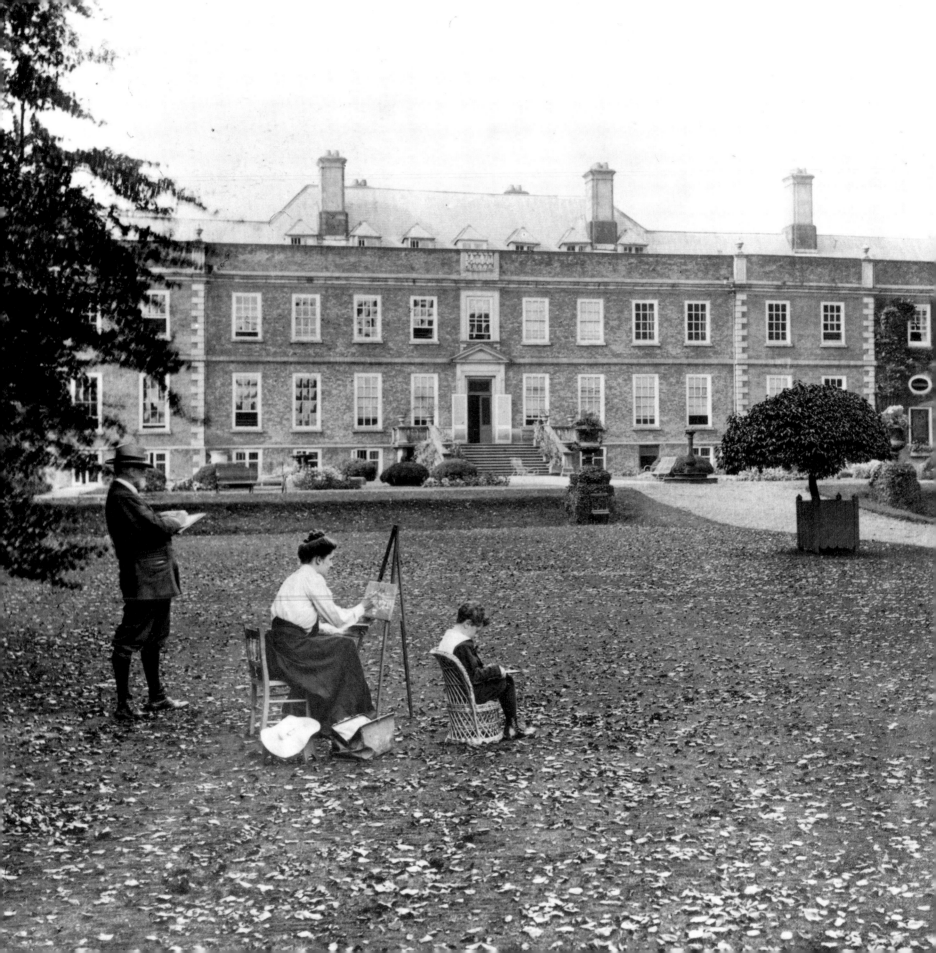

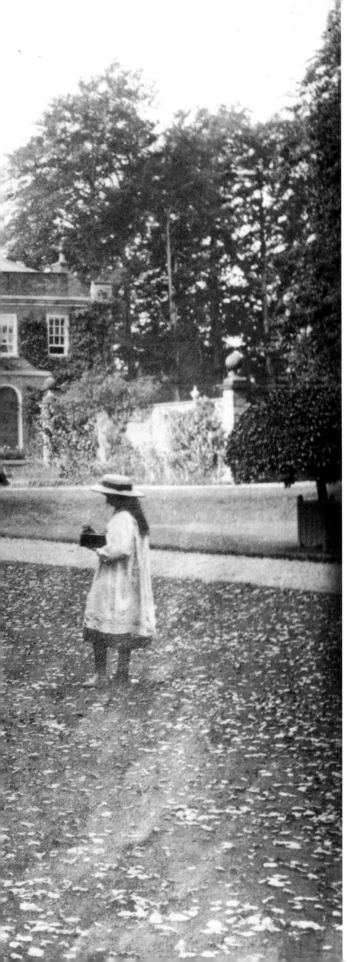

ERDDIG

WREXHAM, CLWYD

The east front of Erddig with a group on the lawn. The man on the left with a beard is Philip Yorke II.

I shall never forget my first of many visits to Erddig. I was staying with friends near by, and we had all been invited to tea by its squire, Philip Yorke. As we passed through the ruined gates and bumped up a drive full of potholes, I realized that it was unlikely to be a run-of-the-mill country house that we were visiting. It was a winter's afternoon and Philip met us on the overgrown front steps, explaining that if we wished to have a look round the house we should hurry up before the light failed. We shuffled round the gloomy, icy-cold rooms, gasping at the dusty treasures and at the dilapidation. In one room, for example, all that stood beneath the open sky was the huge canopy of a magnificent bed, on whose delicate Chinese silk cover buckets were arranged to catch the water that dripped through. Down in the servants' hall – by now illuminated by candles, the house being devoid of electricity – we ate a huge and welcome tea prepared by Philip's friend Mr Heyhoe (to whom he constantly referred as Hoo-ha). After tea I put on some gloves and played the organ in the Hall.

Erddig's early history was inauspicious, to say the least. The house was commissioned in 1684 by Joshua Edisbury, High Sheriff of Denbighshire, and was designed by a mason named Thomas Webb of Middlewich, who built him a plain square house, enlivened only by a cupola. To finance this and other projects, however, Edisbury had been forced to borrow money at exorbitant interest rates, and he soon found himself in dire financial straits. Before Erddig was even half furnished, he fled to London to avoid his creditors, where he eventually died in obscurity. The property was subsequently bought by a prosperous Master in Chancery, John Meller, who added on wings of his own design at each end, refashioned the garden and indulged his own extravagant tastes by furnishing the house with the rarest textiles and furniture from the very finest London cabinet makers. It was inherited by his nephew, Simon Yorke, on his death in 1733, since when it passed by direct descent within the Yorke family till 1973, when the last squire, Philip Yorke III, gave the estate to the National Trust.

When I first used to go there, Philip talked incessantly about the Trust. The reason that the house was then in a terminal state of decay was that his elder brother, Simon, had long since given up trying to cope with the problems which beset him on all sides, in particular the fact that mines being worked directly beneath the house were causing drastic subsidence. He became a complete recluse, living at Erddig with only a housekeeper, Miss Lloyd, to look after him, and a series of strays which she rescued from the local dogs' home. When on one occasion the local postman complained that one of these animals, a particularly bad-tempered specimen called Michael, had bitten him, Simon took the dog's side and decided that thereafter the mail would never again be delivered by the Post Office, but would instead be left at one of the lodges. He fell out with everybody and the house fell down around him. When Philip inherited in May 1966, he at once moved into the house, which had no telephone or electricity. Until a telephone and alarm system were installed, he set up camp in a different room every night, reading by the light of candles reflected in eighteenth-century silver sconces and always listening out for the sound of one of his home-made burglar alarms – such as a table stacked with empty dog-food tins, with one end of a piece of string attached to the table leg and the other to a hook on the passage door. With the help of various estate workers, he instituted his own emergency rescue plan for the house, protecting the furniture from beetle, mending as much of the roof as possible, and importing sheep and goats to act as gardeners. This gave the house valuable breathing space until it was finally taken over by the Trust.

The Cathedral Aisle. 'The gem of Erthig is it's wood,' wrote Charles Apperley in My Life *and* Times. *Perhaps the most impressive feature of the landscaping was the planting of an avenue of beech on top of a narrow ridge. Since this was flanked on both sides by dense woodland, there was fierce competition for light, causing the beeches to grow to a great height. Hence the name.*

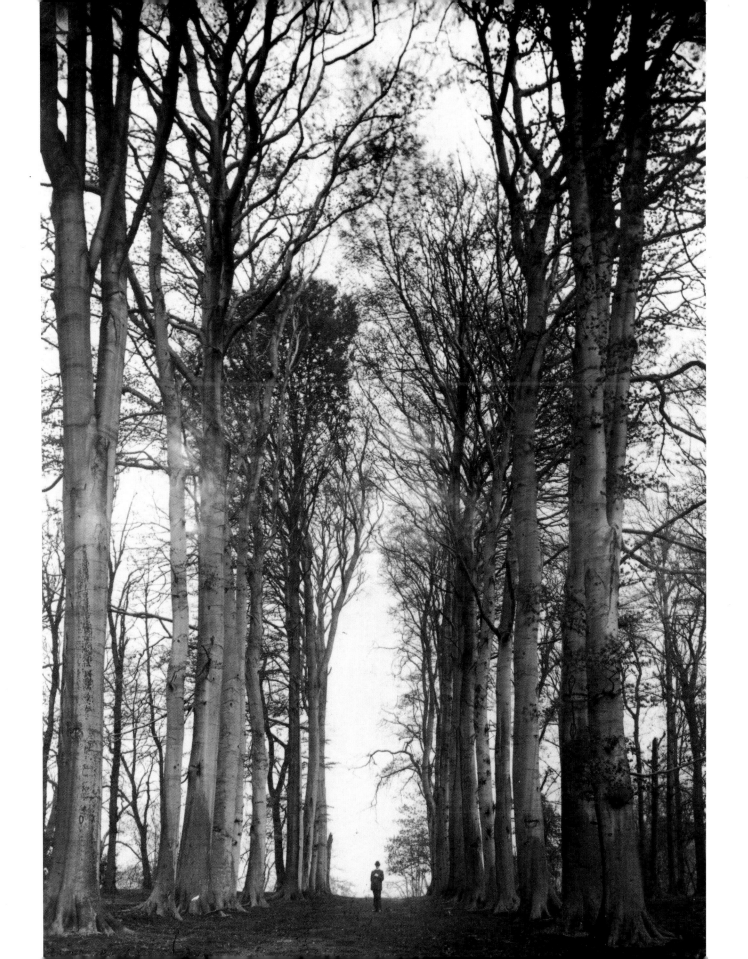

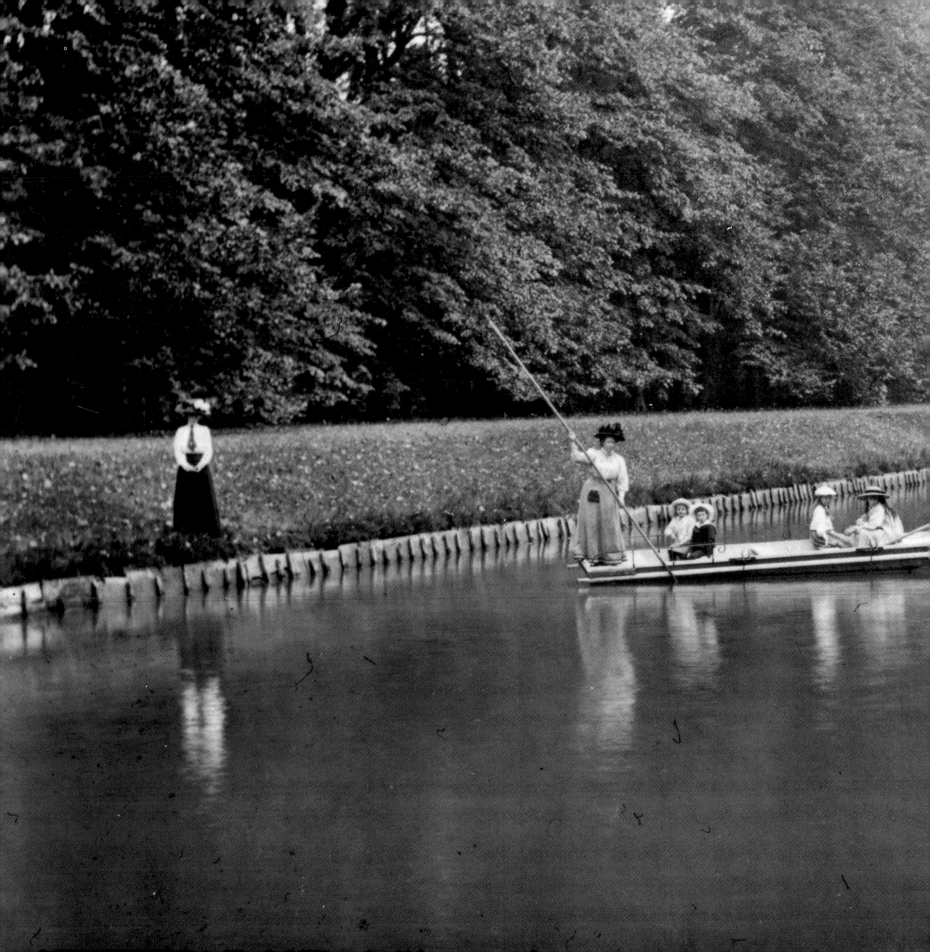

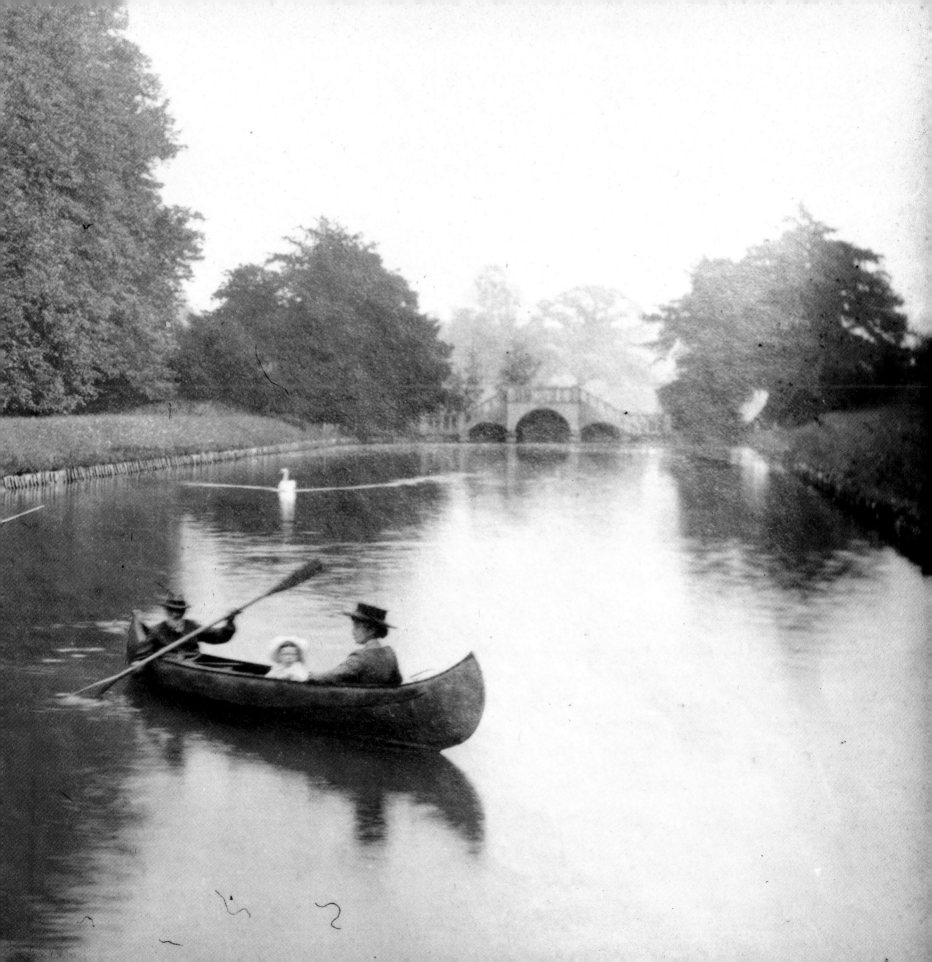

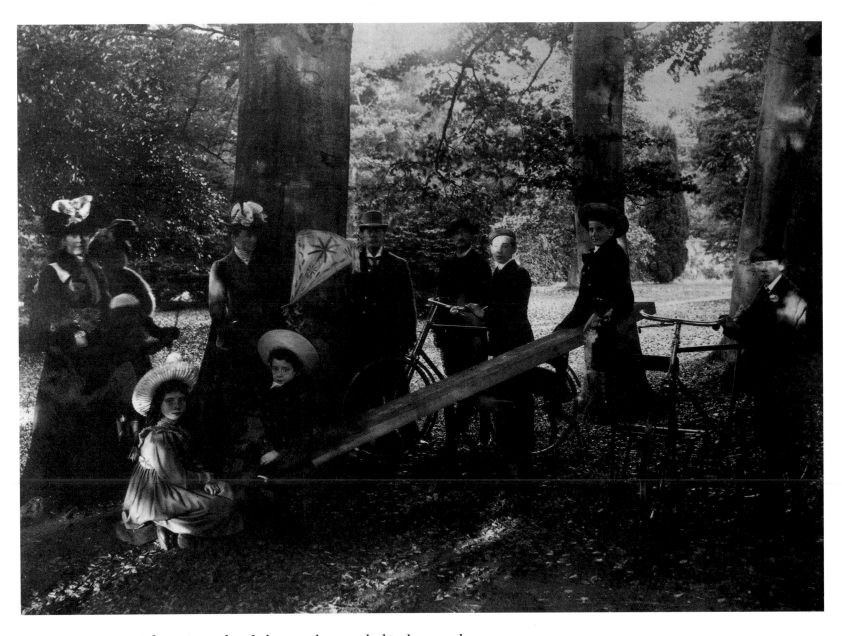

Above: An unidentified group photographed in the grounds.

Opposite: Philip Yorke II on stilts in the garden at Erddig in August 1916. A keen watercolourist, photographer, cyclist and poet, it was he who wrote most of the verses chronicling the lives and duties of the household servants.

Previous page: Punting and canoeing on the canal in the Pleasure Garden.

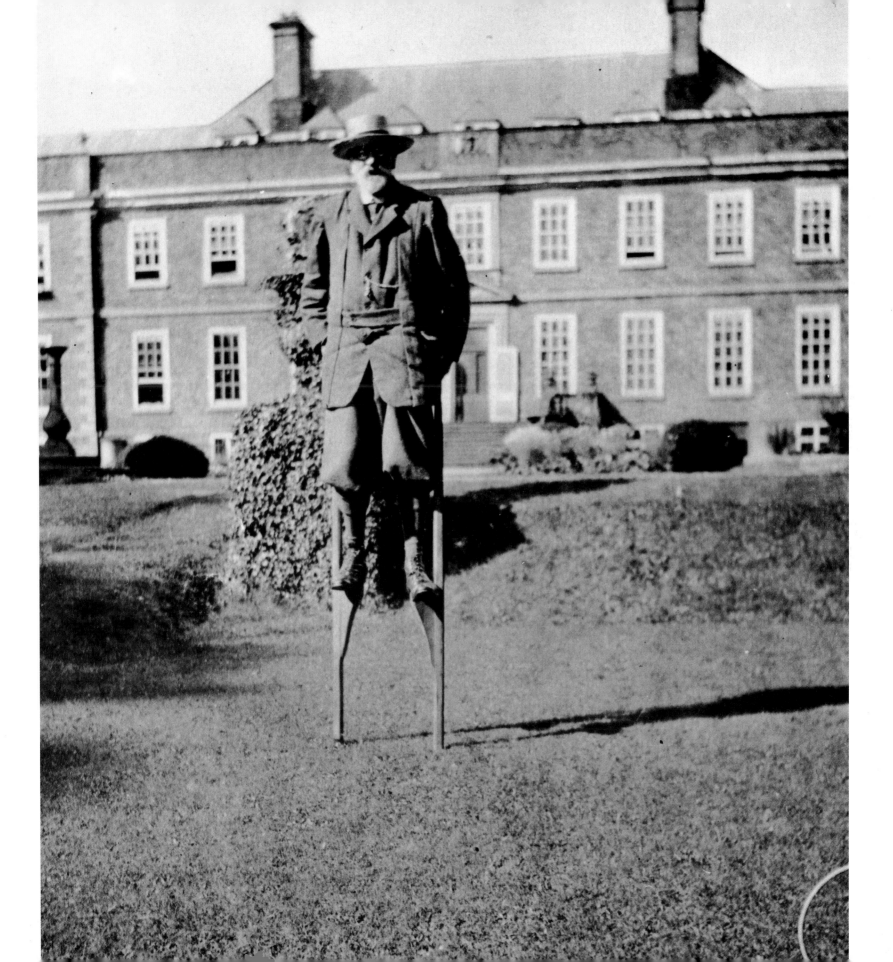

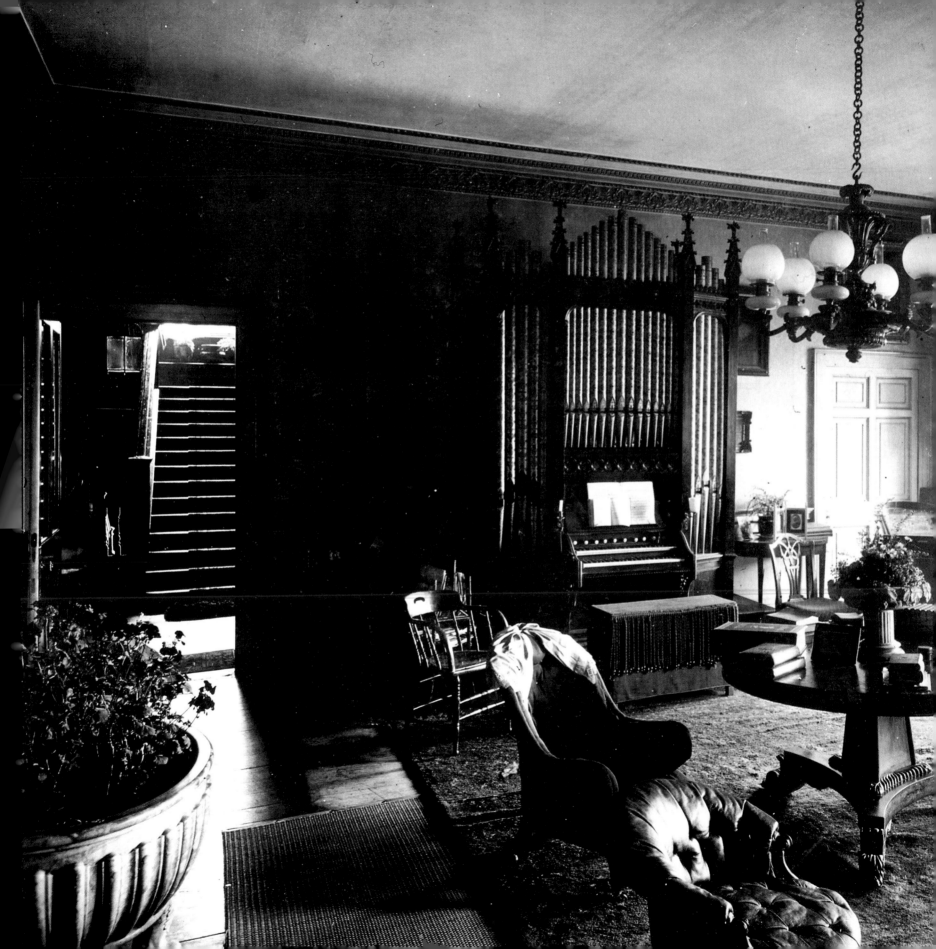

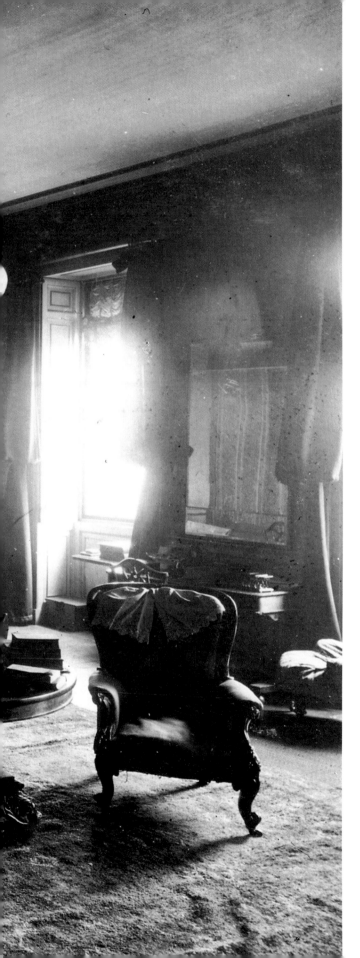

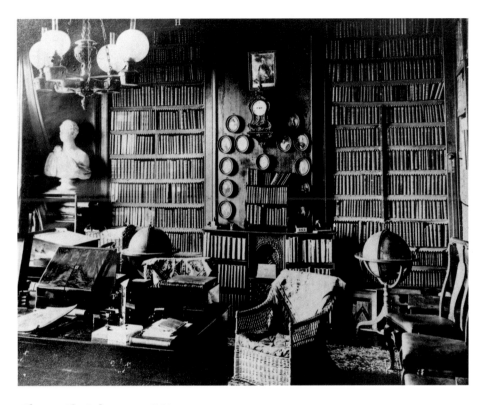

Above: The Library in 1901.

Left: The Entrance Hall, photographed in 1901.

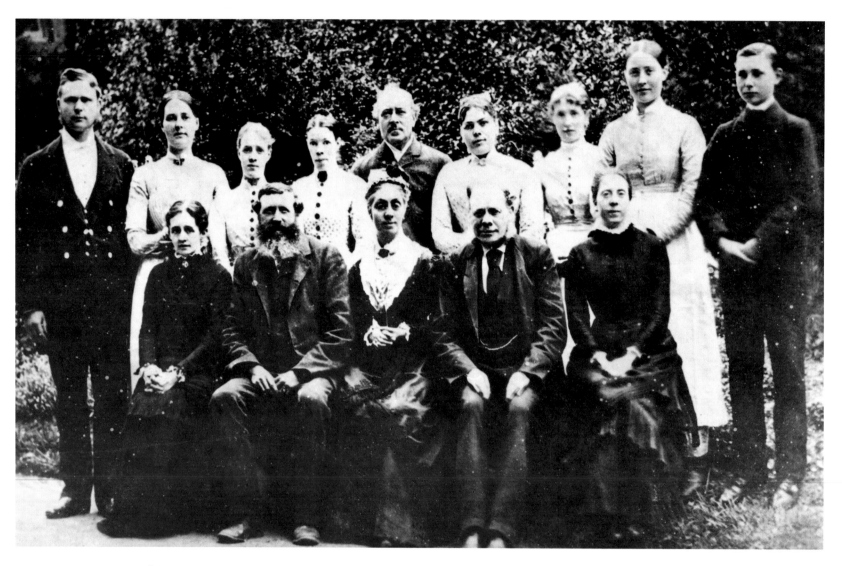

Above: Servants at Erddig in 1887. The bearded gardener Alexander Stirton was to marry Eliza Sumpter, who is standing behind him, next to Meacock, the coachman. On Stirton's left are Harriet Rogers, the housekeeper, and George Dickinson, the butler.

Opposite, clockwise from top left: Mary Webster, housekeeper, mid-Nineteeth Century; Albert Gillam, head gardener; Miss Brown, housekeeper, 1907–14; John Jones, carpenter, 1878–1911.

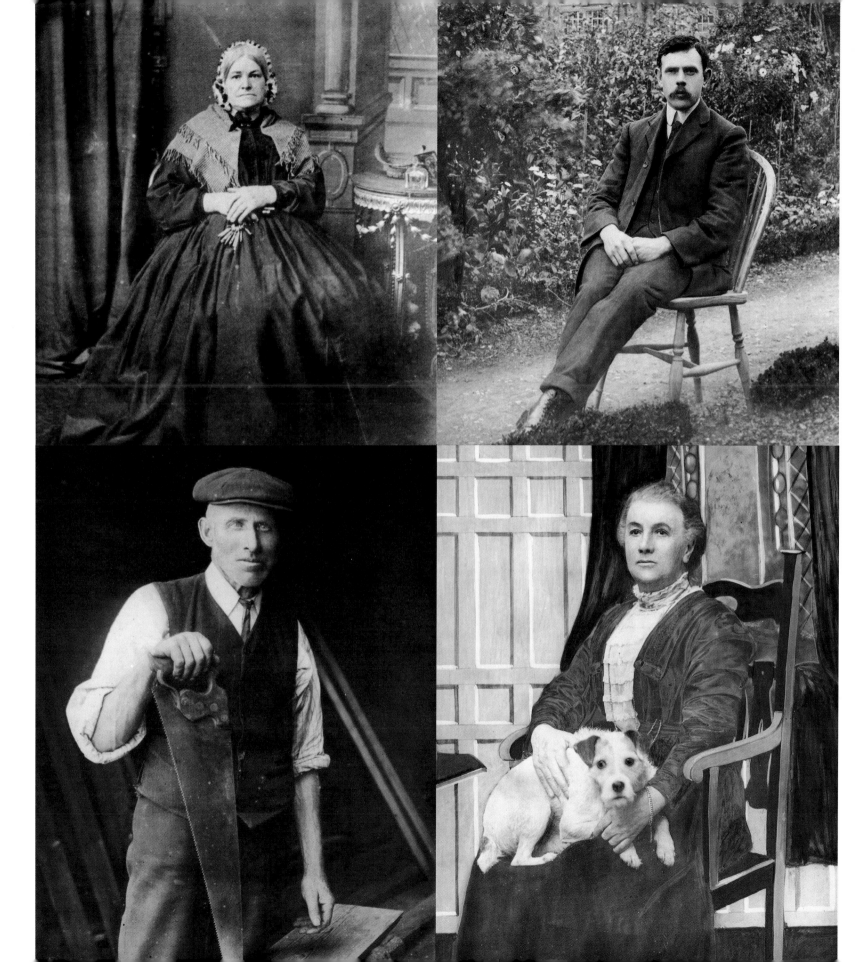

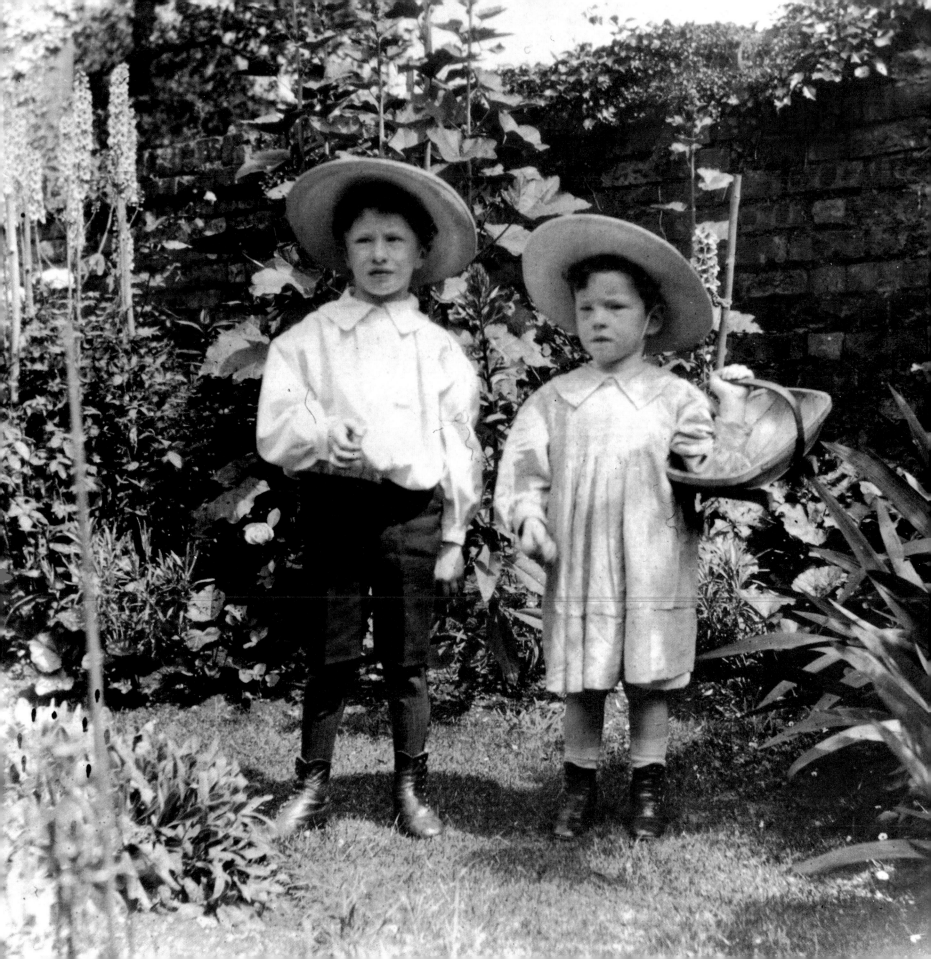

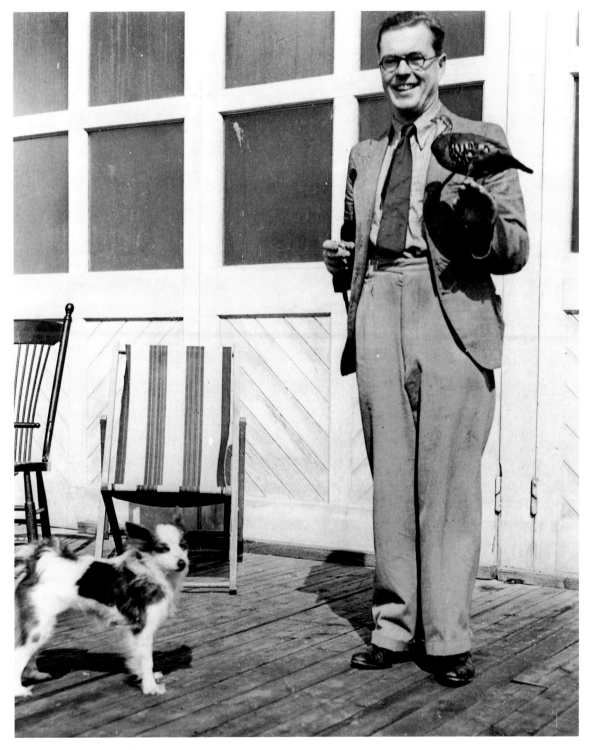

Above: Philip Yorke III, the last squire of Erddig.

Left: Simon and Philip Yorke dressed in the typical attire of Edwardian children. Both grew up to be eccentric.

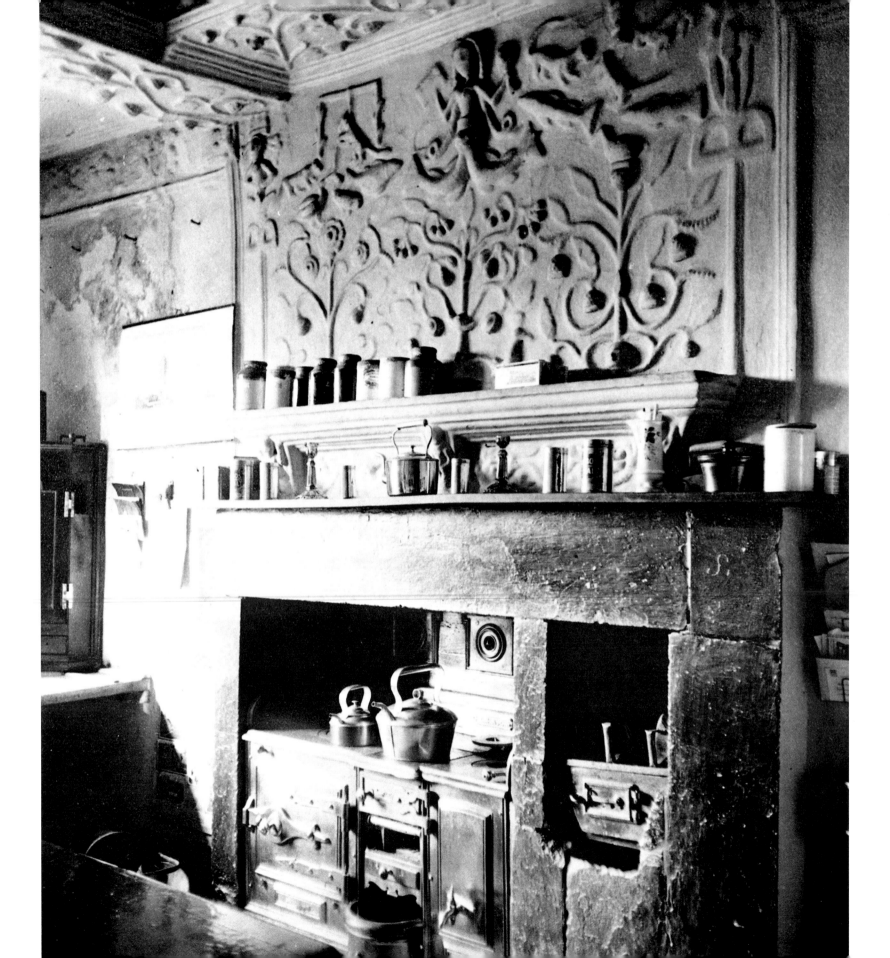

WESTWOOD MANOR

BRADFORD-ON-AVON, WILTSHIRE

Westwood is a hauntingly beautiful English manor house which has survived through the ages virtually unscathed. Its history divides into three periods, none later than the Seventeenth Century. The earliest part goes back to 1480 when Thomas Culverhouse, a prosperous farmer, built himself a house on the site of an earlier building, which may have been the home of the parish priest. Then in about 1518, Thomas Horton, a rich West Country cloth merchant, bought the property and enlarged it, his two best rooms being the Solar, the present sitting room, whose fireplace still bears his initials, and a little panelled room above it. Finally, a century after Horton's arrival, the last of his descendants, Toby Horton, sold Westwood to his brother-in-law, John Farewell, who made further alterations which included the horizontal division of the two-storey hall. He created the two most beautiful rooms in the house, the Great Parlour and the King's Room, both memorable for their superb and exuberant plasterwork. The Farewell connection with the house was severed at the end of the Seventeenth Century, and in the succeeding two hundred years, when it was mostly in the hands of various tenant farmers, Westood sunk into a gradual decline.

It was finally rescued in 1911 when it was bought by Edgar Graham Lister, a Wiltshire antiquarian, for whom it was love at first sight. At that time, as the photographs show, the King's Room was in use as a kitchen, while the Great Parlour had been divided into two, with one half being used as an apple store. Lister, who was a man of considerable taste, set about a sensitive programme of restoration, creating a home for himself which was a perfect evocation of the past. 'Each time I come here I am overwhelmed by the perfection of this house,' wrote James Lees-Milne after a visit to Westwood Manor in August 1942. 'Everything Ted has done to it is in the best possible taste and proves his astonishing, instinctive understanding of the late medieval and Jacobean periods. He has restored the interior porches, the late Gothic mullions and glazing bars, the stucco and stonework, with a restraint and sensitivity which I have never experienced in any English country house of these early dates. Even the patchy rendering of the outside walls, washed over with a primrose to russet harl, rough and broken, with an occasional rambler rose lolloping over the upper windows, is contrived to perfection.' On his death in 1956, Lister bequeathed Westwood Manor to the National Trust.

The east wall of the King's Room when it was in use as a kitchen, 1909.

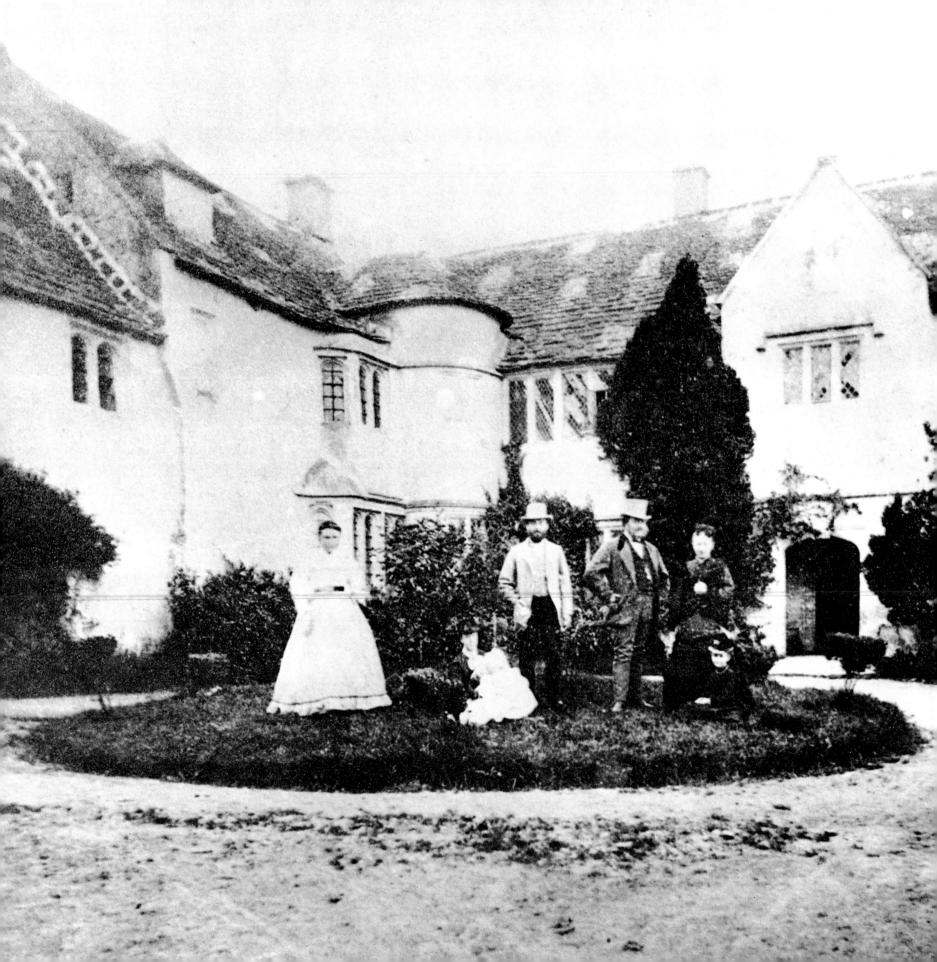

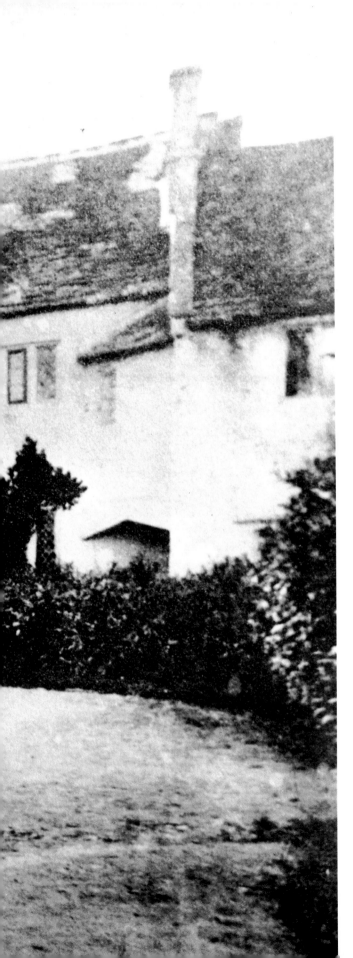

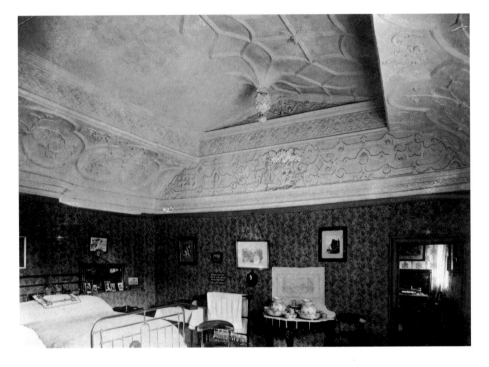

Above: The Great Parlour when it was divided up and one side was used as a bedroom, 1909.

Left: An unknown group in front of the house, c.1860, taken just before the wing on the far right of the photograph was demolished.

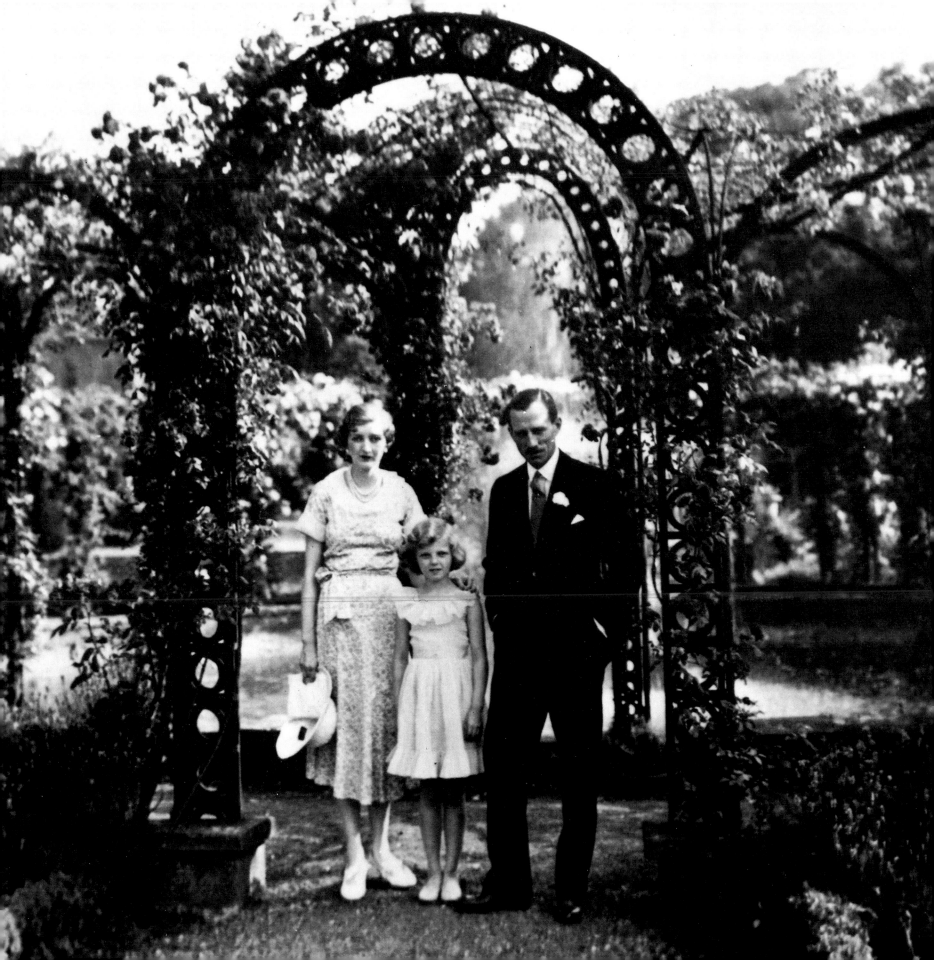

BELTON

GRANTHAM, LINCOLNSHIRE

On 29 October, 1695 the diarist De La Pryme recorded that King William III was 'mighty nobly entertained at Sir John Brownley's . . . Sir John killed twelve fat oxen and 60 sheep besides other victuals for his entertainment . . . The King was exceeding merry and drank freely which was the occasion that when he came to Lincoln he could eat nothing but a mess of milk.' The house where this great feast took place was Belton, the recently completed home of Sir John Brownlow, known as 'Young' Sir John to distinguish him from his great-uncle of the same name. He was the descendant of Richard Brownlow, a shrewd and ambitious London lawyer who had flourished during the reigns of Elizabeth I and James I, and with the enormous salary he earned as Chief Protonotary to the Court of Common Pleas – some £6,000 per annum – had bought himself a country house at Enfield and property in Lincolnshire, including the manor of Belton. Both these estates he had cherished, and on his death, in 1638, his bowels were buried in Enfield Church, while his body was carried to Belton. Here there stood a manor house which 'Young' Sir John found far too modest and old-fashioned when he eventually inherited in 1680, aged nineteen. He therefore decided to demolish it and erect a grand new country house in its place. The work began in March 1685, in the very last days of the reign of Charles II, when the steward at Belton noted in his journal that he 'Gave the Mason to drinck att Laying the first ston on the new house, 5s.'

The style of Belton, with its hipped roof, balustrade and wooden cupola, is Anglo-Dutch, and though no one man is recorded as having been its architect, the likelihood is that it was built by a master mason, William Stanton, from designs provided by Captain William Winde, the gentleman architect who most probably designed Ashdown and whose Combe Abbey, built the previous year for the Earl of Craven, bears a striking resemblance to it. It took three years to build, and is generally regarded as being the finest surviving house of the period. It evidently brought little happiness to its owner, however, for in July 1697 it was reported by Narcissus Luttrell that 'Sir John Brownlow, member of Parliament for Grantham . . . last week shott himself at Mr Freakes in Dorsetshire; but the reason not known.' Though his descendants, in particular the first and second Lord Brownlows, made considerable alterations to both the exterior and the interior of the house between 1776 and 1853, if Sir John were to return to Belton today, he would find it remarkably little changed. This is because between 1867 and 1921 the then Lord Brownlow and his wife, Lady Adelaide Talbot, carried out a brilliant programme of restoration using the elevation engraved in *Vitruvius Britannicus* as their model. Many of the original features which had been removed in previous years, such as the balustrade and the cupola, were replaced; the old formal gardens were recreated, while inside plasterwork was restored to its former glory. The house was acquired by the National Trust in 1984.

The 6th Baron Brownlow, Peregrine Adelbert Cust, and Katherine Lady Brownlow, with their daughter Caroline, 1936.

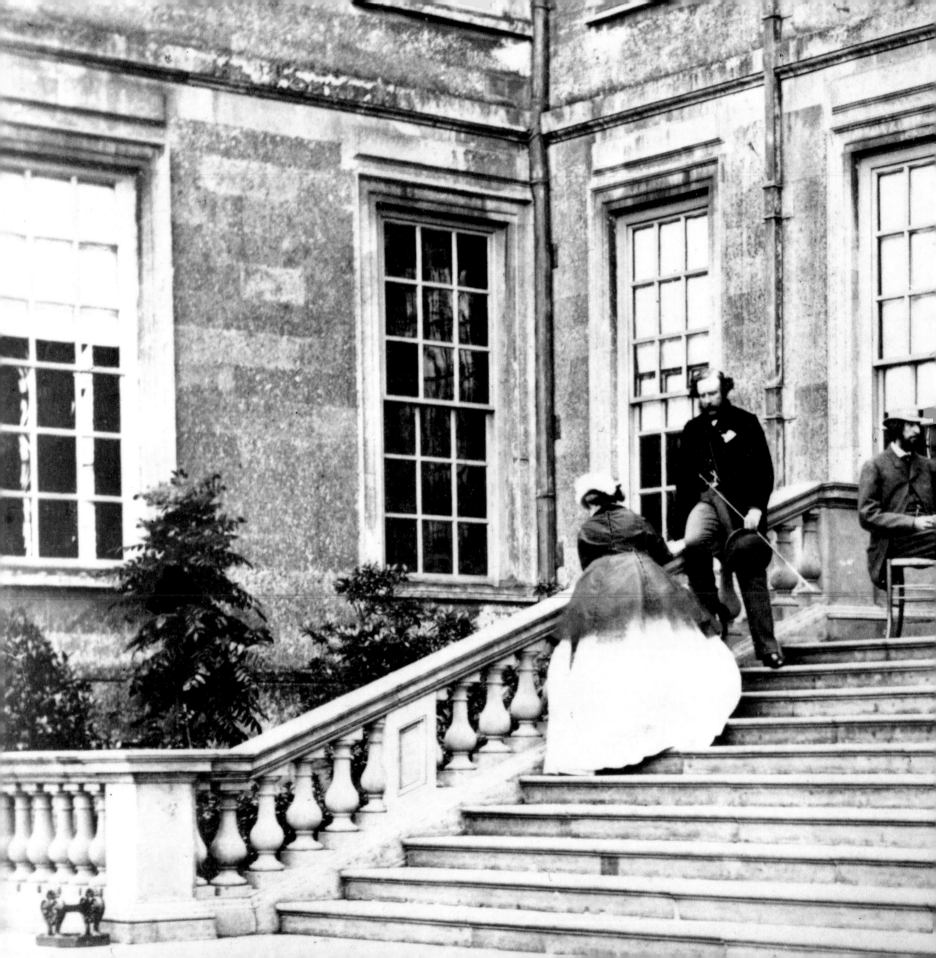

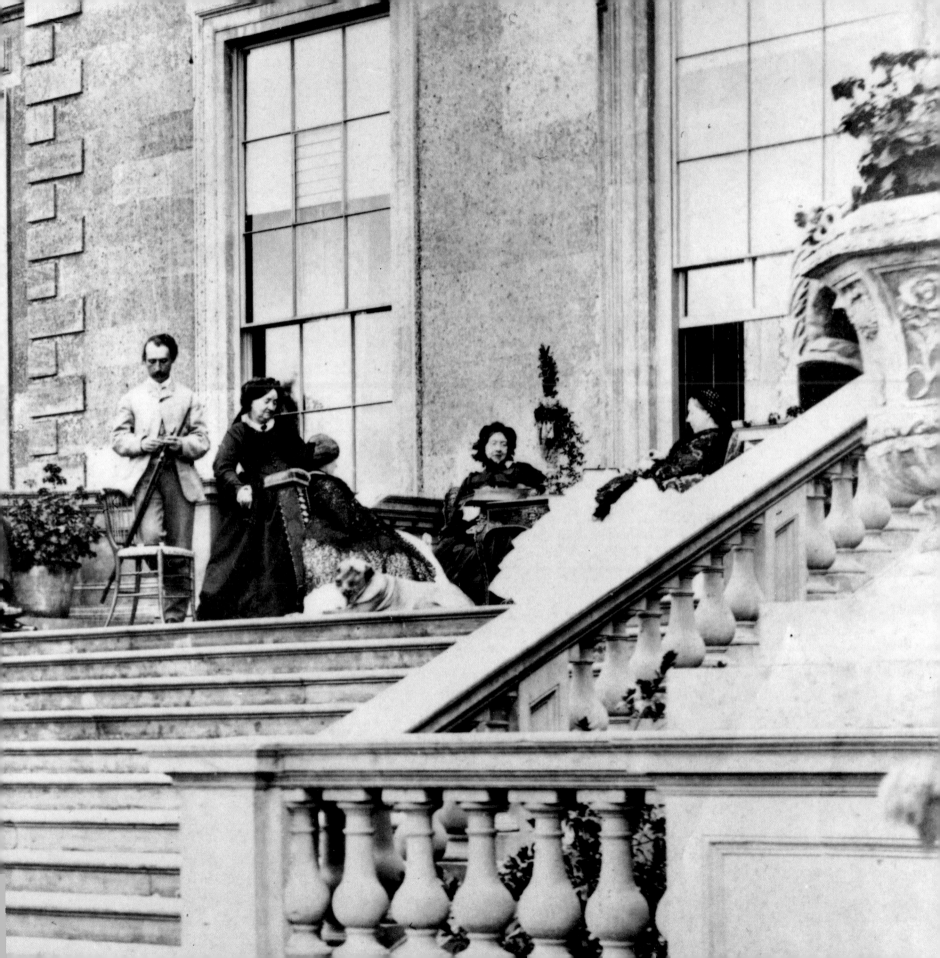

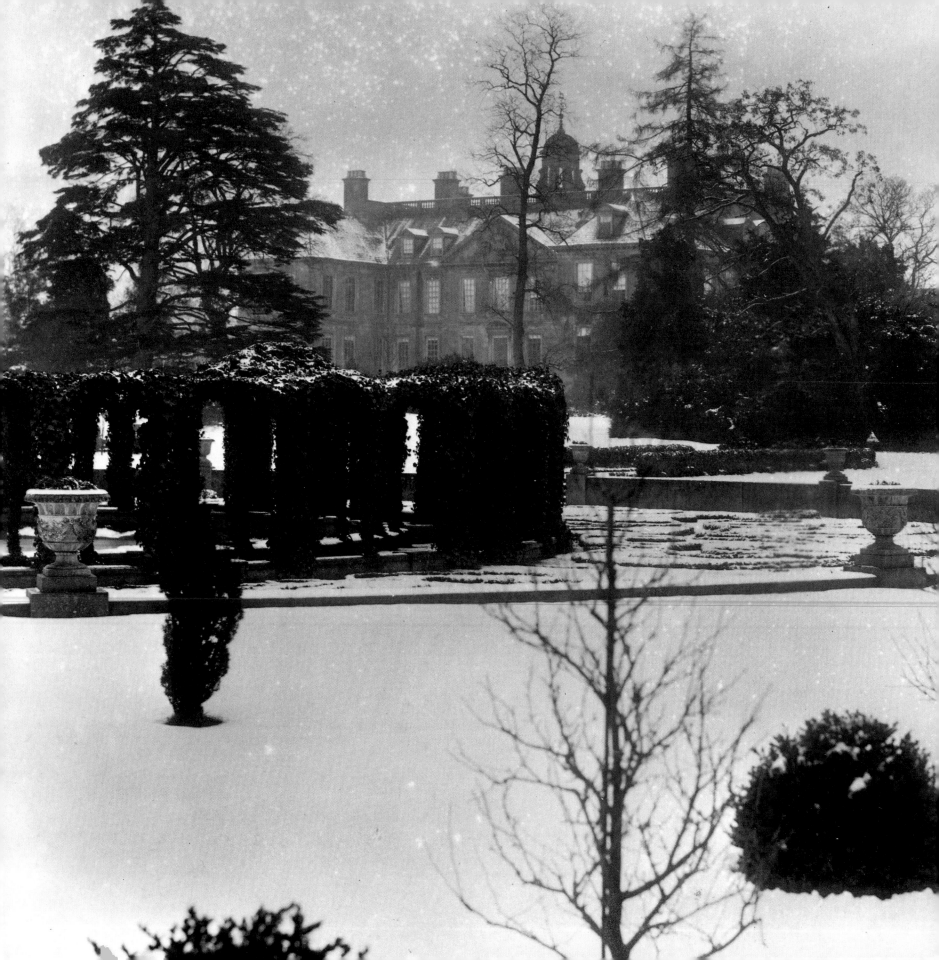

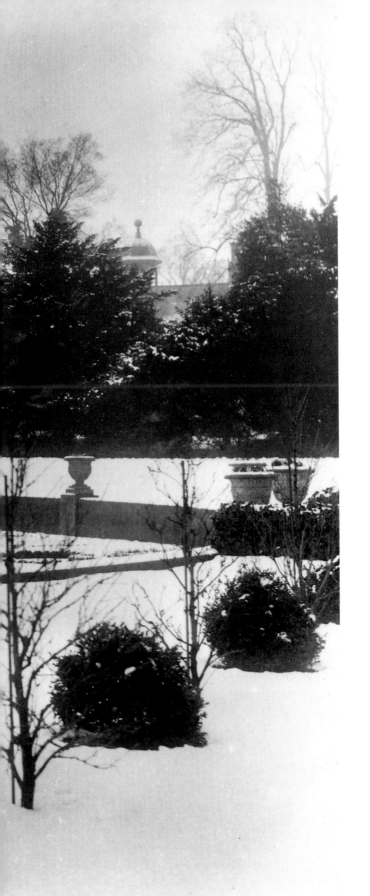

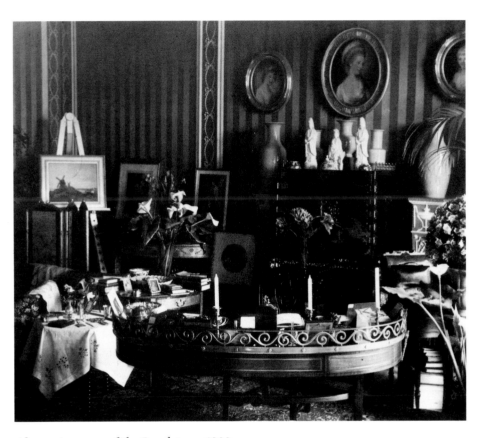

Above: A corner of the Boudoir, c.1900.

Left: The south front in winter.

Previous page: A group on the north steps, c.1860. The 2nd Earl is seated third from the left, his brother, who succeeded him in 1867 as 3rd Earl, is second from the left, and Lady Marion Alford, their mother, is seated second from the right.

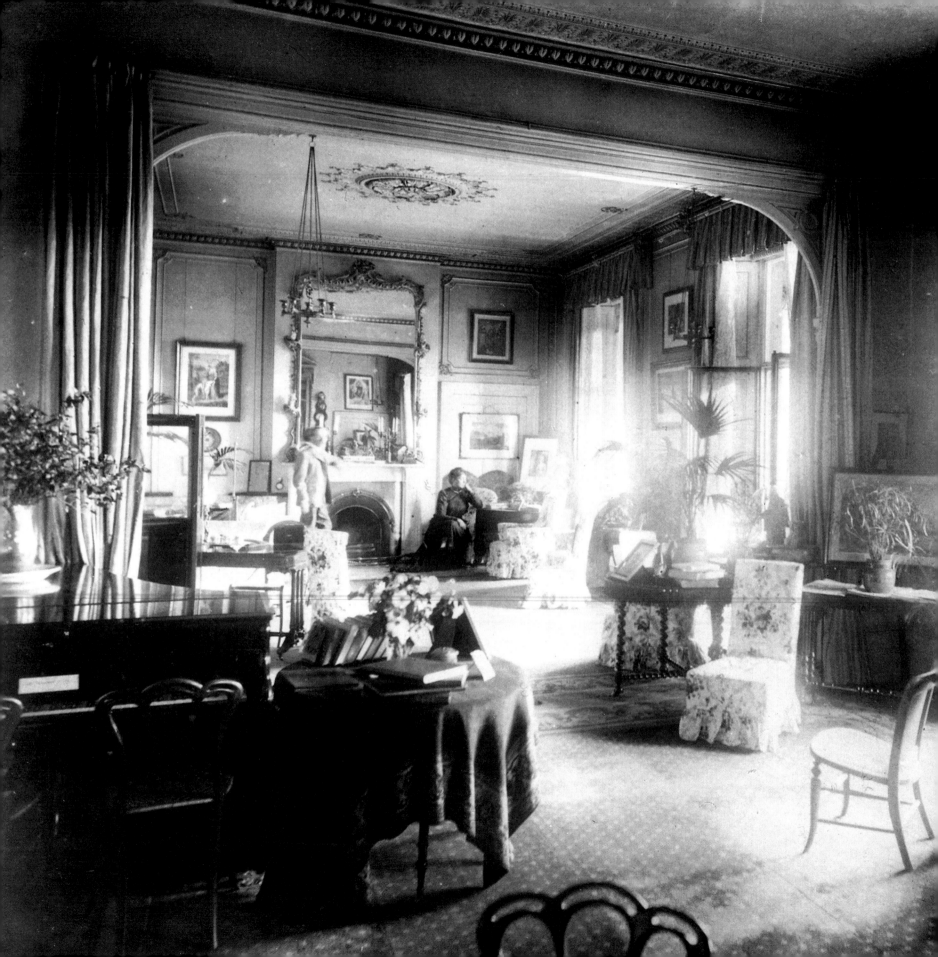

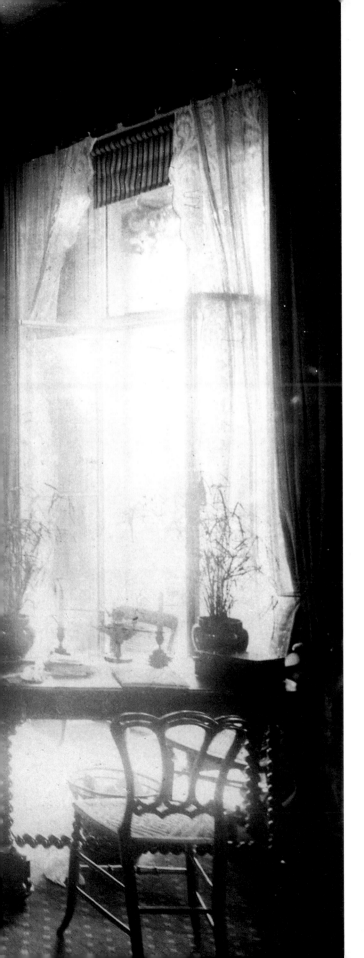

POLESDEN LACEY

DORKING, SURREY

The Drawing Room in the Nineteenth Century, before Mrs Greville's alterations.

Today Polesden Lacey is far better known for having been the sumptuous Edwardian home of Mrs Ronnie Greville than for either its architecture or its collection of pictures and French furniture. This is a tribute to Mrs Greville's success as one of the leading hostesses of the first three decades of this century. Born Maggie MacEwan, she was the illegitimate daughter of William MacEwan, a former Edinburgh MP who founded the MacEwan Brewery and was known thereafter as the 'Bass of Scotland'. It was his fortune which assisted her determined rise in society. This began in 1891 when she married the Hon. Ronald Greville, a Captain in the Life Guards and the best friend of George Keppel, husband of one of Edward VII's favourite mistresses. She thus secured herself a place both in society and in the fashionable Marlborough House set. From that moment on there was no stopping her.

She entertained lavishly, both at her London house, 16 Charles Street, and at a rented house in the country, Reigate Priory, employing her own press-cuttings agency to keep abreast of her public progress. The time soon came when a rented country house was no longer enough, so she persuaded her husband to buy Polesden Lacey, a house which had twice been remodelled since its ownership by Richard Brinsley Sheridan at the turn of the Nineteenth Century. The Caroline house which Sheridan had occupied was rebuilt in 1821 as a Regency villa by Thomas Cubitt. Latterly Sir Clinton Dawkins, a rich socialite, had commissioned Sir Ambrose Poynter to carry out substantial alterations and extensions, but he had died before he was able to take up residence. Mrs Greville's architects were Mewes and Davis, fresh from their completion of the Ritz Hotel in Piccadilly, who gave the house a dramatic succession of styles: a Georgian dining room, a William and Mary library, a Wren hall, an opulent Italian drawing room and a charming French tearoom. The latter played an important role in weekend parties, as Beverley Nichols describes in *Down the Kitchen Sink*. 'Tea is at 5 o'clock . . . and not five minutes past . . . which means that the Spanish Ambassador, who has gone for a walk down the yew avenue, hastily retraces his steps, and that the Chancellor of the Exchequer . . . hurries down the great staircase, and that the various gentlemen rise from their chaises-longues . . . and join the procession to the tea-room. The tea-pots, the cream jugs, the milk-pots and the sugar basins are of Queen Anne silver; the tea service is Meissen; and the doyleys, heavily monogrammed, are of Chantilly lace.'

Mrs Greville's house-parties were justifiably famous. Kings and queens, politicians and potentates, film stars and socialites all fill the pages of her visitors' books and photograph albums, the latter being also sprinkled with groups of the endless servants required to keep the show on the road. On her death in 1942, she bequeathed Polesden Lacey to the National Trust. In *School for Scandal*, Beverley Nichols, who had been a frequent weekend visitor, recalled his feelings on his first visit to the house as a member of the public. 'There stands the nice old Tudor table on which every evening at six o'clock the footmen used to lay out the drinks . . . but it is an uncanny experience to visit, as a tourist, a house where one has often stayed as a guest, to be greeted by a stern custodian of the State, instead of by old Bowles, the Head Butler . . . It is impossible to believe that in a moment the familiar figure will not appear at the top of the staircase, and demand in the gentlest of tones, "My dear, what are these extraordinary people doing in my house?"'

A house-party for the King of Egypt.

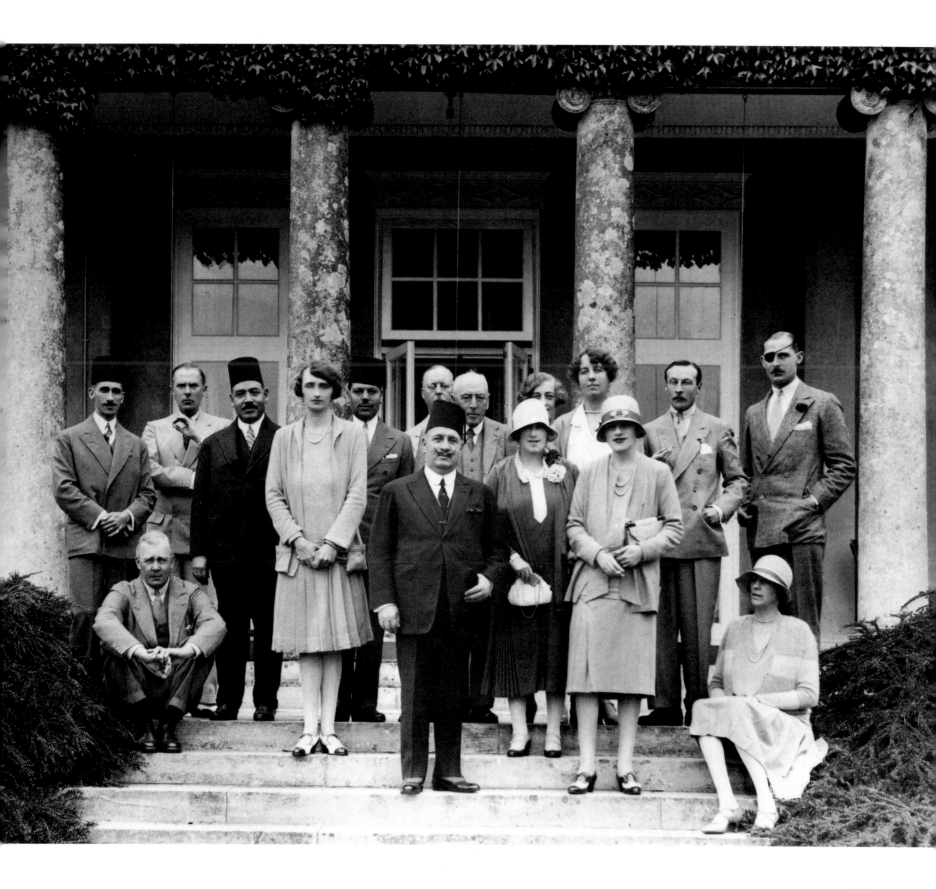

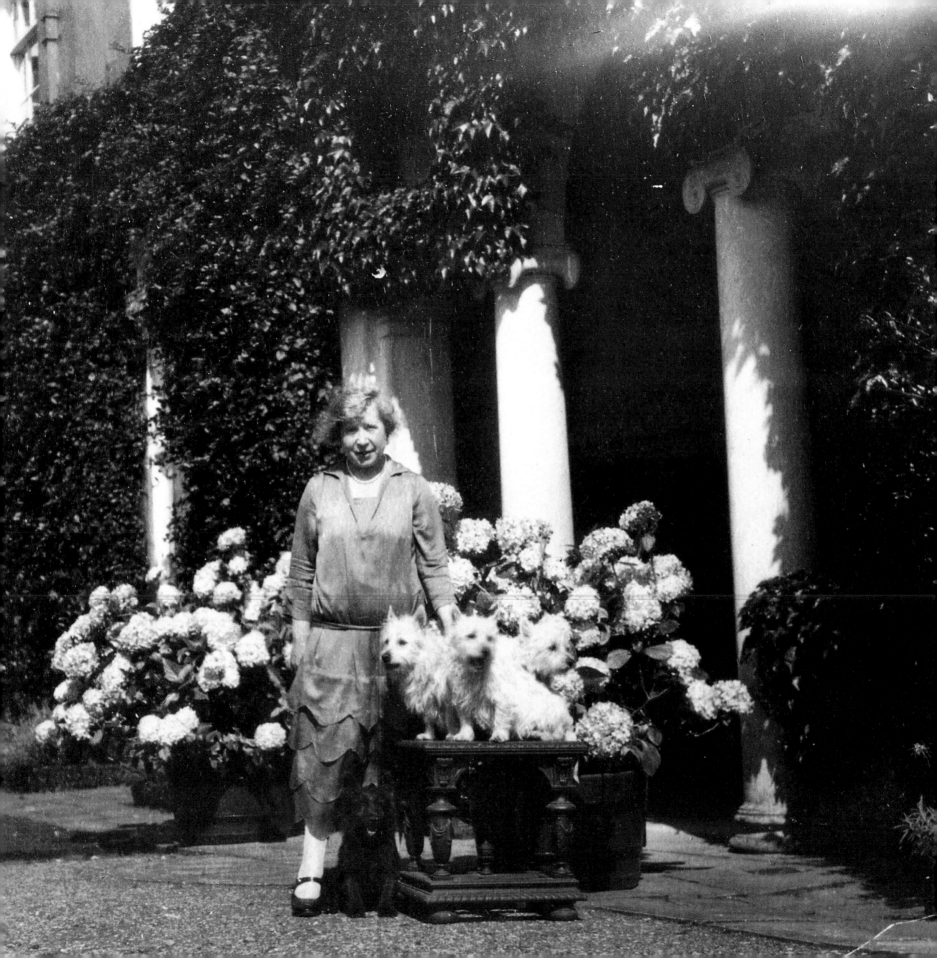

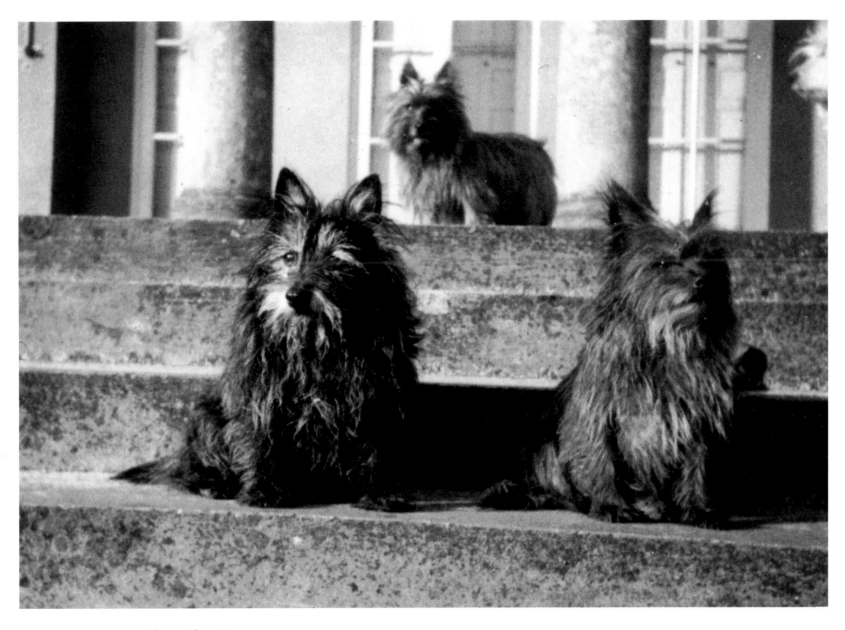

Above: The cairns.

Left: Mrs Greville and her dogs.

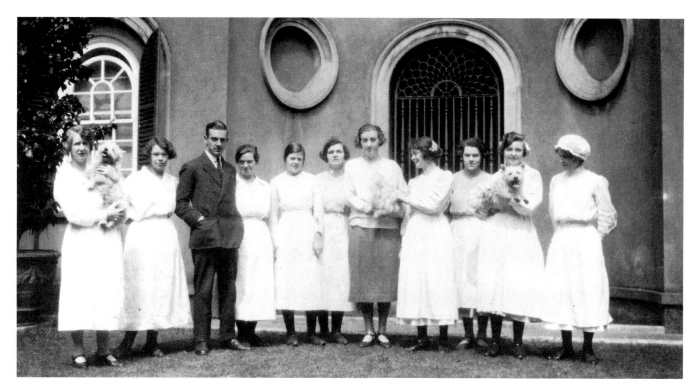

The steward and housekeeper with the housemaids.

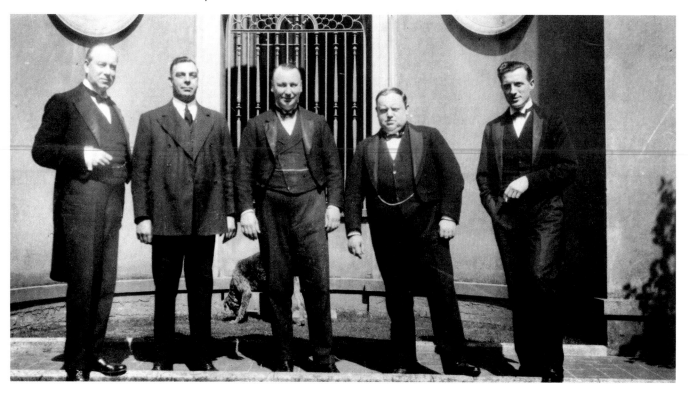

The butler and footmen.

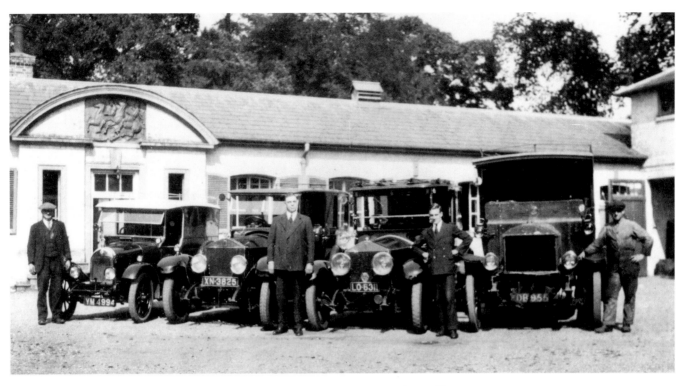

Chauffeurs and mechanics with Mrs Greville's fleet of cars in the stables.

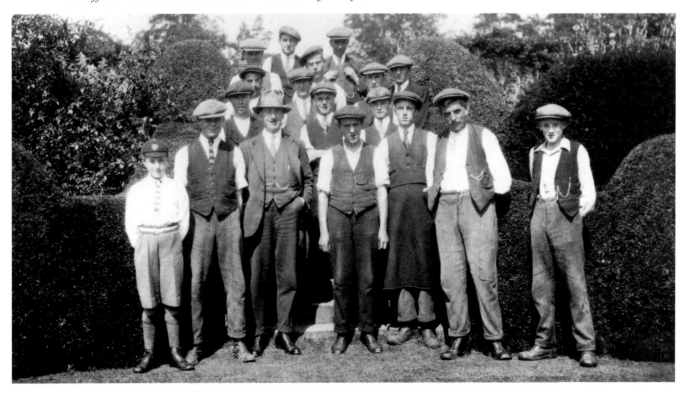

The gardeners.

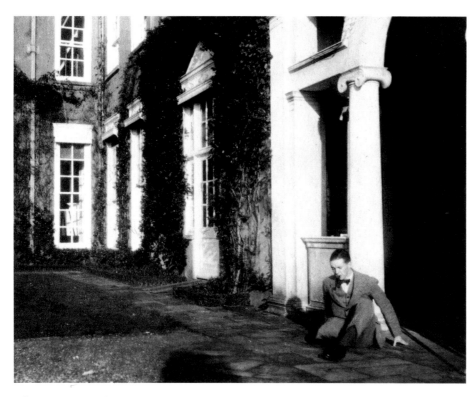

Above: During the First World War, the house was used as a convalescent home for officers.

Opposite: The Duke and Duchess of York on their honeymoon.

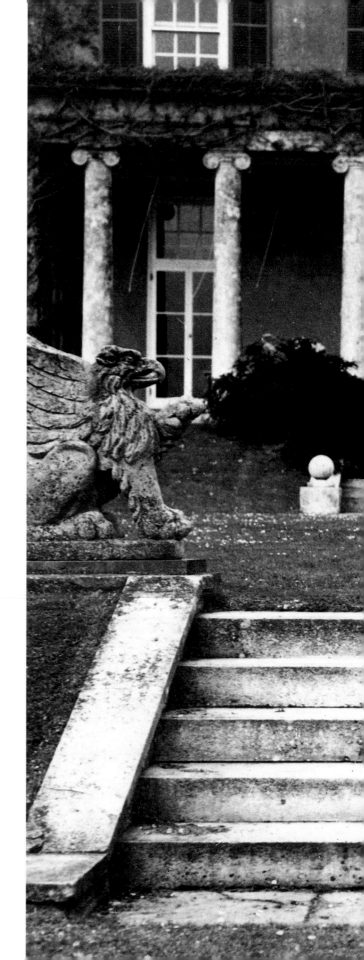

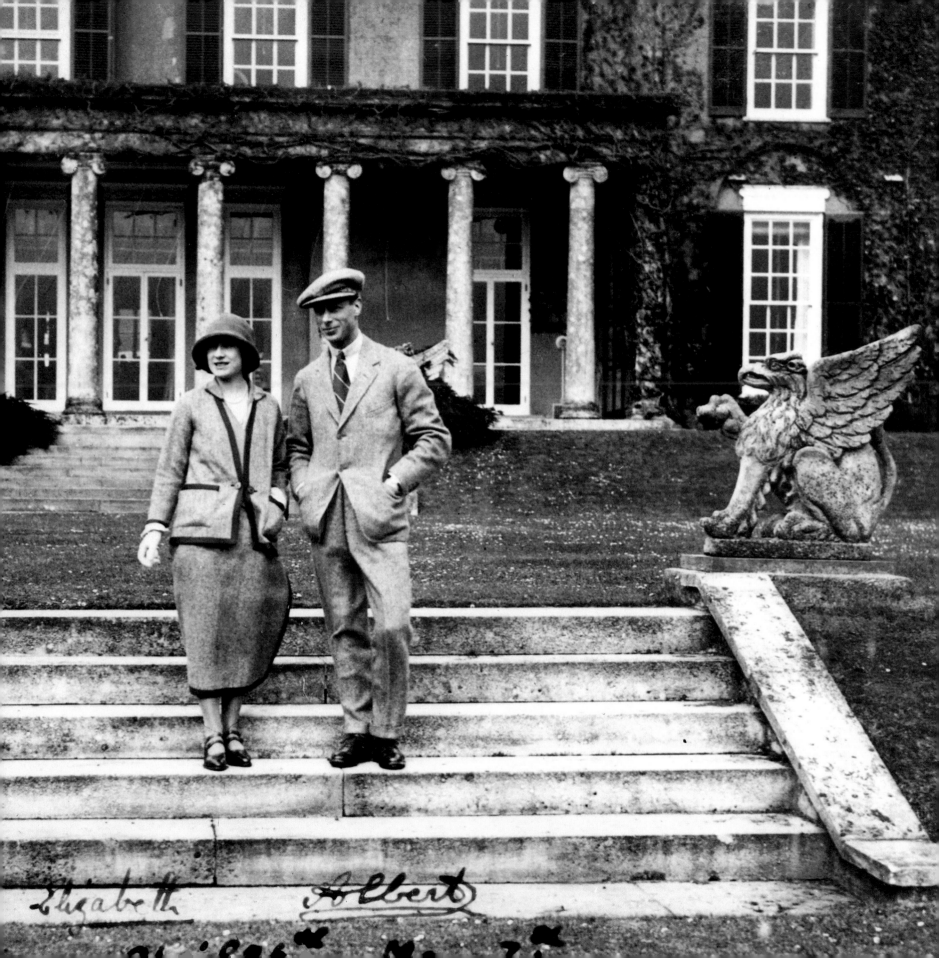

Elizabeth   Albert

GREAT CHALFIELD MANOR

MELKSHAM, WILTSHIRE

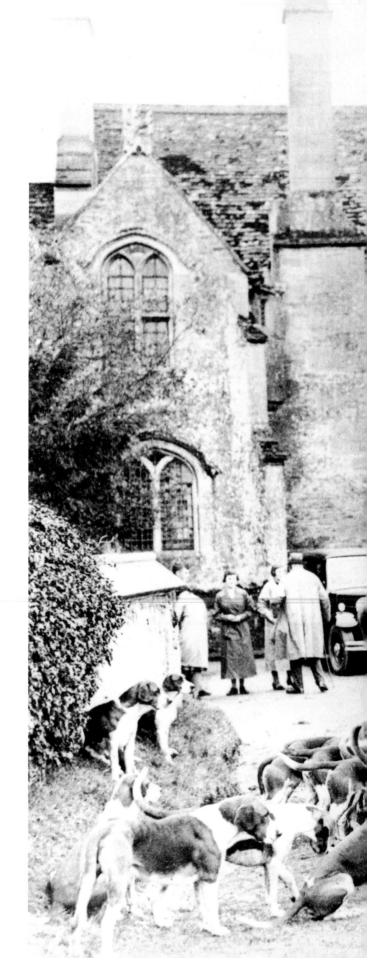

A lawn meet in the 1930s.

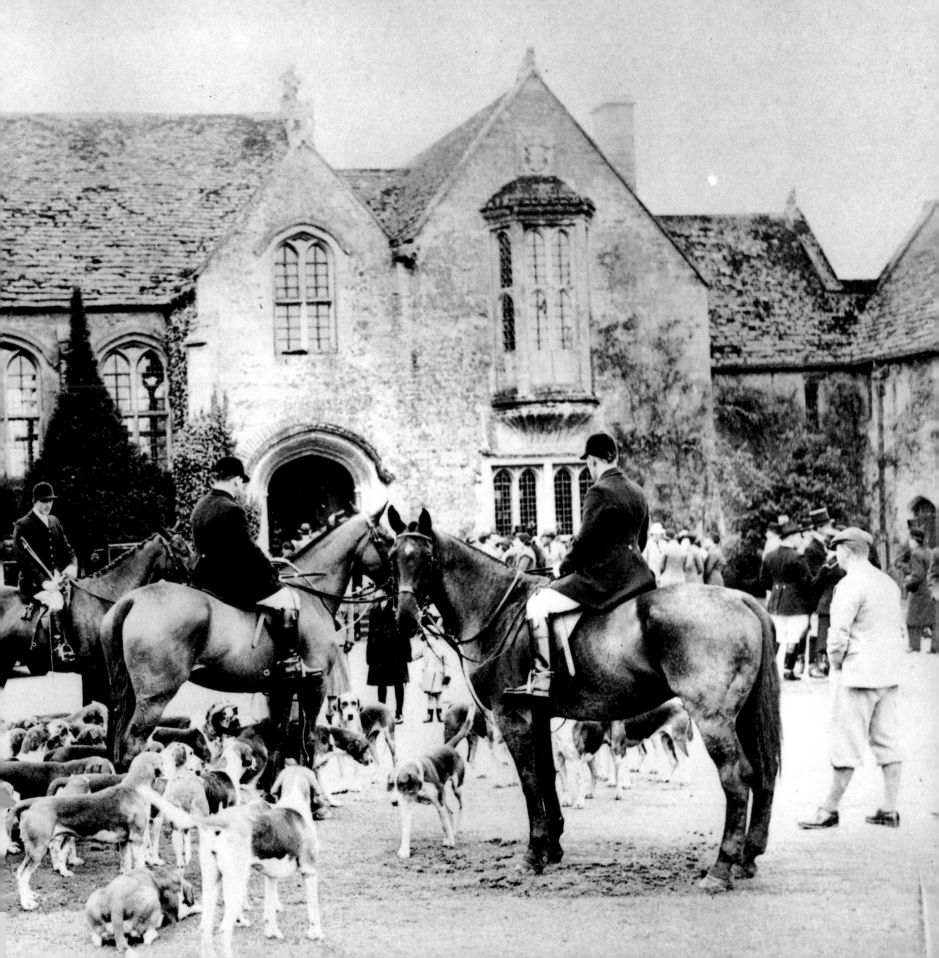

The north front of Great Chalfield Manor, with the little parish church of All Saints beside it, stands today just as it did in 1480, when it was newly built for Thomas Tropnell. He was a shrewd local businessman who during the Wars of the Roses had built up his holds of land to include seven Wiltshire manors. His fortune had increased correspondingly, so that when he inherited Great Chalfield, a manor house which had come into his family through marriage, he could afford to alter it substantially to his own taste. Being a man of vision, he managed to combine many of the traditional arrangements with an architectural approach far ahead of its time. Thus while retaining the central Great Hall, lit by high windows, at either end he placed identical projecting wings, each with an outer and inner gable, which contained not only the traditional first-floor rooms for family and guests, but also some quite new ideas, such as a Dining Room beyond the screens end of the Hall. This gave the house, too, a strikingly symmetrical appearance which anticipated later styles. Sadly, fate allowed Tropnell's heirs a painfully short ownership, for the last of them, Giles Tropnell, died young and without issue sometime before 1550 when 'as hunting putting one end of a paire of Dogg Couples over his head running after his sport and leaping over a hedge, the end of ye Dogg Couple which hung at his back tooke holde of a boughe, kept him from touching ye ground until hee was strangled.'

In the succeeding centuries Great Chalfield passed through the hands of three different families and changed little. For much of the Eighteenth Century it was uninhabited, and by the time Thomas Larkin Walker, a pupil of Pugin, made drawings of it in 1836, it had fallen into a sorry state of disrepair. Its wonderful medieval atmosphere, however, remained intact. 'It cannot be doubted,' wrote a visitor for *The Gentleman's Magazine* in 1838, 'that the curious and reflecting visitor of Chalfield Manor-House and its appurtenances, will feel his imagination somewhat excited, when they carry back his thoughts to the aera of their freshness; to the inartificial manners of that early age; and to the scenes of hospitality and merriment, which then gladdened the venerable pile. He will, for a moment, at least, feel inclined to believe, that these "good old times" teemed with joys, of which we, of the present day, have only the tradition:- the simplicity of the rustic; the generosity of the Lord; the feast in the hall; the Yule log, throwing a bright blaze through its vast extent; the harper and the mime in its gallery; and the stranger or beggar receiving his dole at the gateway; the charms of feudal priviliges; and the dignity of local jurisdictions – are images which will naturally crowd upon his fancy, when he stands within this magic precinct.' Whoever this anonymous visitor was, he must have been among the last persons to have seen Great Chalfield in its original state, for soon after the east wing was demolished. Much of the house we see today is a careful reconstruction, based on Walker's drawings, carried out by Sir Harold Brakspear between 1905 and 1912 for the new owner, Robert Fuller, who gave it to the National Trust in 1943.

Opposite: A door on the stairs, before Brakspear's restoration.

Overleaf: The north front in 1900.

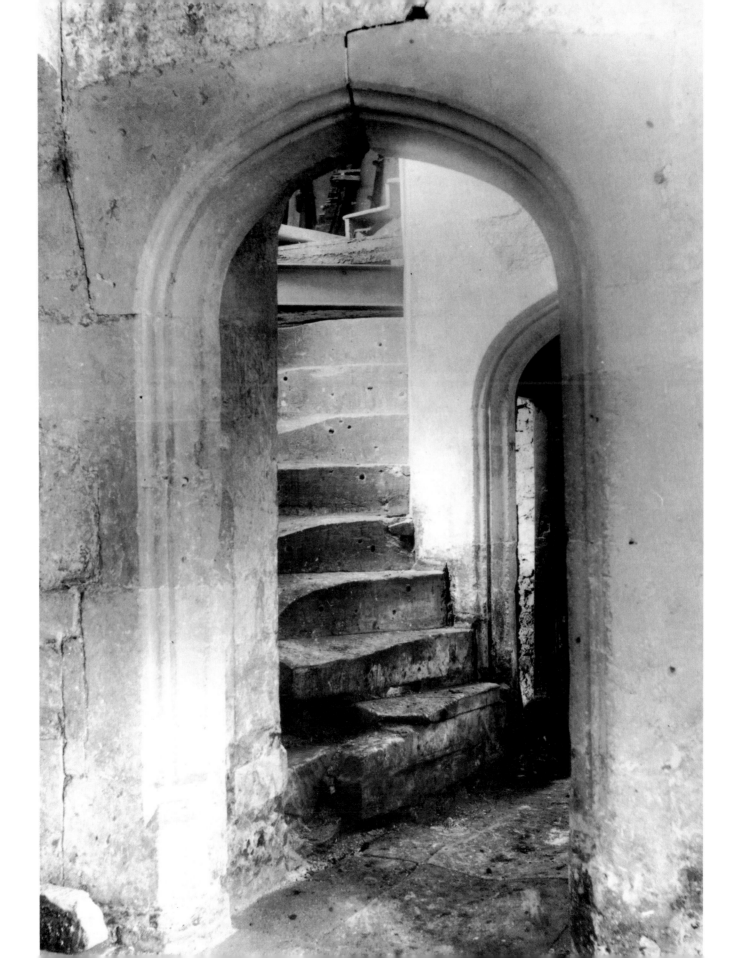

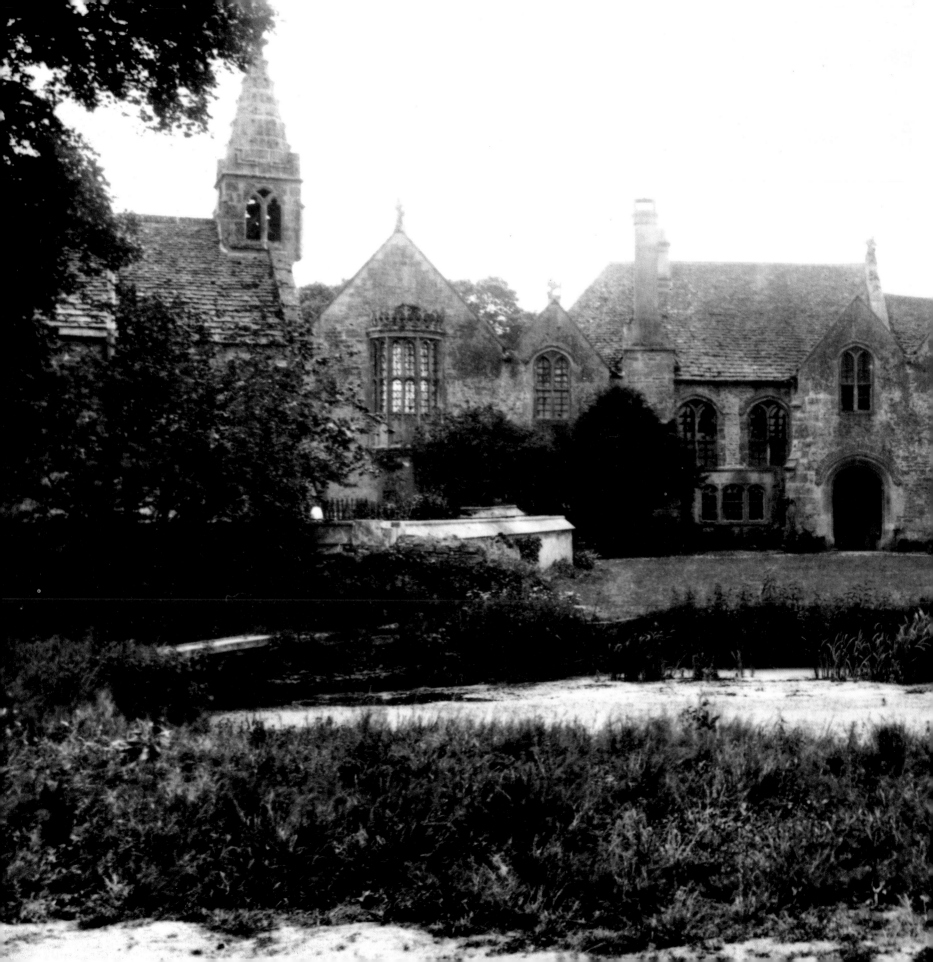

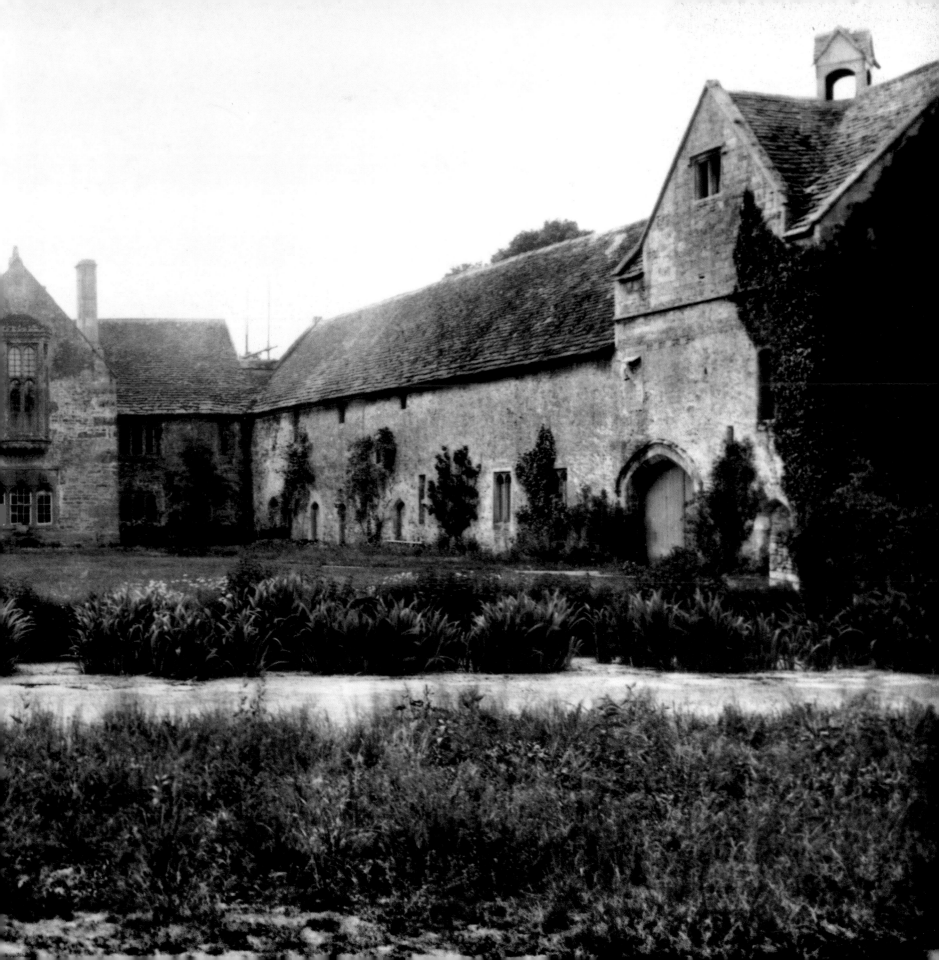

STOURHEAD

STOURTON, WILTSHIRE

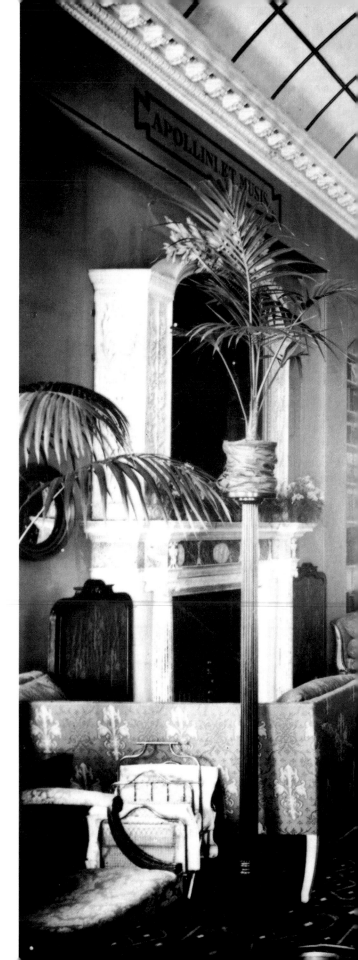

The Library in 1901.

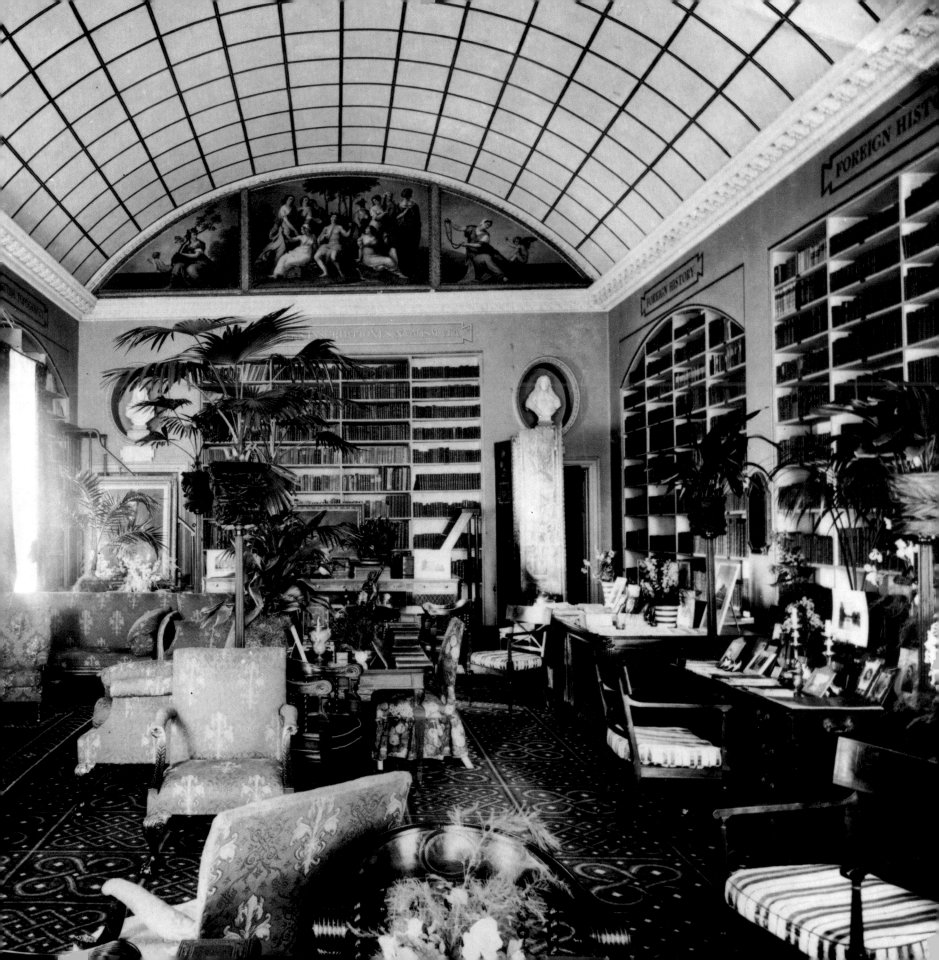

On Wednesday 21 May, 1947, James Lees-Milne visited Stourhead, the eighteenth-century seat of the Hoare family, newly acquired by the National Trust. 'We reached Stourhead at 3 o'c.,' he wrote in his diary. 'By that time the sun had penetrated the mist, and was gauzy and humid. The air about lake and grounds of a conservatory consistency. Never do I remember such Claude-like, idyllic beauty here. See Stourhead and die.' Stourhead was built by Henry Hoare, nicknamed 'Good' for his charitable works, the second son of Sir Richard Hoare, the founder of Hoare's Bank. Being a man of taste and fashion, he employed the leading architect of the new Palladian style, Colen Campbell, who built him one of the first Palladian villas in the country, based on the Villa Emo at Fanzolo. Since then each generation of the family has altered the house in some way, quite destroying the original intent. His son Henry, for example, creator of the landscape garden for which Stourhead is so famous and thus known as 'Henry the Magnificent', upset the balance of the façade by extending the West Front in the 1740s. His son Colt Hoare, celebrated antiquary and author of *The Ancient History of Wiltshire*, further disrupted the symmetry when he added the Library, jutting out from the original building and obliterating two bays. When the house was gutted by fire in 1902 and subsequently rebuilt, Sir Henry Hoare, 6th Baronet, extended the south façade westwards with another two bays rising the full height of the house.

The 6th Baronet and his wife Alda lived at Stourhead for fifty-three years, the longest single occupancy of any member of the family. James Lees-Milne's description of his visit to see them in 1942, soon after Sir Henry had decided to hand over the house to the Trust, is unforgettable. 'Sir Henry is an astonishing nineteenth-century John Bull, hobbling on two sticks. He was wearing a pepper-and-salt suit and a frayed grey billycock over his purple face. He had a very bronchial cough and kept hoiking and spitting into an enormous carrot-coloured handkerchief. En route for Stourhead I sat in the back of the car beside him . . . Sir Henry talked about his bad knee, and told me he had lost a knee-cap. I found myself shouting, for he is rather deaf. "Do you find it much of a handicap having no kneecap?" After the third repetition I decided that my remark was inept. Lady Hoare is an absolute treasure and unique . . . She said to me [at dinner], "Don't you find the food better in this war than in the last?" I replied that I was rather young during the last war, but I certainly remembered the rancid margarine we were given at my prep school when I was eight. "Oh!", she said. "You were lucky. We were reduced to eating rats." I was a little surprised, until Sir Henry looked up and said, "No, no, Alda. You keep getting your wars wrong. That was when you were in Paris during the Commune."'

The following day James Lees-Milne was up bright and early for a tour of the grounds. 'It is a beautiful morning and Sir Henry gets into his electric chair, and I accompany him to the lakes and the temples; or rather I gallop at breakneck speed behind him. He is quite unaware that his chair goes the devil of a pace and I have the utmost difficulty in keeping up. As he presses the accelerator he asks me questions which demand answers and intelligent comments. He keeps saying "Where are you? Why don't you say something?" When I do catch up I am so out of breath I can't get the words out. All he says (to himself) is, "I don't understand what's come over the boy." . . . They are the dearest old couple.' Four years later, Sir Henry made his gift to the National Trust, and the following year he died, on Lady Day, 1947. His wife, who had always dreaded being left alone, died six hours later.

The Picture Gallery in 1901.

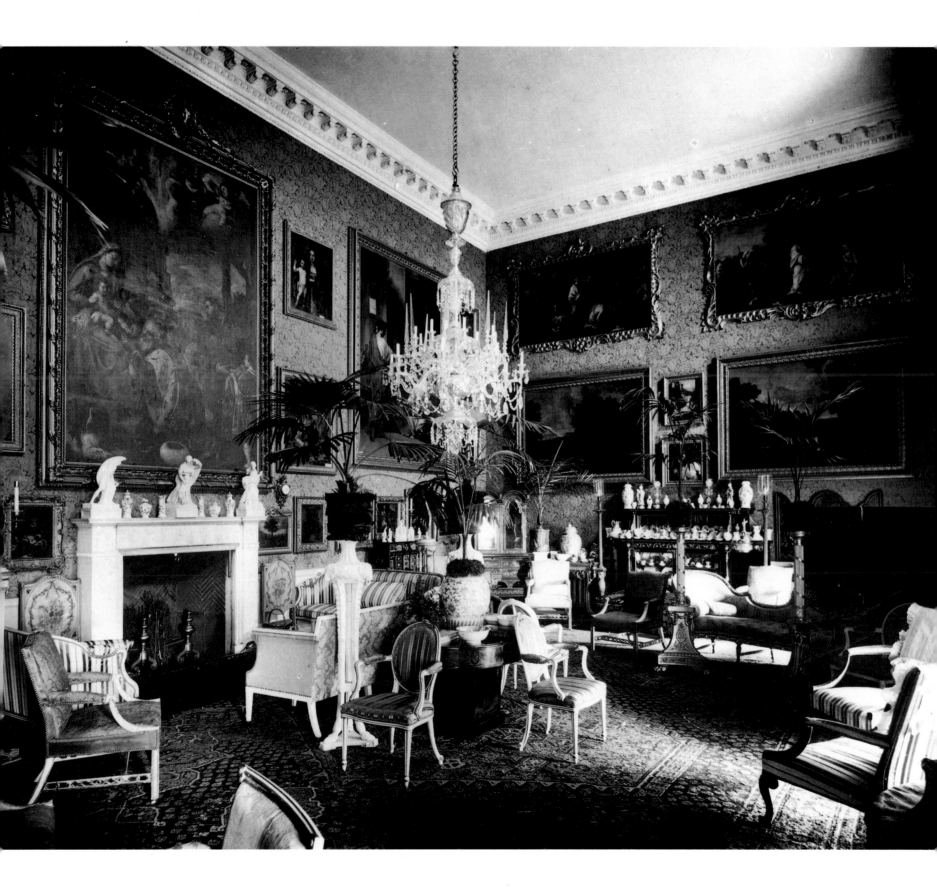

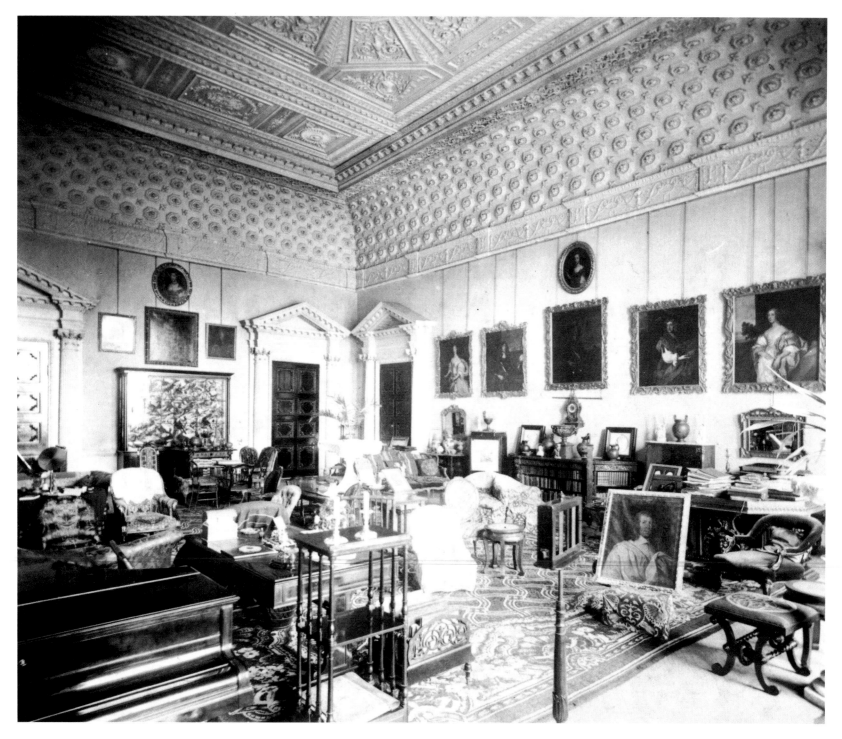

Above: The Saloon in 1901.

Opposite left: Alda, Lady Hoare.

Opposite right: Henry Hugh Arthur Hoare, 6th Baronet.

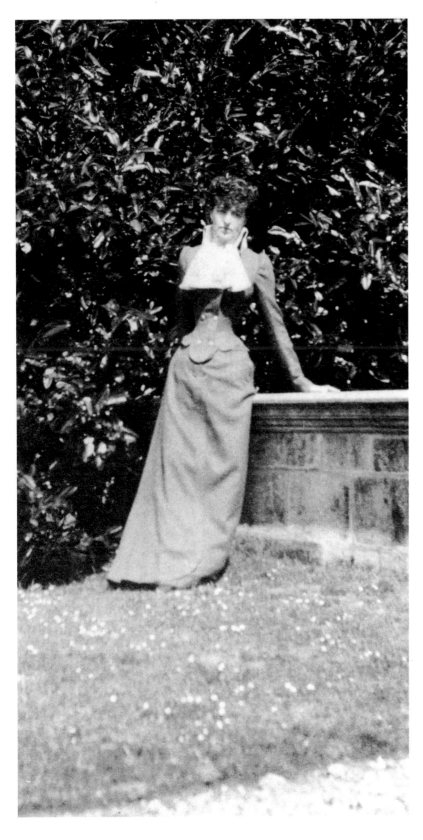
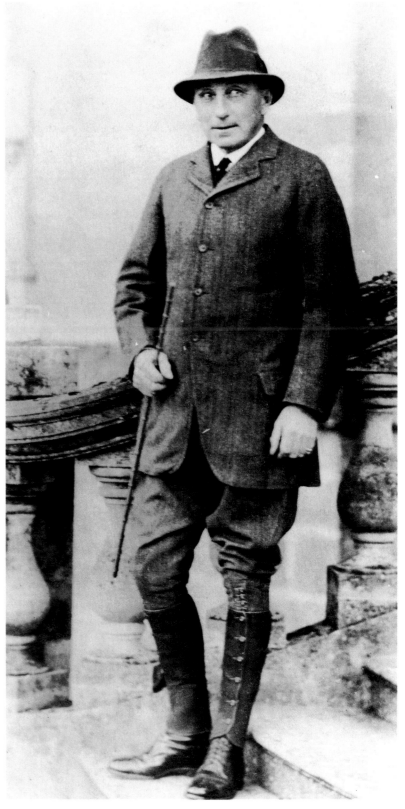

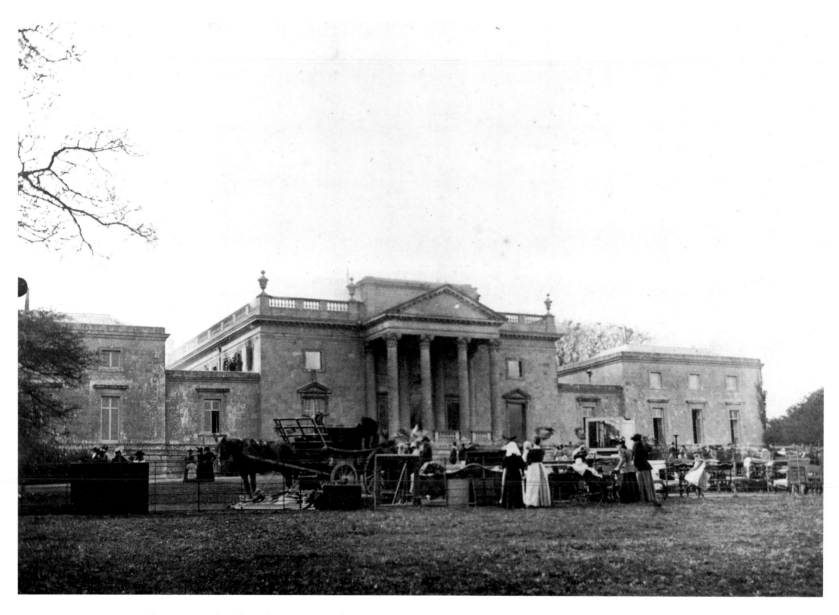

Above: Stourhead on the morning after the fire, 1902.

Opposite: The Entrance Hall, photographed the morning after the fire, 1902.

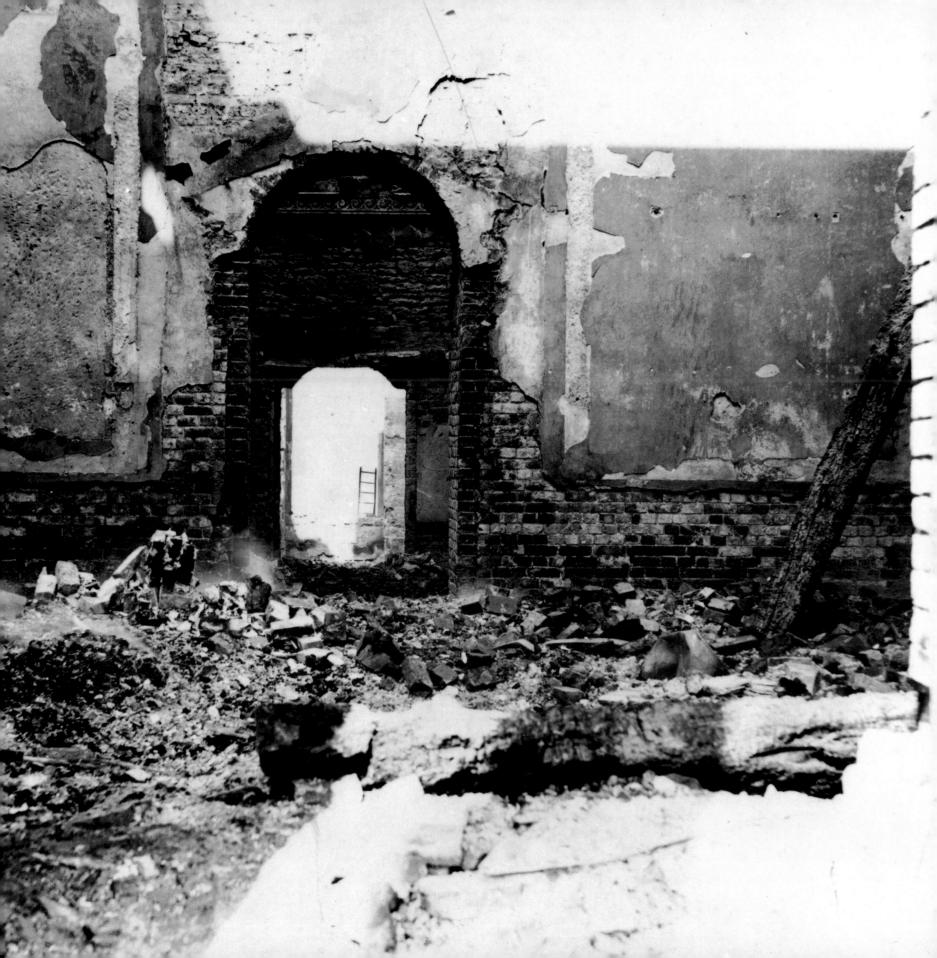

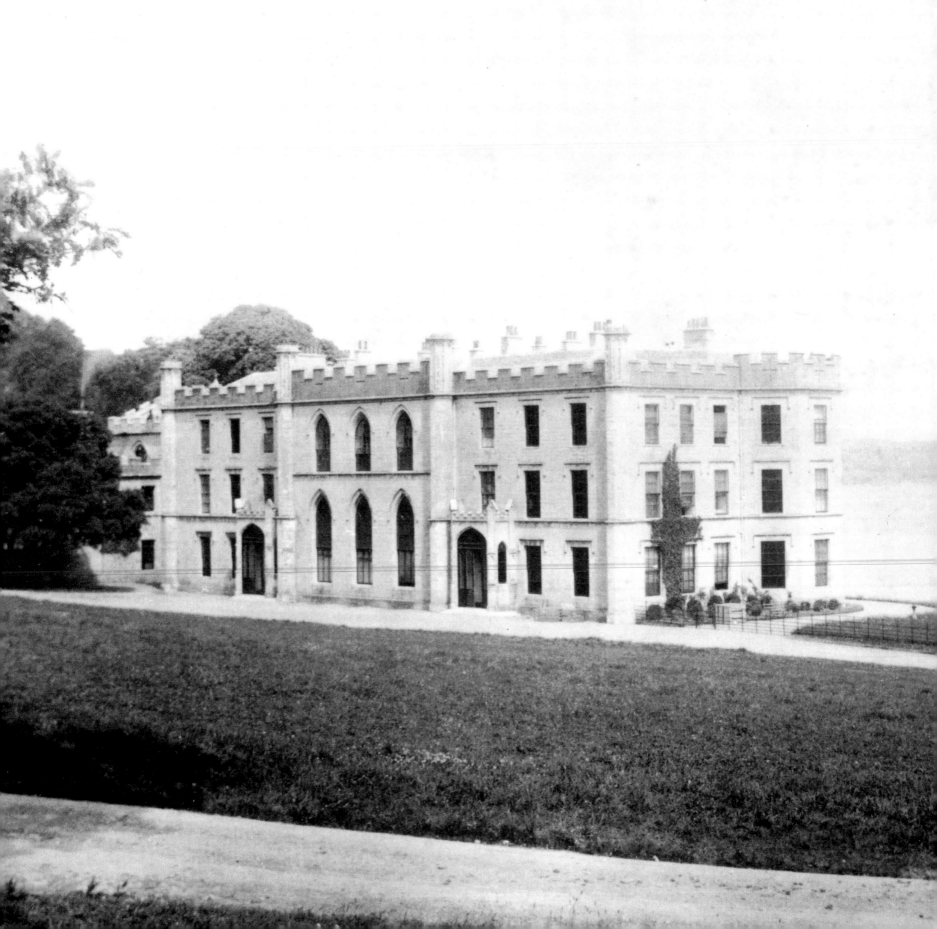

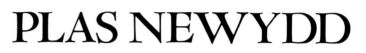

PLAS NEWYDD

LLANFAIRPWLL, ANGLESEY, GWYNEDD

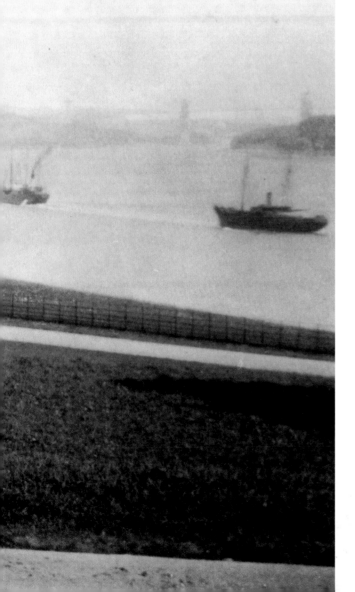

Plas Newydd looking east.

Sometime early in 1901, a Dresden newspaper carried the following report: 'In the Central Theatre last Sunday, a new artist appeared under the name of "San Toi". In a dark house and on a dark stage he produces kaleidoscopic pictures in life size. In quick succession San Toi appeared in the costumes of the different nationalities and in all sorts of fancy dress. The splendour and the brightness of the colours, the tasteful combination, and the constant change of the beautiful pictures thrown by electric light on the slender form of the artist, clothed in white, gladdened the eyes. The likeness of the German Emperors, William I, Frederick III and William II, of the German heroes of the last decades, and of the Saxon royal couple were beautifully rendered. The production was without any flaw, and was received with great applause. The artist himself is a most interesting personality. He is Lord Anglesey, an English marquis, the head of a noble and well-known English family with a seat and a vote in the House of Lords.' Henry Cyril Paget, 5th Marquis of Anglesey, was the great-grandson of the 2nd Earl of Uxbridge, whose exploits on the battlefield of Waterloo, as the right-hand man of the Duke of Wellington, had earned him the title of 'the most perfect hero that ever lived'. No two men could have been more different, for while the latter was a red-blooded soldier, who had undergone the amputation of his leg during the battle 'without flinching and without complaint', Henry Cyril was a lily-livered fop with a penchant for dressing up in drag.

In fact the two men were not blood relations, the 5th Marquis being the illegitimate son of a French actor, Coquelin. He was brought up in France in the theatrical world, and it was only when he inherited in 1898 that he came to live on the family estate at Plas Newydd, on the Isle of Anglesey. This beautiful eighteenth-century Gothic house stands in a setting which is unsurpassed for its beauty and drama, perched as it is on the edge of the Menai Strait, overlooking the water with the mountains of Snowdonia in the background. It evidently appealed to Henry Cyril's sense of theatre – he renamed it Anglesey Castle – and he at once set about spending his inheritance to indulge his art. He converted the early nineteenth-century Chapel into a Theatre, 'The Gaiety', modelled after Sarah Bernhardt's in Paris, and here he staged lavish productions, in all of which he took the leading roles, supported by prominent actors and actresses from London. On 26 December 1901, for example, in a production of Aladdin staged by 'Mr Alex Keith's London Company' he took the part of Pekoe, the Vizier's Son (a bit Moony on Yummy-Yum). 'In Scene 4', the programme proudly announced, 'will be introduced The Butterfly Dance by The Marquis of Anglesey', and he has thus been known forever after in the family as 'The Dancing Marquis'. His extravagance knew no bounds. He lavished huge sums on jewellery and clothes, buying up the entire window display of Van Cleef and Arples in Paris on his honeymoon. In winter he kept braziers alight along the woodland paths in case he should wish to warm himself while out walking, and there is a story that on one occasion he threw a £3,000 bejewelled fur coat into one of these because he was too hot. He died bankrupt in 1905, at the Hotel Royale in Monte Carlo, aged only thirty. His successor, his first cousin Charles, the 6th Marquis, destroyed all evidence of his existence. The photographs reproduced here were gathered together from friends and neighbours by the present incumbent, the 7th Marquis, who gave Plas Newydd to the National Trust in 1976.

Opposite: The Saloon, 1890.

Overleaf: Henry Cyril Paget, 5th Marquis of Anglesey (standing in the centre) with one of his theatrical companies.

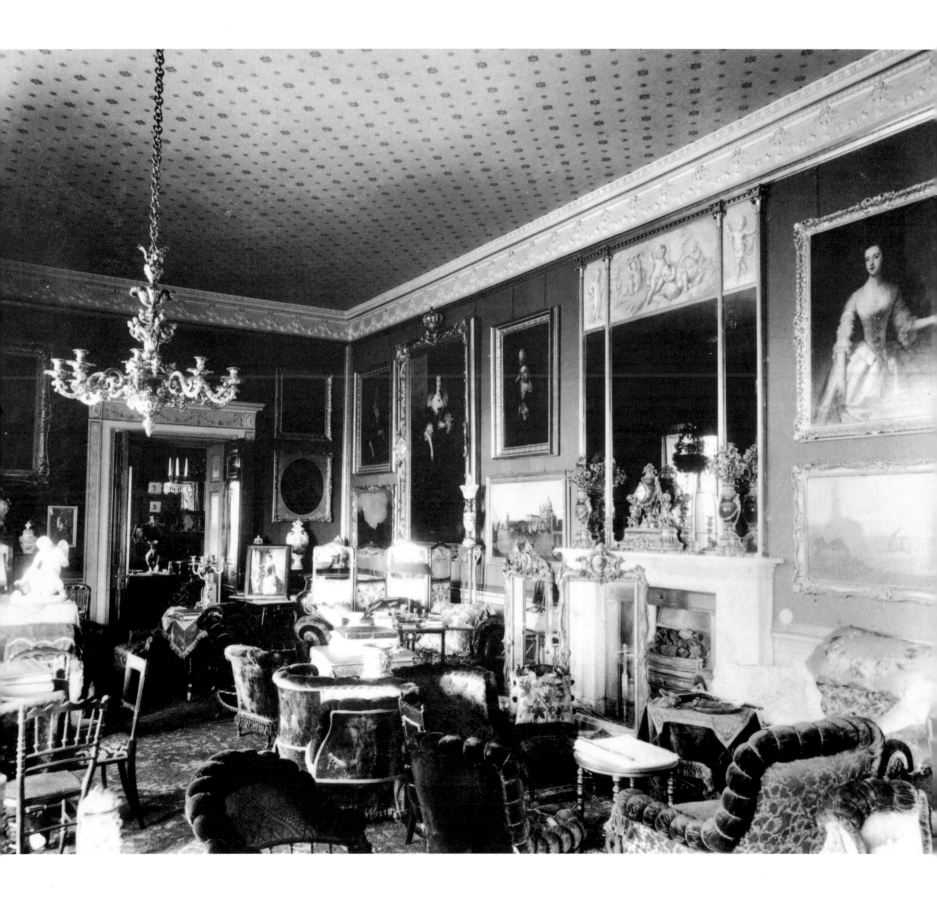

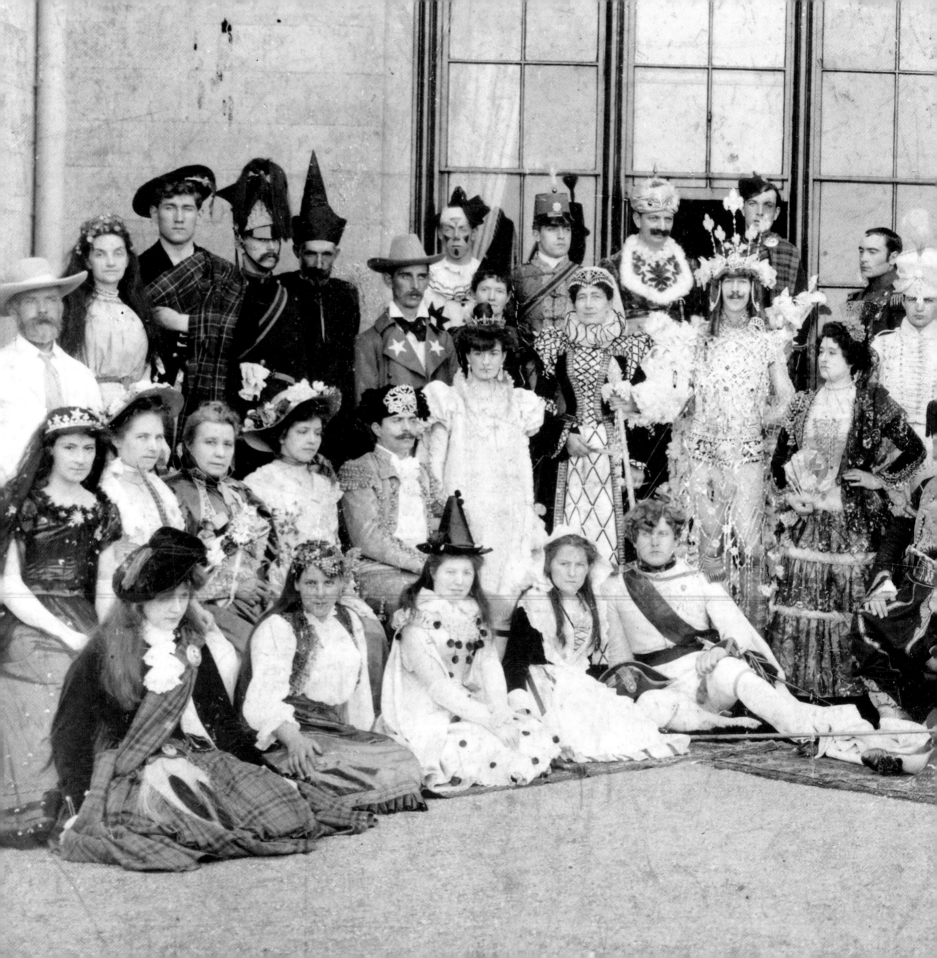

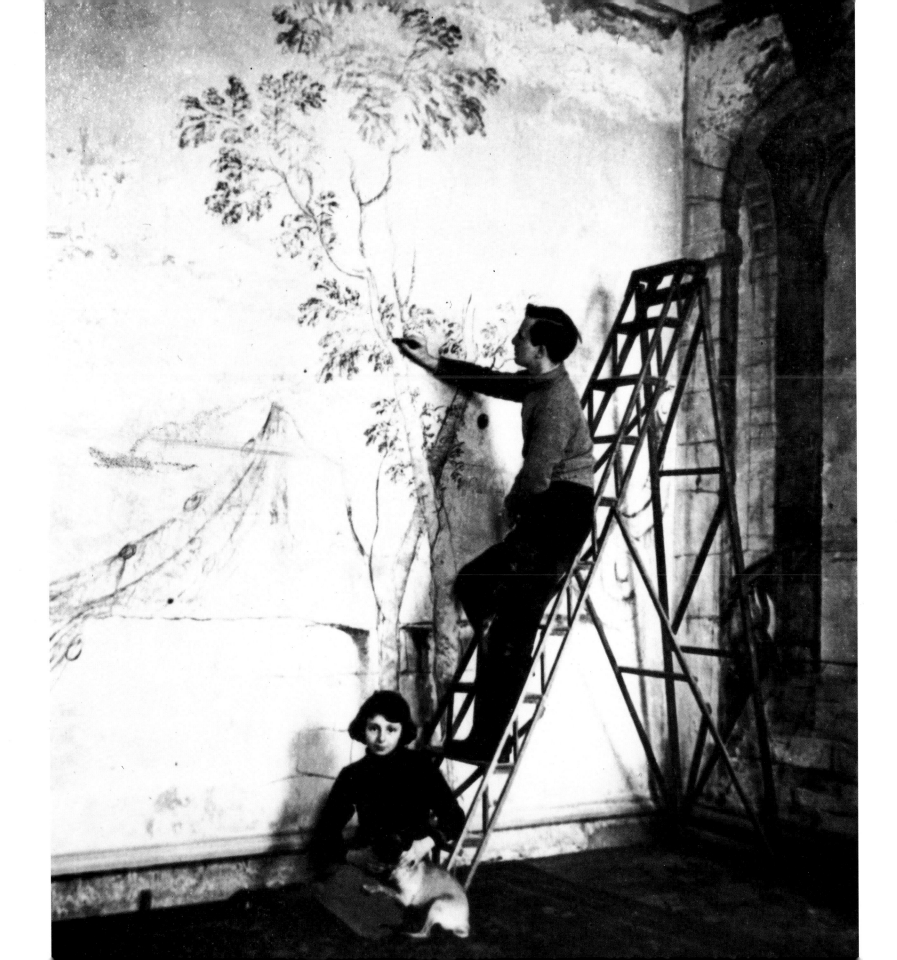

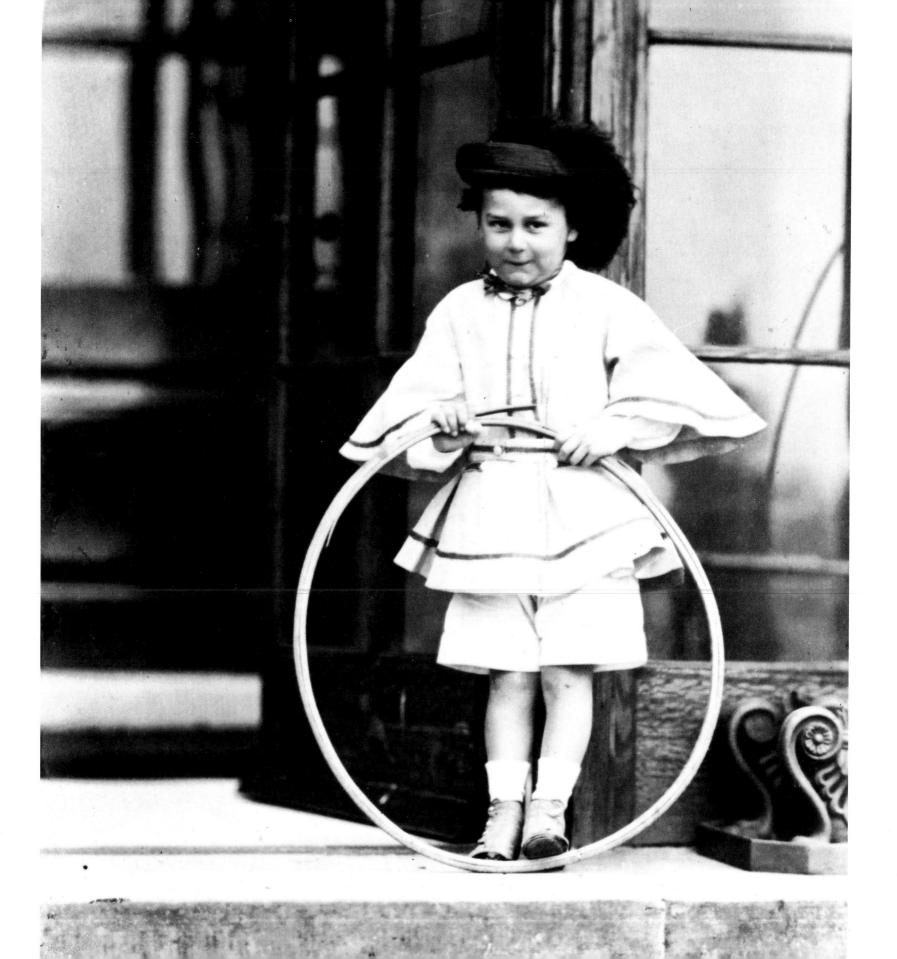

SUDBURY HALL

SUDBURY, DERBYSHIRE

When George Vernon, an ambitious Derbyshire squire, began work on building himself a new house to replace the modest manor house he had inherited on his father's death, he recorded a detailed account of the progress he made in a manuscript book kept between 1659 and 1701. Since the house remains little altered, one can read, among other entries, that on 20 October 1668 Thomas Phillips was paid 16 shillings for '16 big stones for cullomes' and know that these are the very columns which grace the façade of the house today. Little is known about what part the old house played in the building of the new, but the likelihood is that no more than the foundations were included. The family had advanced a great deal since the beginning of the century, when they were of little consequence, and by the time George Vernon began what was to be a lifetime's work they were one of the principal families in the county. He was High Sheriff in 1664 and was elected Member of Parliament for Derby in 1670. He was a good friend of the Earl of Devonshire, the most important man in Derbyshire, and was a frequent visitor to his house at Hardwick. He had inherited land from his mother, and gained a fortune on marriage to Margaret Oneley, an heiress. He needed a grander house which would be in keeping with his new status.

Vernon appears to have been his own architect, no doubt following the advice of his contemporary Roger North, who wrote 'a profest architect is proud, opinionative and troublesome, seldome at hand, and a head workman pretending to ye designing part, is full of paultry vulgar contrivances; therefore be your owne architect, or sit still.' The result is a fascinating house, the style of which develops in accordance with Vernon's burgeoning skills as an architect. Thus the upper parts of the exterior are very much more advanced in style than the lower, where the E-shaped plan, the diapered pattern of the brickwork, the tracery in some of the windows, the suggestion of strapwork in the lower cornice and the two-storey porch are all much closer in spirit to the Jacobean era than the Restoration. He also included a 138 foot Long Gallery on the first floor of the house which, magnificent though it is, is most unusual for the period. By the time he got to the roof, however, he was evidently becoming more sophisticated, for it is hipped and with a cupola, both thoroughly up-to-date features. The interior tells the same story, for while he began the work using local craftsmen such as Samuel Mansfield, the plasterer, and William Wilson, the carver, by the mid-1670s they had given way to more fashionable London men, namely Edward Pierce and Grinling Gibbons, carvers, and James Pettifer and Robert Bradbury, plasterers. For £101 2s. 0d. the latter decorated in the Long Gallery what is perhaps the finest ceiling of its kind in England. It is a dazzling display of the plasterer's art featuring dragons, wild boars, emperors' heads, shells, grasshoppers and much more along its entire length. Remarkably, for there were many ambitious plans in the Nineteenth Century to alter the house, if George Vernon were to visit Sudbury today, he would find it little changed. It became the property of the National Trust in 1967.

George William Henry Vernon, 7th Baron, aged 4 in 1858.

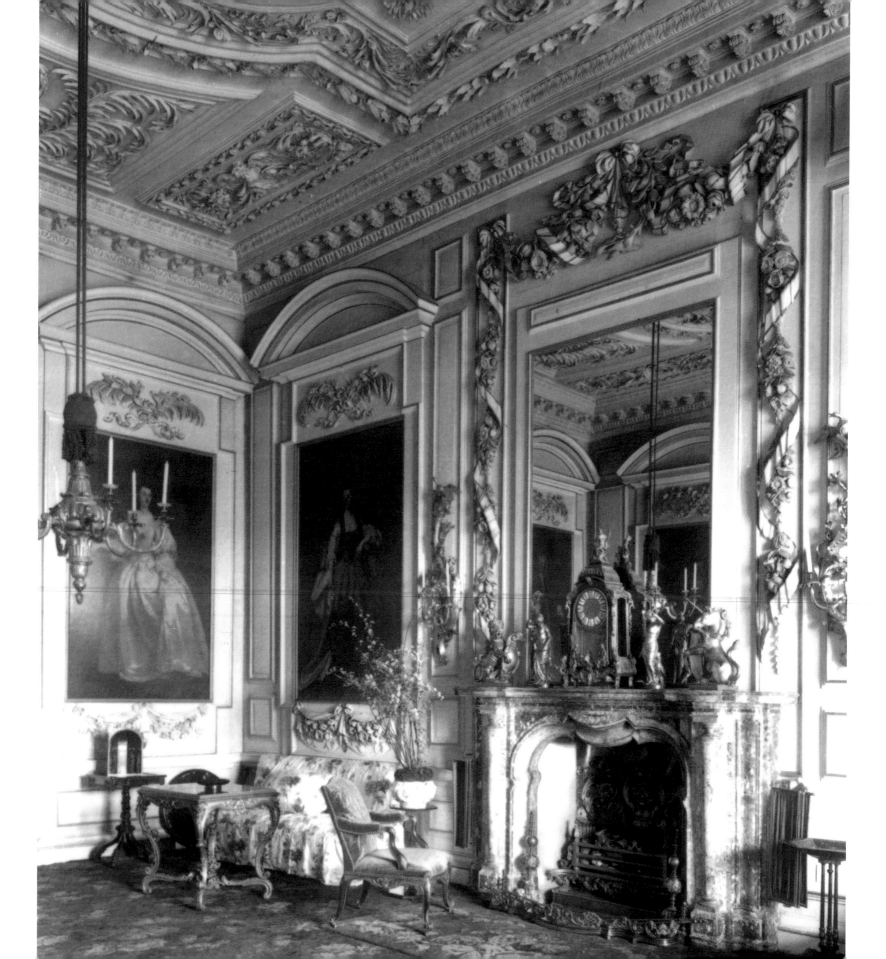

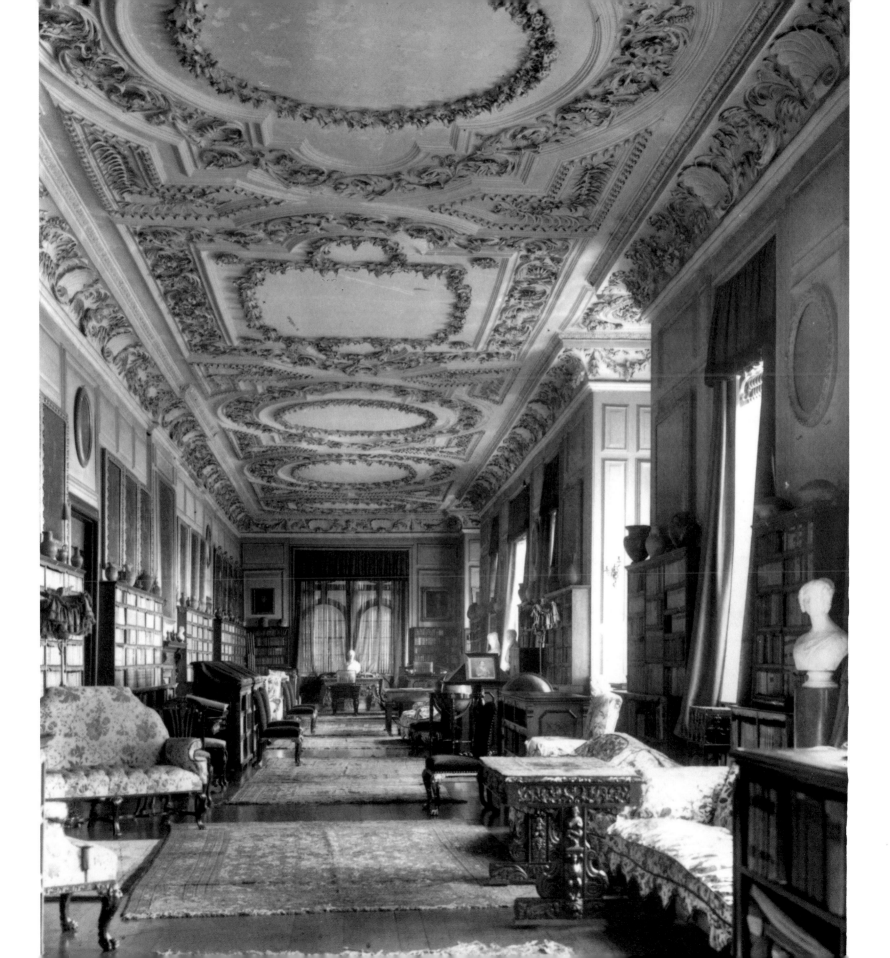

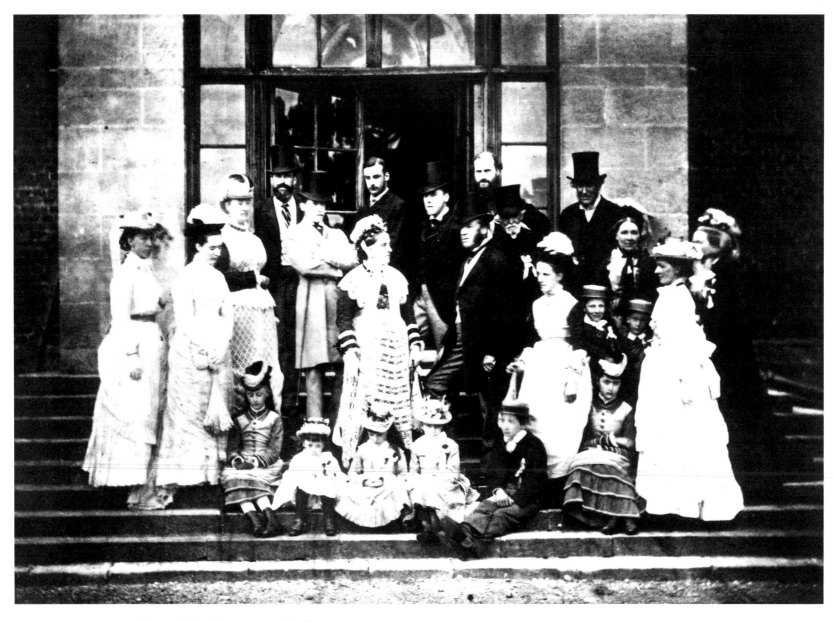

Above: A family group on the front steps.

Previous pages: (Left) The Saloon in the Nineteenth Century, with its plasterwork by Bradbury and Pettifer. (Right) The Long Gallery in the Nineteenth Century, Robert Bradbury completed this ceiling alone.

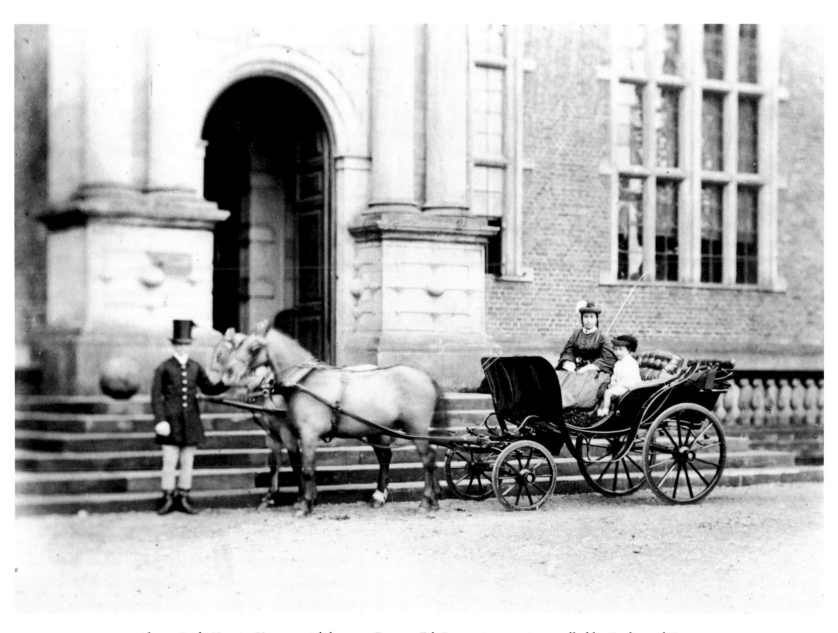

Above: Lady Harriet Vernon with her son George, 7th Baron, in a carriage pulled by Frolic and Fun.

Overleaf: Sudbury from across the lake.

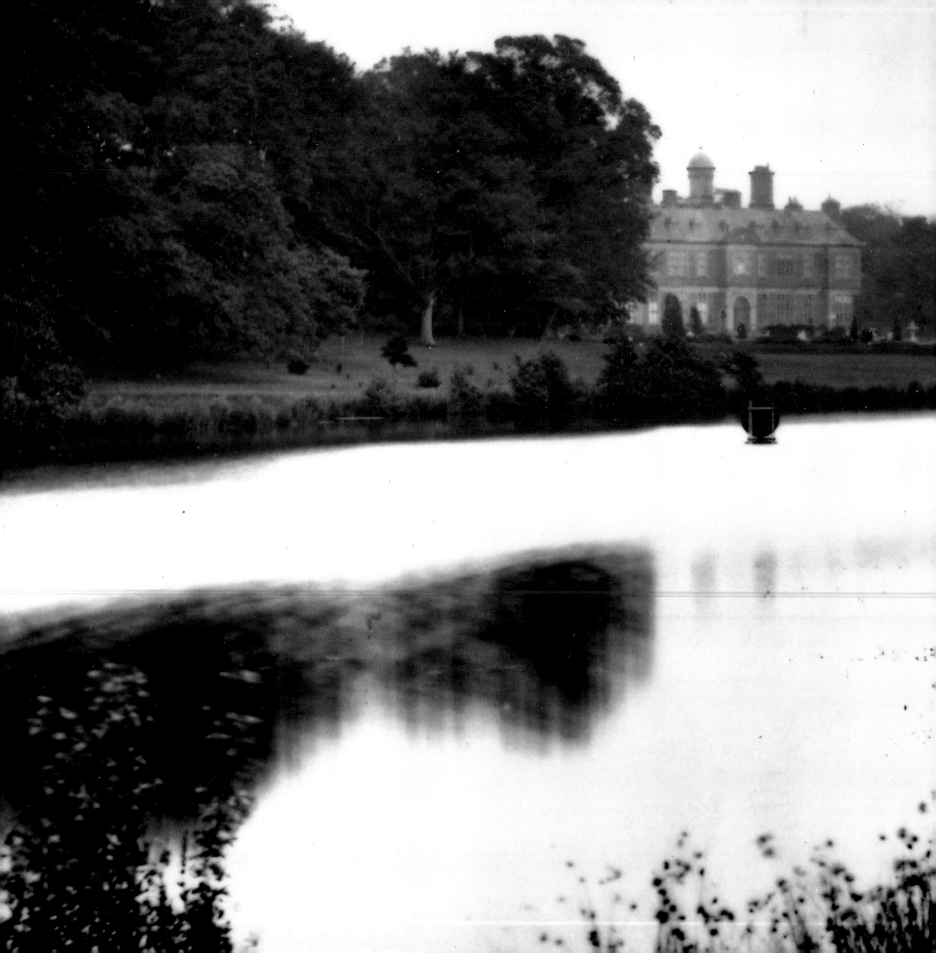

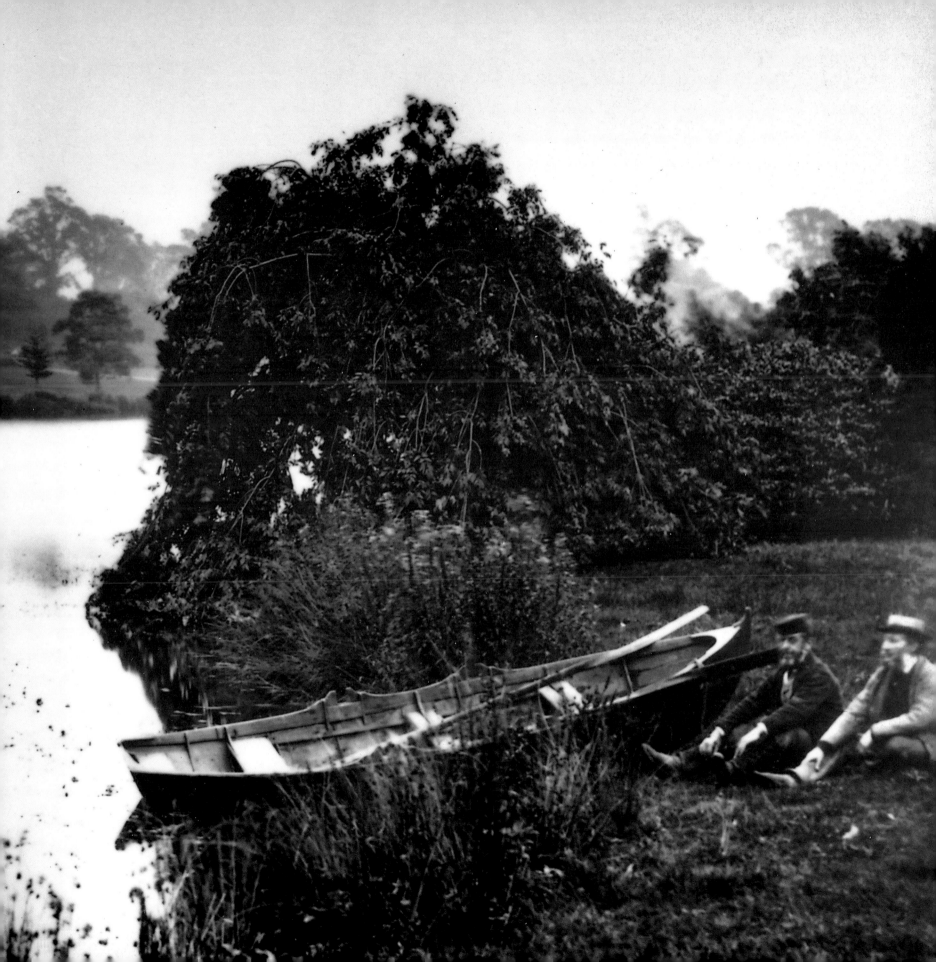

PETWORTH

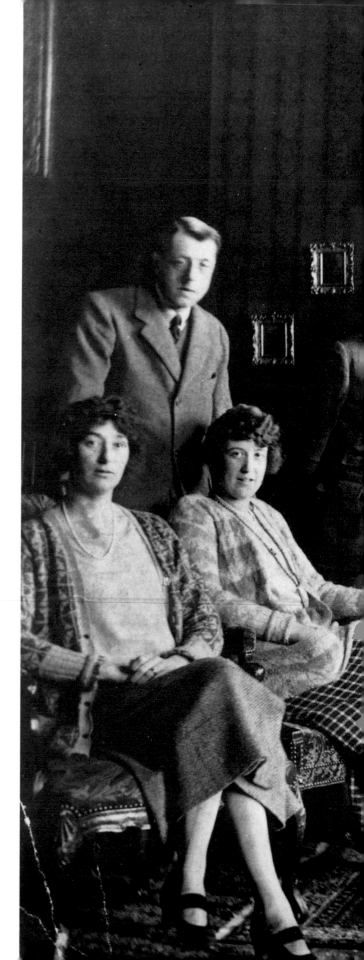

Left to right: The Hon. Mrs Edward Wyndham, the Hon. Edward Wyndham, Lady Leconfield, The Hon. Hugh Wyndham, The Hon. Humphrey Wyndham (seated by fire), The Hon. Mrs Hugh Wyndham, The Dowager Lady Leconfield (in chair), The Hon. Mrs Humphrey Wyndham, Lord Leconfield.

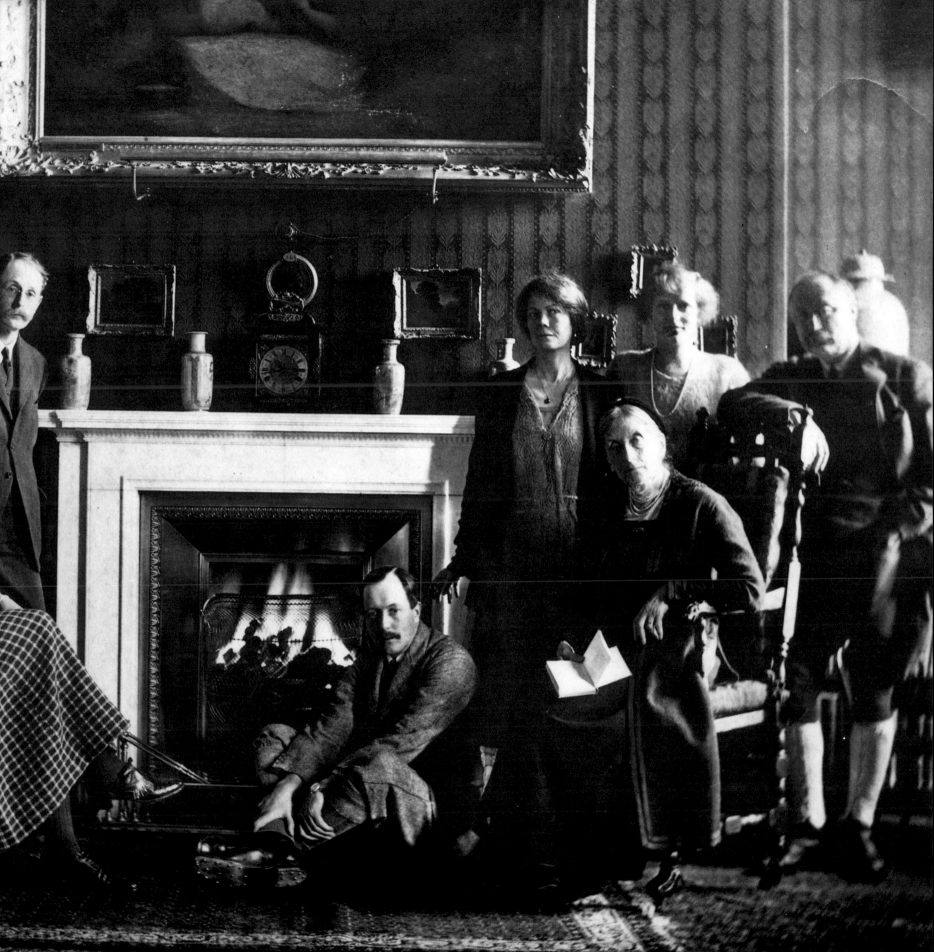

It was for a good reason that Charles Seymour, 6th Duke of Somerset, was known as 'The Proud Duke'. He took his obsession with his lineage and his position to ridiculous lengths, insisting on being served on bended knee and never addressing servants directly. Even his children were expected to stand in his presence, and he is said to have disinherited one of his daughters after he had fallen asleep and woken to find her seated. Jeremiah Milles, who visited him in 1743, wrote that 'The Duke spends most of his time . . . in a grend retirement peculier and agreable only to himself. He comes down to breakfast at 8 of ye clock in the morning in his full dress with his blue ribbon; after breakfast, he goes into his offices, scolds and bullys his servants and steward till dinner time; then very formally hands his Duchess downstairs. His table, tho' spread in a grand manner as if company was expected consists of his own family ye Duchess and his 2 daughters; and when he has a mind to be gracious the chaplain is admitted. He treats all his country neighbours, and indeed everybody else, with such uncommon pride, and distance, yt none of them visit him.' It was thus quite in character that he should have built at Petworth one of the grandest houses in England.

Lady Elizabeth Percy was only fifteen when she made her third marriage to the Duke of Somerset, bringing with her Petworth, a fortified manor house which was the ancient seat of the Percy family. Apart from the traceried east window of the chapel and part of the cellars, none of this remains, for as soon as his wife came of age in 1688, the Duke embarked upon a complete reconstruction of the old building, turning it into a palace with a 320 foot long façade, the inspiration for which undoubtedly came from France. Though there have been various alterations in the succeeding years, the house we see today is basically still that built by the 6th Duke. On his death, Petworth passed first to his son Algernon, who died without a male heir, and subsequently to his daughter Catherine, the wife of a Norfolk landowner, Sir William Wyndham, in whose family (later created Earls of Egremont and Barons Leconfield) it remained till 1947, when the 3rd Lord Leconfield made it over to the Trust.

'I arrived at Petworth at 3.30,' recalls James Lees-Milne of 19 July 1945. 'I stopped at the street entrance, walked through a long, gloomy passage, crossed a drive, passed under a *porte-cochère* into a hall, and was ushered into Lord Leconfield's presence. He gave me a hurried handshake without a smile, and told the housekeeper to show me round the inside . . . She and one housemaid look after this vast palace . . . Then I was handed back to Lord Leconfield . . . He was highly suspicious. He looked up and said, "Understand, this visit commits me to nothing. I much doubt whether the National Trust can help me." . . . He walked me very slowly round the park . . . He said that the Victorian architect Salvin, when summoned by his father, stood on the mound in the park, and pointing to the house said, "My Lord, there is only one thing to be done. Pull the whole house down and rebuild it." His father replied, "You had better see the inside first." At 5.45 Lord Leconfield, tired out, led me to the street door where he dismissed me. Pointing to a tea house with an enormous notice CLOSED hanging in the window, he said, "You will get a very good tea in there. Put it down to me. Goodbye." Had I not been forewarned I would have concluded that my visit was a distinct failure.'

Opposite above: George Wyndham, son of the 2nd Lord Leconfield, and his tutor, Mr Robinson, in the schoolroom, 1878.

Opposite below: George, Charles and Mary Wyndham with their governess in the schoolroom, c.1875.

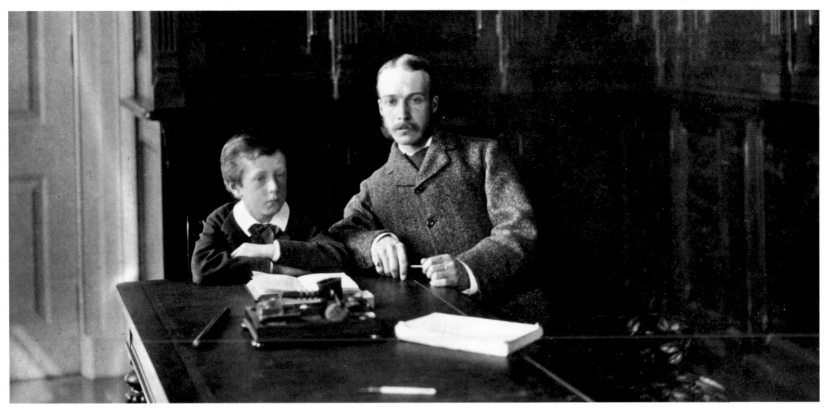

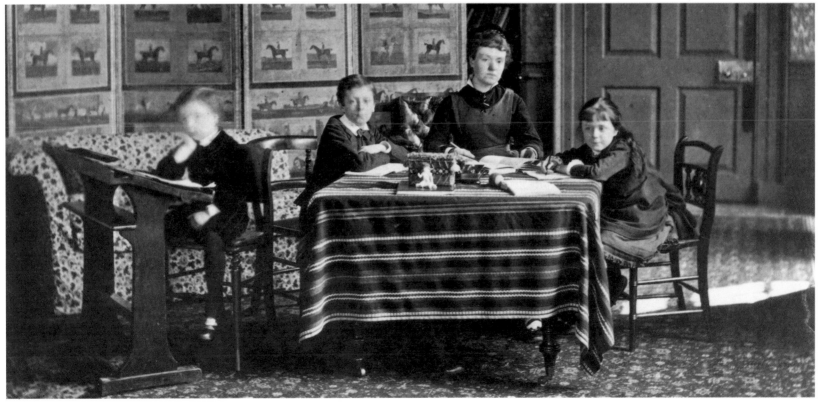

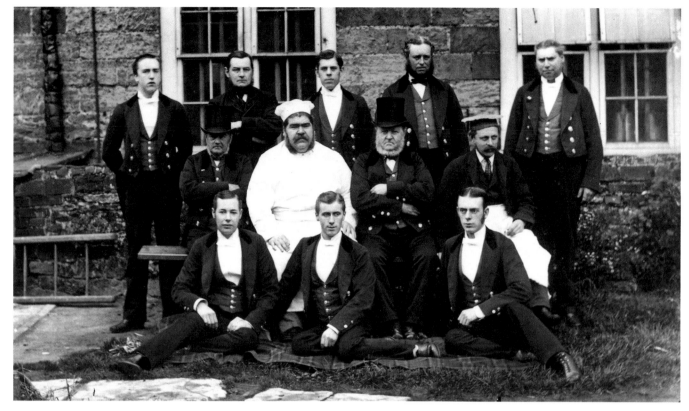

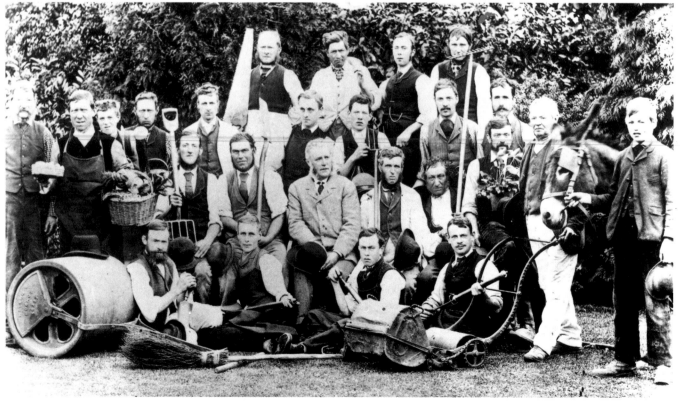

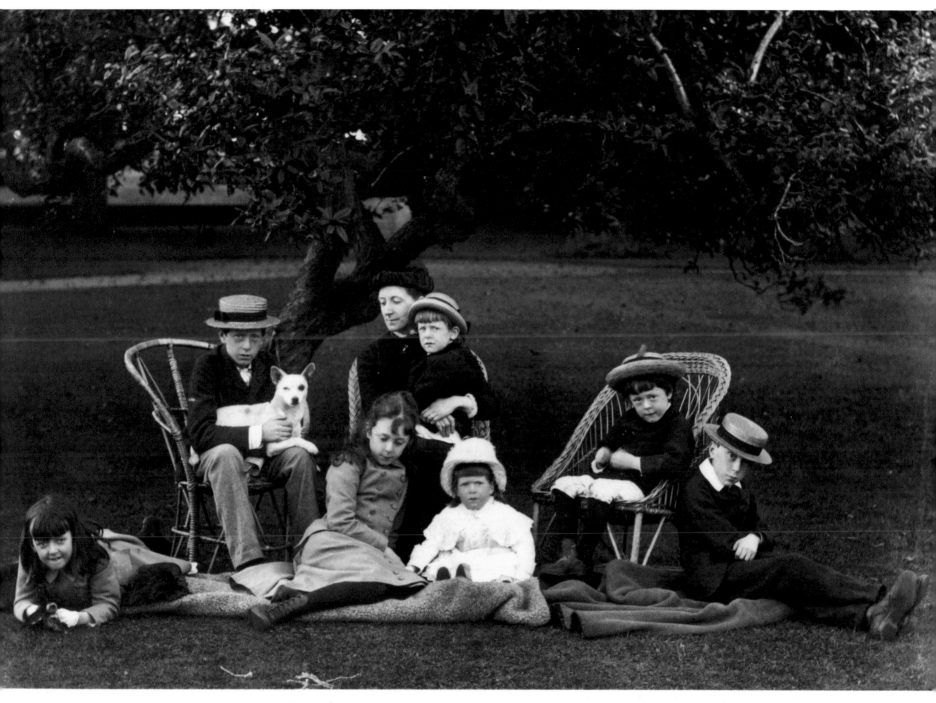

Above: The family of the 2nd Lord Leconfield.
Back row, seated in chairs, left to right: George, Lady L., Hugh, William.
Seated on ground, left to right: Maud, Mary, Margaret, Charles.

Left above: Household servants at Petworth, 1883.

Left below: The gardeners at Petworth, 1880s.

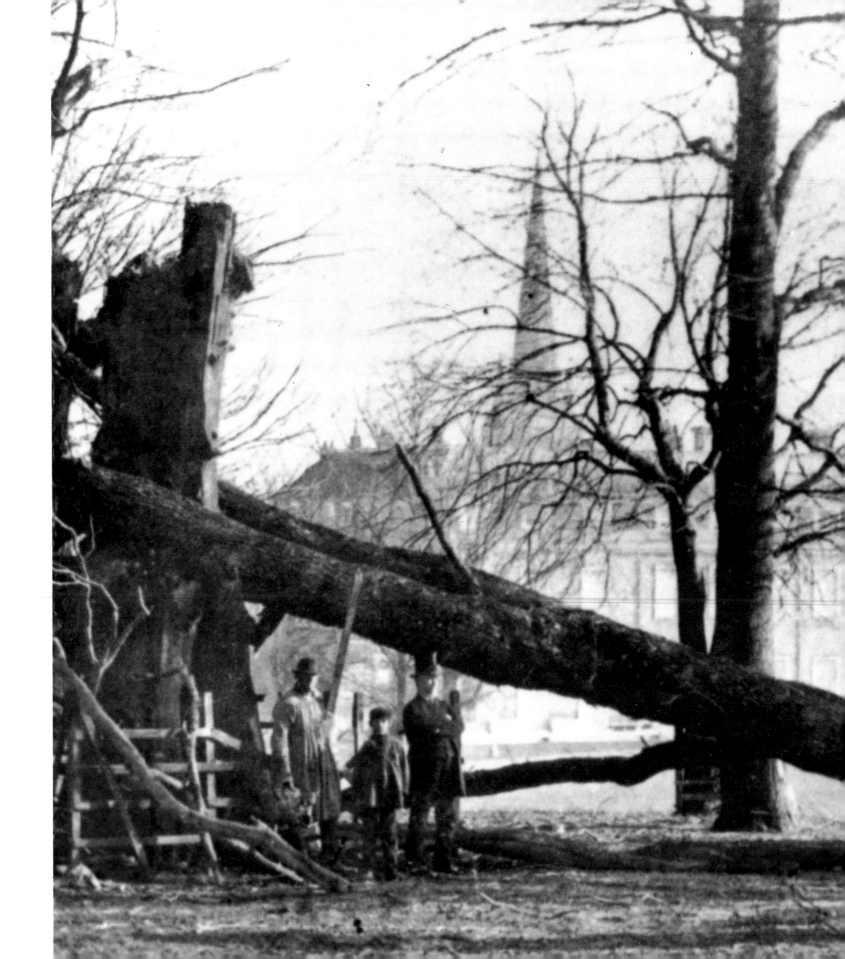

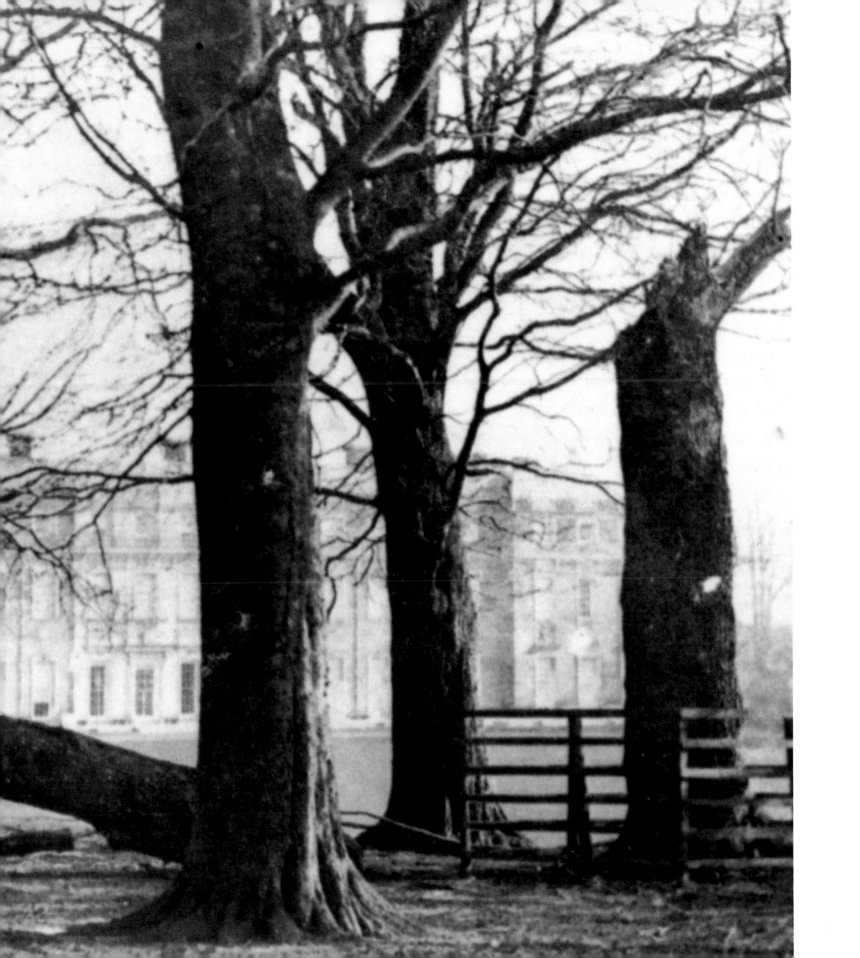

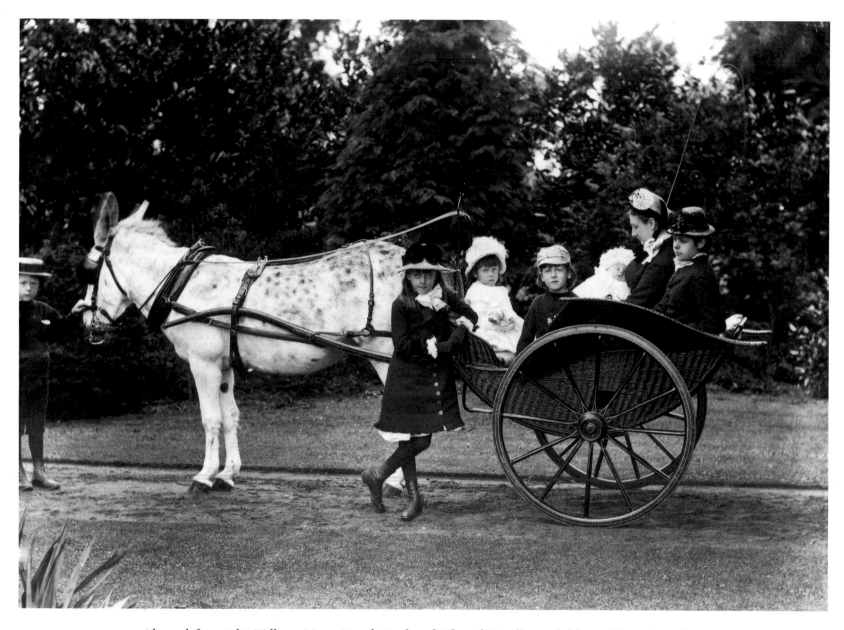

Above, left to right: William, Mary, Maud, Hugh and Edward Wyndham, children of the 2nd Lord Leconfield with Lady L. and nursemaid, 1883.

Opposite: John Maxse, grandson of the 2nd Lord Leconfield, on his pony.

Previous page: A fallen tree in the park, c. 1860.

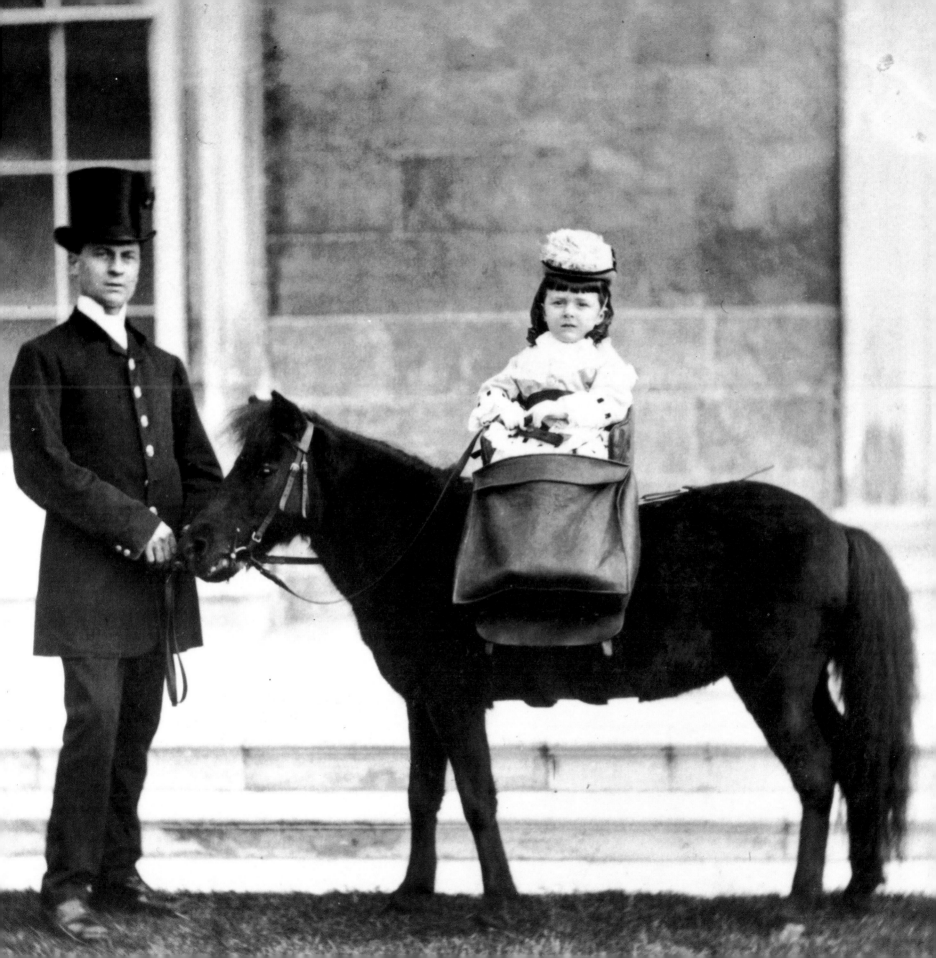

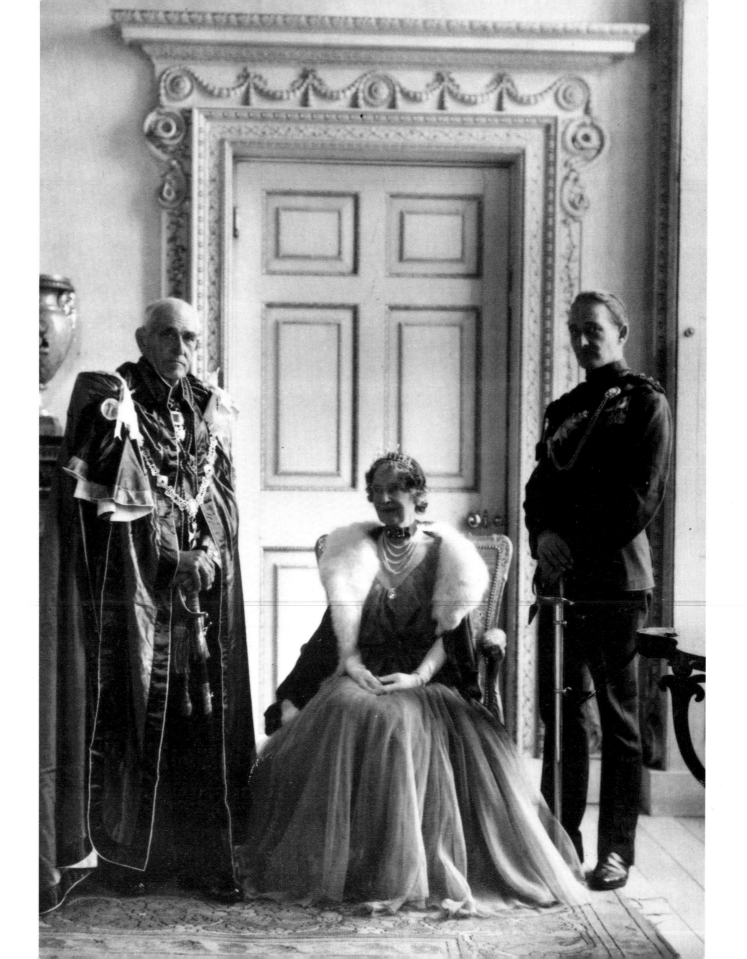

UPPARK

'**Motored** in the office Morris to Uppark in Sussex,' wrote James Lees-Milne in his diary of 12 January 1947. '. . . The country here is heavenly, rolling downs under a pellucid sea-light. Backed by a belt of trees the house commands a panoramic view of sheep-cropped sward and the sea. A romantic house . . .' Uppark is an unspoiled gem, and has been called 'the Sleeping Beauty House'. It was built, *c.* 1690, for the Earl of Tankerville to the designs of William Talman, but its heyday was from 1747 to 1846 when it was owned by the Fetherstonhaughs. Sir Matthew, a keeper of meticulous accounts, estimated that in the years up to 1759 he spent £16,615 on Uppark, which included the creation of a great white and gold Saloon on the south side of the house; the redecoration of many of the state rooms, and the furnishing of the house with pictures, books and furniture bought on a Continental tour which he made between 1749 and 1751. The house has changed remarkably little since.

Sir Harry Fetherstonhaugh, Sir Matthew's only son and heir, was an immensely rich and cultivated young man, with a wild streak. In 1780, six years after his father's death, he caused a considerable stir in the neighbourhood by bringing home to live with him an ill-educated fifteen-year-old dancing girl called Emma Hart – better known by her later name of Emma Hamilton – whom, a year later, he kicked out into the arms of Charles Greville. He then threw himself into society, becoming a close friend of the Prince Regent. In July 1785 a certain Miss Iremonger wrote to a friend, 'I have been staying with my Aunt at Uppark, and are now come here to vacate our places to the Prince and his Party. The Entertainment was to last three days; great preparations were making to render it completely elegant. Races, of all sorts, were to be upon the most beautiful spot of ground I believe England can produce, and three hot dishes of meat were to form a regular part of each morning's breakfast . . .' For twenty-five years Uppark was the setting for many a brilliant occasion. After that Sir Harry fell out with the Prince. The lavish parties stopped. He retired from society and in 1825, at the age of seventy, surprised the neighbourhood once again by marrying his head dairymaid, Mary Ann Bullock, the daughter of the Uppark poulterer. After Sir Harry died in 1846, she and her younger sister, Frances, lived on in the house until their respective deaths in 1874 and 1895, when the estate was left to Colonel Keith Turnour, the son of an old family friend, and thence to Admiral the Hon. Sir Herbert Meade, both of whom adopted the name of Fetherstonhaugh.

When James Lees-Milne visited Uppark in 1947, negotiations were already under way for the Trust to take it over. He was touched by the Meade-Fetherstonhaugh's devotion to the house. 'Lady M-F showed me all round. She has done wonders repairing the curtains and stuffs and bringing back their old colours by dye from her herb garden . . . There are no servants in the house now at all. Lady M-F and the Admiral gave us luncheon and tea in the basement. Their lives are completely and utterly sacrificed to the house, and they and their son love it.'

Admiral the Hon. Sir Herbert and Lady Meade-Fetherstonhaugh with their son Richard, dressed for the Coronation of Queen Elizabeth II.

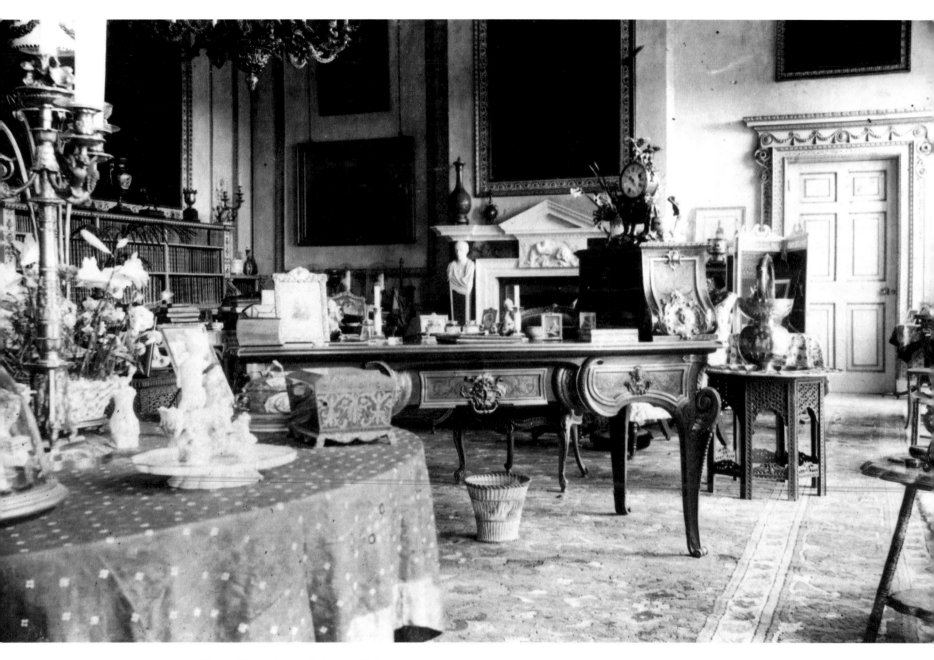

Above: Uppark, the Saloon, 1908.

Opposite above: Mrs Turnour-Fetherstonhaugh in front of the west façade.

Opposite below: Colonel Keith Turnour-Fetherstonhaugh and his retrievers.

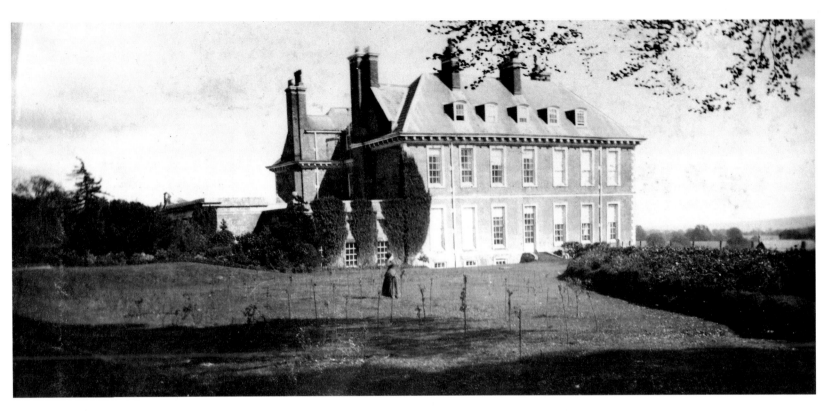

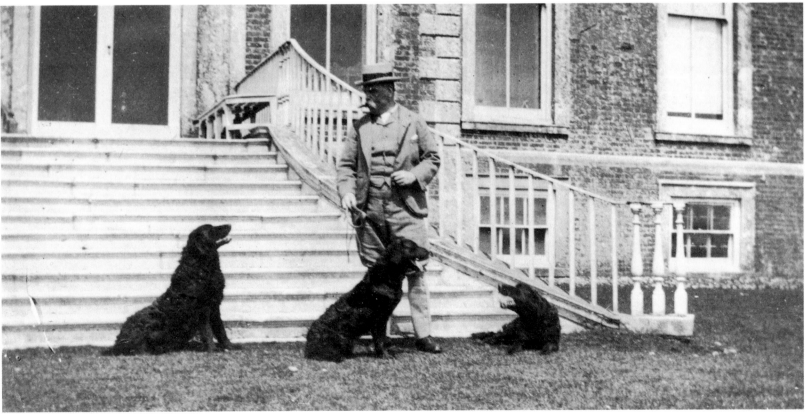

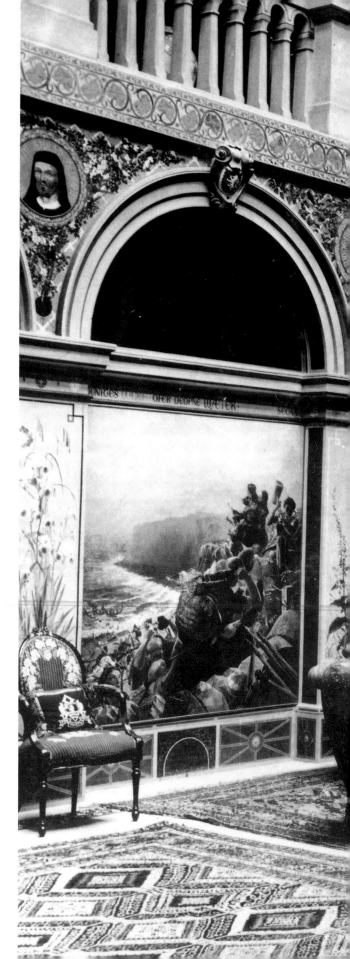

WALLINGTON

CAMBO, NORTHUMBERLAND

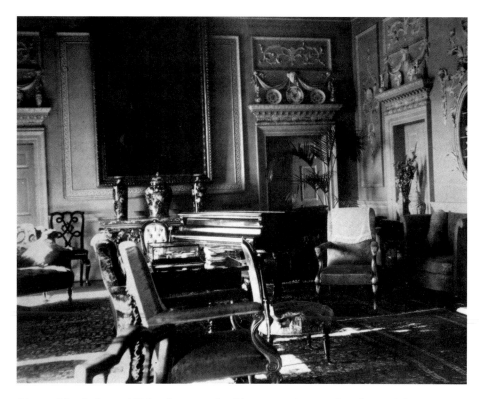

Above: The Saloon, 1899, photographed by Miss Choate, daughter of the American Ambassador.

Opposite: The Hall, 1894. The painted panels, depicting scenes from Northumberland history, were the work of William Bell Scott.

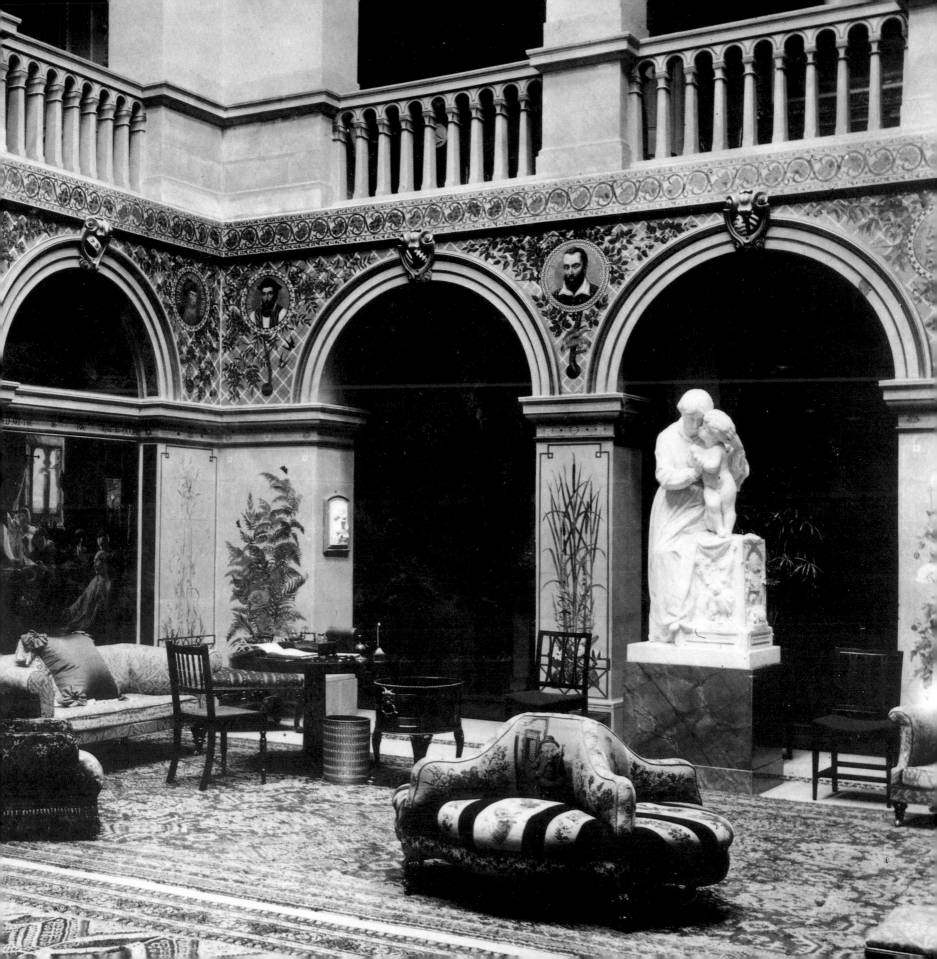

'Such a curious place this is! and such curious people!' wrote Augustus Hare of a visit to Wallington in 1862. 'I get on better with them now, and even Sir Walter is gruffly kind and grumpily amiable . . . His conversation is so curious that I follow him about everywhere, and take notes under his nose, which he does not seem to mind in the least, but only says something more quaint and astonishing the next minute. Lady Trevelyan is equally unusual. She is abrupt to a degree, and contradicts everything. Her little black eyes twinkle with mirth all day long, though she says she is ill and has "the most extraordinary *feels*"; she is "sure no one ever had such extraordinary feels as she has." She never appears to attend to her house a bit, which is like the great desert with one or two little oases in it, where by good management you may possibly make yourself comfortable.' He also complained that the house was haunted; 'awwful noises are heard all through the night; footsteps rush up and down the untrodden passages; wings flap and beat against the windows; bodiless people unpack and put away their things all night long, and invisible things are felt to breathe over you as you lie in bed. I think my room is quite horrid . . . I have pushed the heavy dressing-table with its weighty mirror, etc., against [the door] to keep out all the nasty things that might try to come in.'

Wallington is a solid and gentlemanly house which sits above the river Wansbeck near Cambo in Northumberland. Though originally built in 1688 by Sir William Blackett, a Newcastle merchant, it is predominantly a Georgian house, remodelled in the 1740s, for Sir Walter Calverly Blackett, by Daniel Garrett. He gave it some fine rococo rooms, notably the Saloon which, with its magnificent plasterwork by Pietro Francini, can claim to be one of the most beautiful eighteenth-century rooms in England. Sir Walter died childless in 1777, and Wallington passed to his nephew Sir John Trevelyan, with whose family it has been associated ever since. When Augustus Hare visited his son, what is perhaps the most extraordinary room in the house, the central Hall, had only just been completed. This was the work of John Dobson, then the leading architect in the north-east, and was created by roofing over a central courtyard. The decoration, by the Pre-Raphaelite painter William Bell Scott, is a manifestation of the taste of Sir Walter's wife Pauline, nineteen years his junior, who had many friends in the Brotherhood, including Ruskin, Millais, Holman Hunt and Swinburne, all of whom were frequent guests at Wallington.

Wallington remained in the possession of the Trevelyans till 1941, and in all that time an intellectual tradition survived there. Sir Charles Edward, the successor of Sir Walter, was married to the sister of Lord Macaulay. His son, Sir George Otto, was a distinguished man of letters and historian, the editor of his uncle's *Life and Letters*. Sir Charles, his son, was a great reformer, who sat in the House of Commons both as a Liberal and a Socialist, and was twice President of the Board of Education. When James Lees-Milne visited there in September 1942, after Sir Charles had handed the whole place over to the Trust, he found it all just a little too much. 'After dinner I am worn out, and long for bed. But no. We have general knowledge questions. Lady T. puts the questions one after the other with lightning rapidity. I am amazed and impressed by her mental agility, and indeed by that of the daughters, who with pursed lips shoot forth unhesitating answers like a spray of machine-gun bullets. All most alarming to a tired stranger. At the end of the "game" . . . they allot marks. Every single member of the family gets 100 out of 100. The son-in-law gets 80, Matheson (who is also a clever man) gets 30. I get 0 . . . Deeply humiliated I receive condolences from the Trevelyans and assurances that I shall no doubt do better next time. I make an inward vow that there never will be a next time.'

A tea party in the Central Hall, 1899.

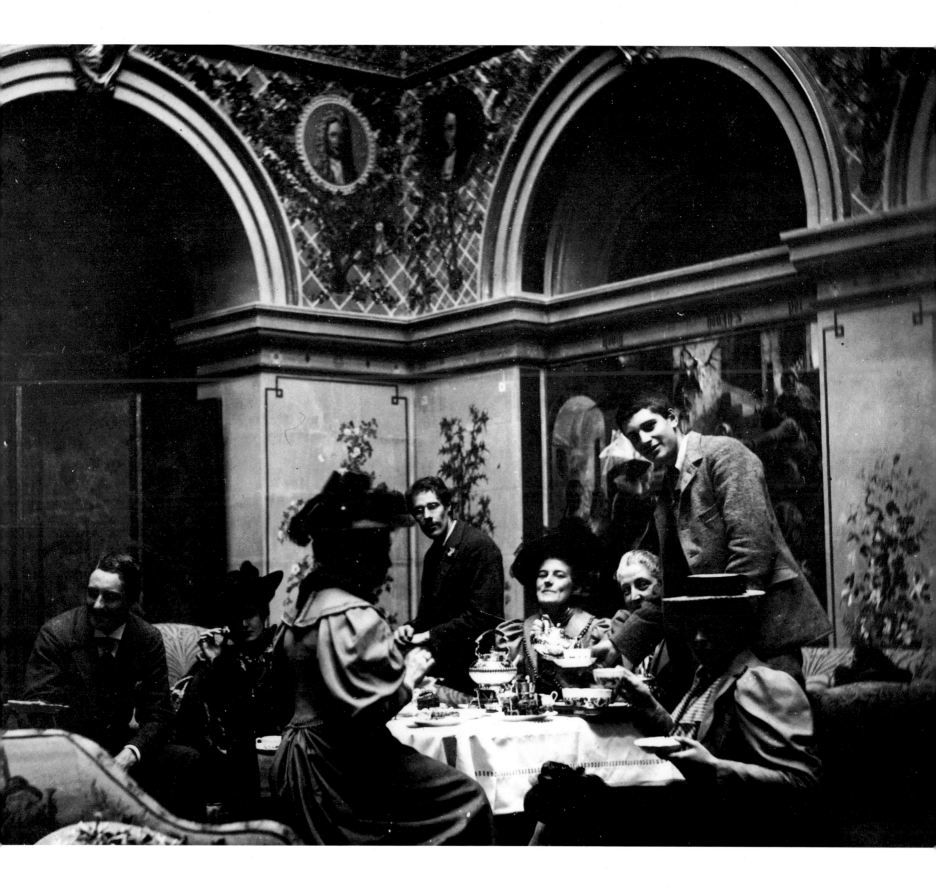

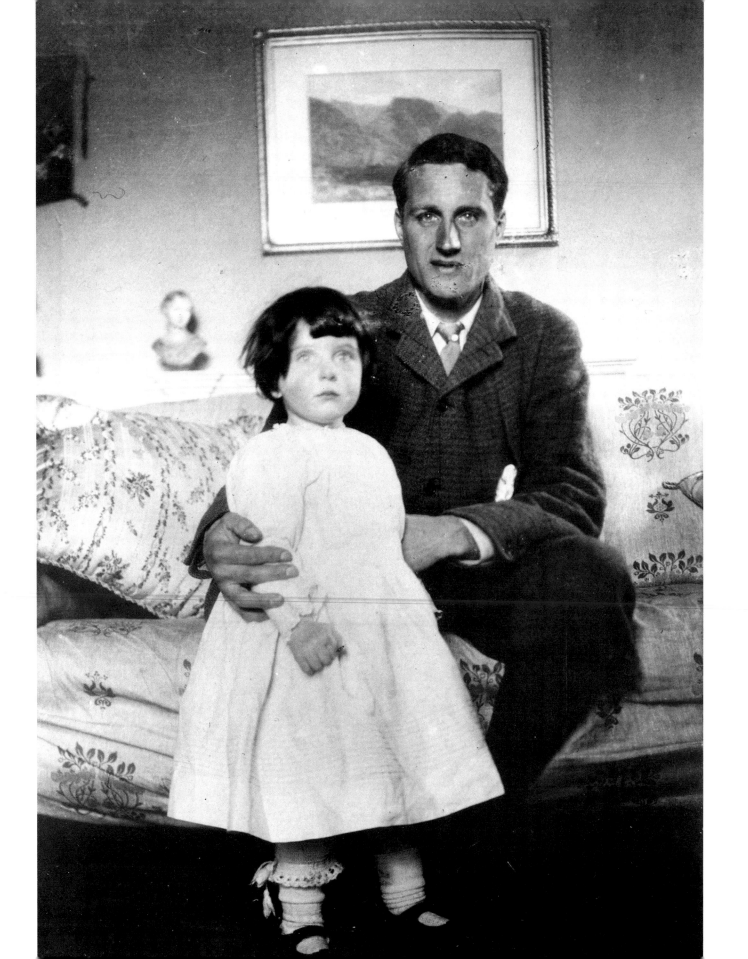

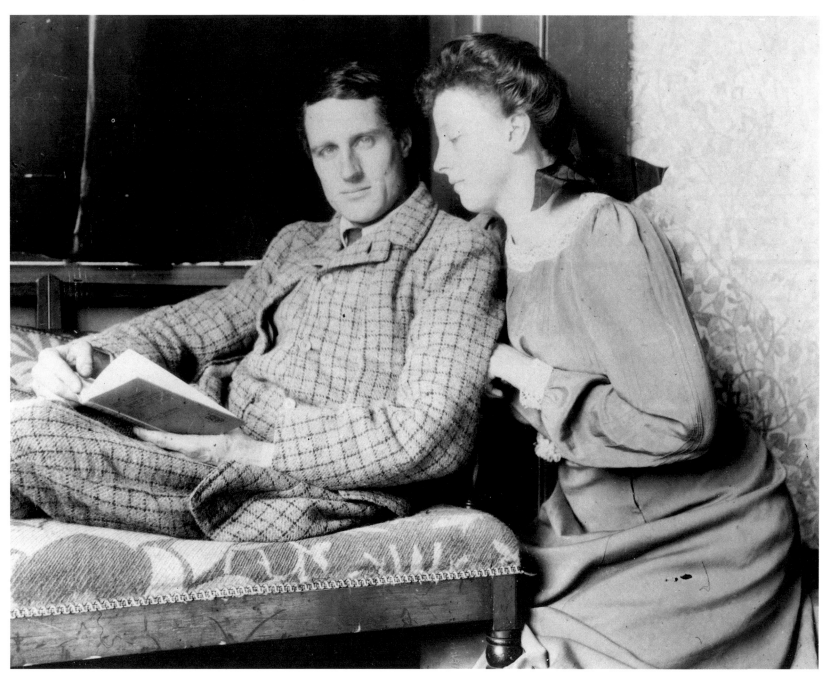

Above: The engagement photograph of Sir Charles Trevelyan and Miss Mary Bell, September 1903.

Left: Sir Charles Trevelyan with his daughter, Pauline, August 1907.

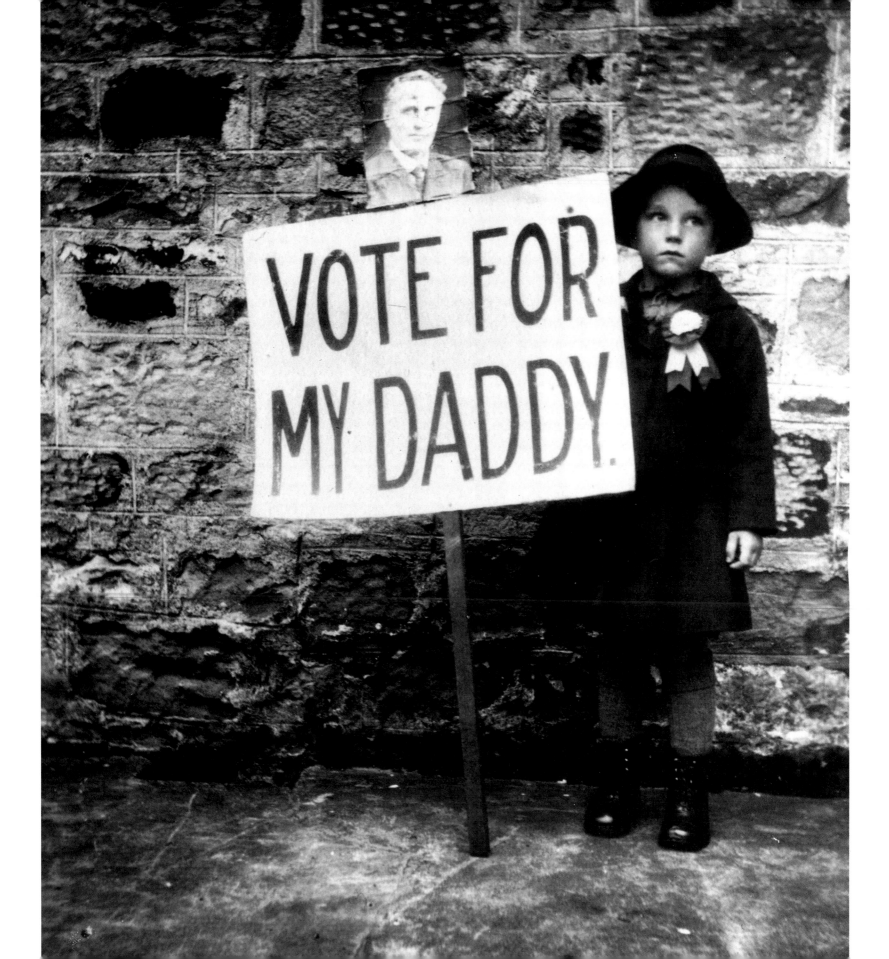

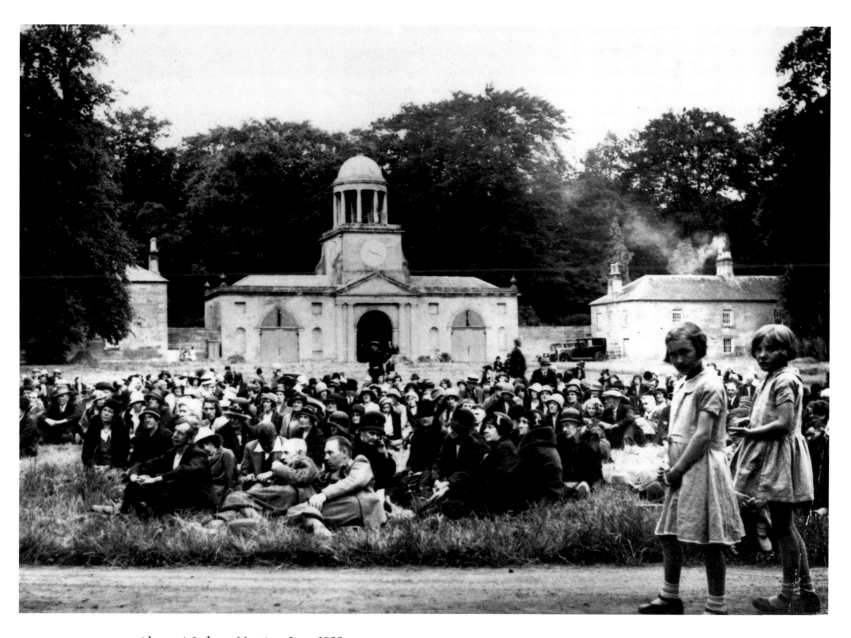

Above: A Labour Meeting, June 1933.

Left: Geoffrey Trevelyan holding a placard encouraging people to vote for his father who was standing as a Labour candidate in Newcastle Central, December 1923.

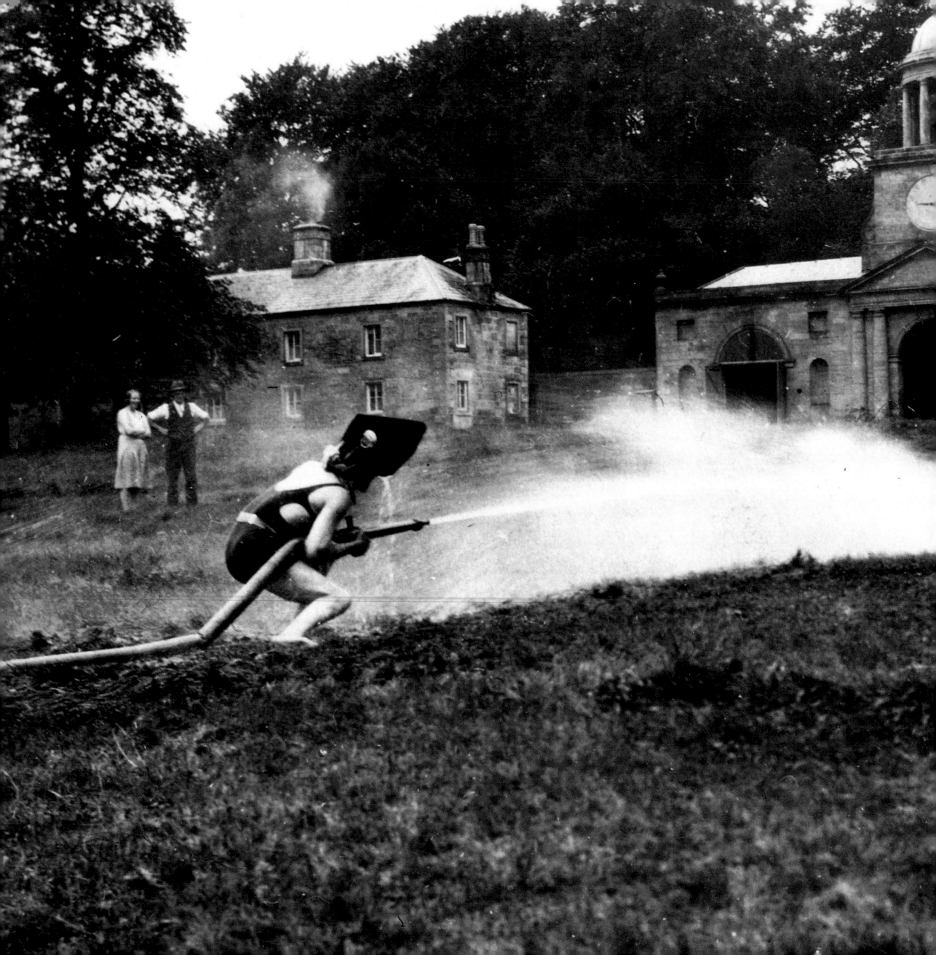

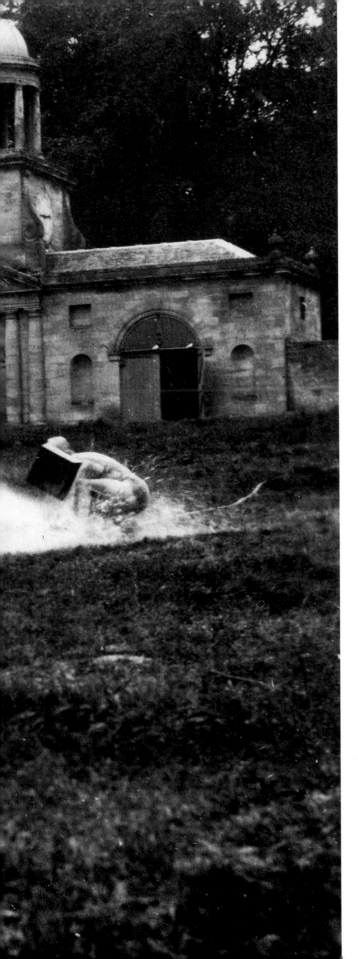

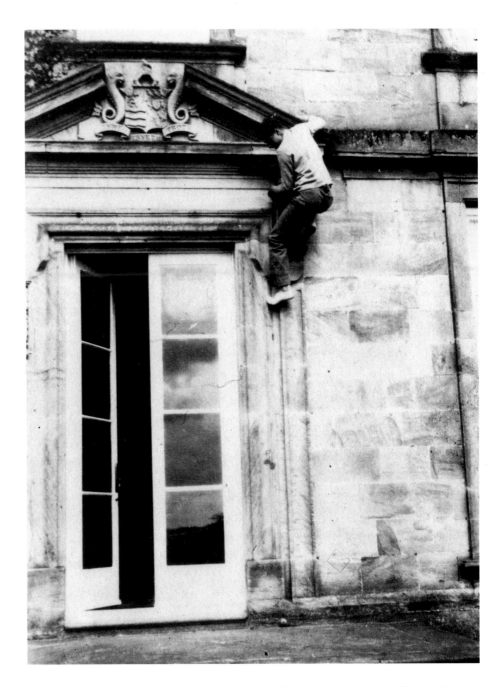

Above: 'How the family obtains the most complete knowledge on Wallington'. George Trevelyan, September 1929.

Left: A battle with hosepipes between George Corderoy and George Trevelyan.

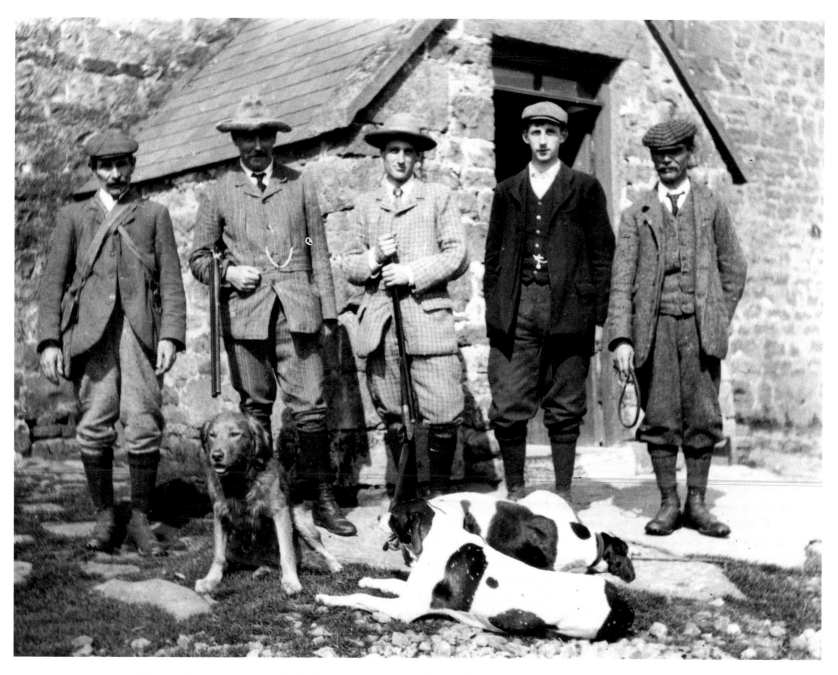

Above: Shooting party at Redpath, August, 1904. Left to right: Shade (Keeper), H. Watson, Charlie T., Baxter (Keeper), Howie (Keeper). Dogs: Cronje, Shot and Ben.

Opposite: Three gardeners, May 1954. Herdman, Armstrong and Parker.

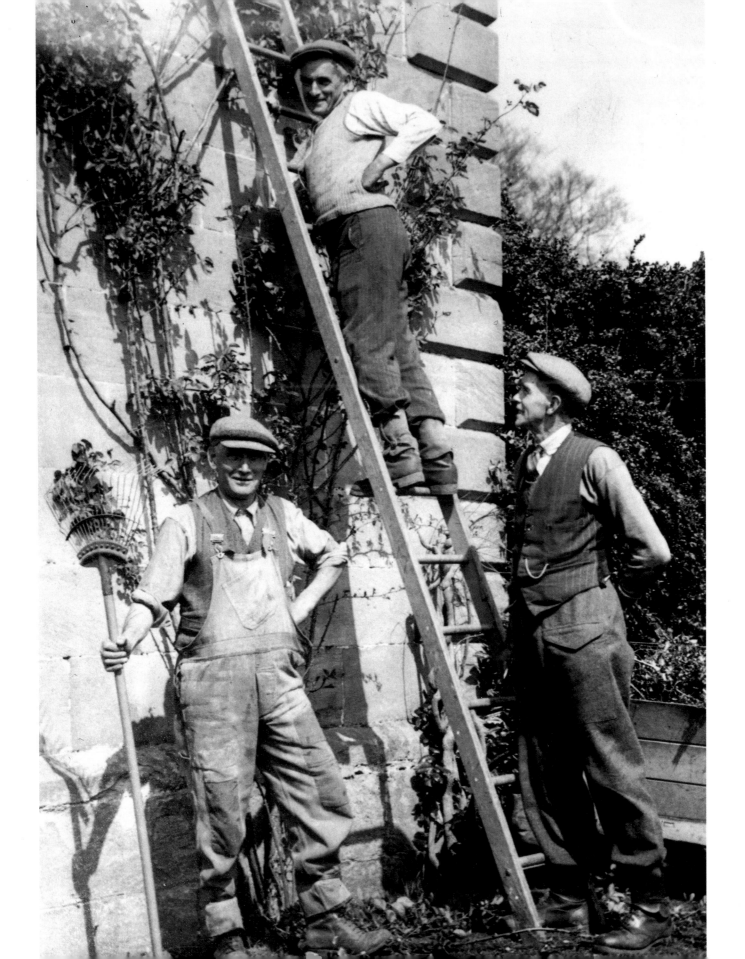

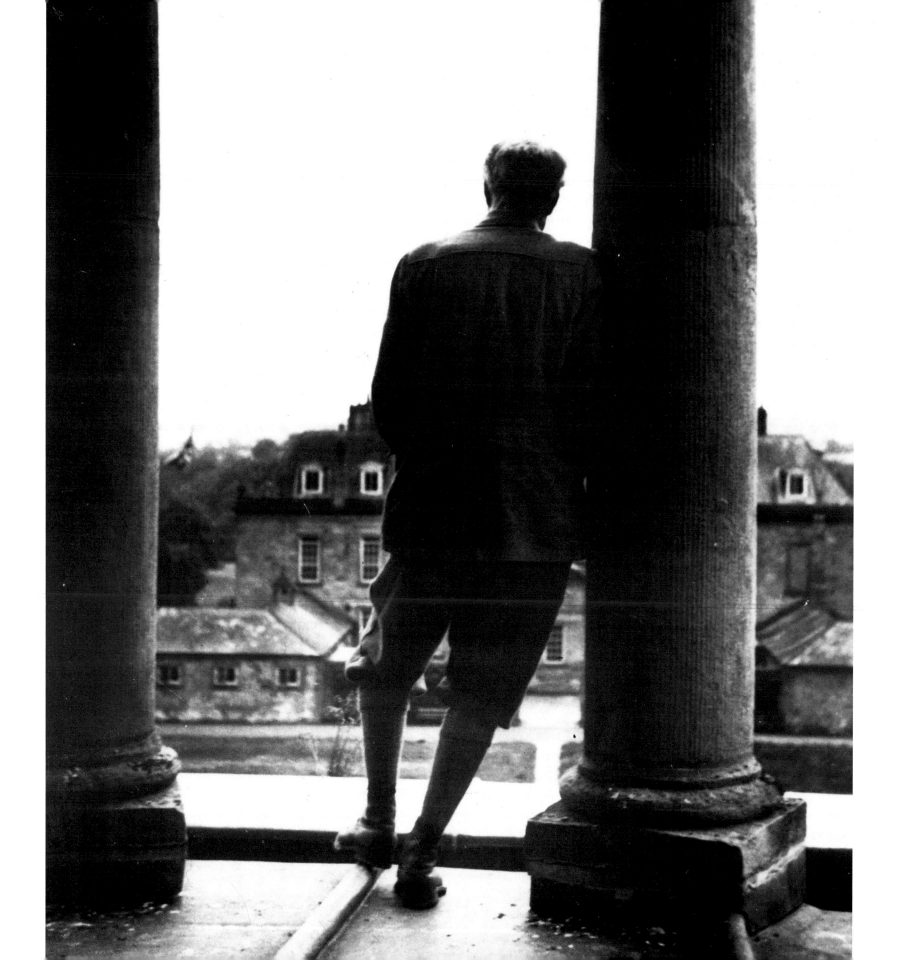

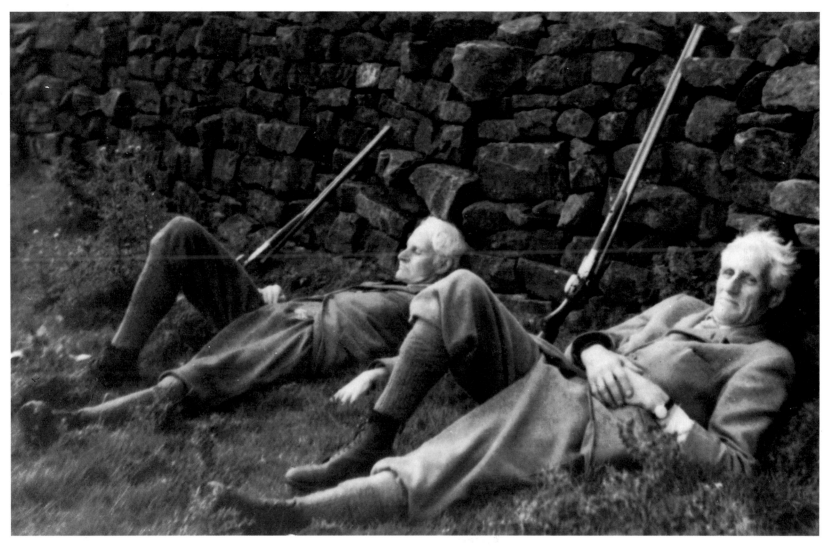

Above: Summer 1945, at Fallowlees, George and Charles Trevelyan, resting after lunch.

Left: The Master of the House. Sir Charles Trevelyan surveys his domain from the stable bell tower, August 1932.

CLEVEDON COURT

BRISTOL, AVON

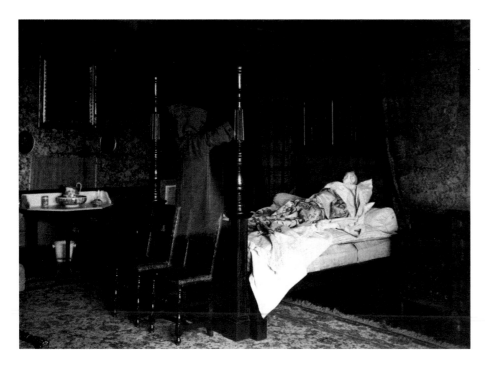

Above: The Clevedon ghost.

Opposite: The Great Hall as furnished by Dame Rhoda Elton in the Nineteenth Century.

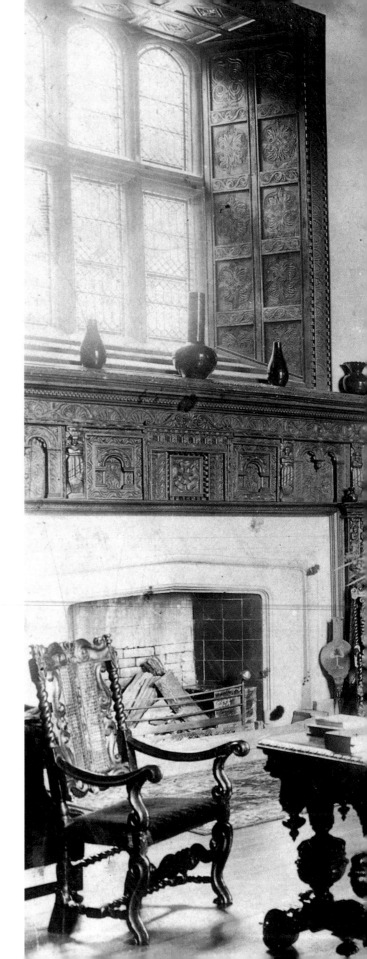

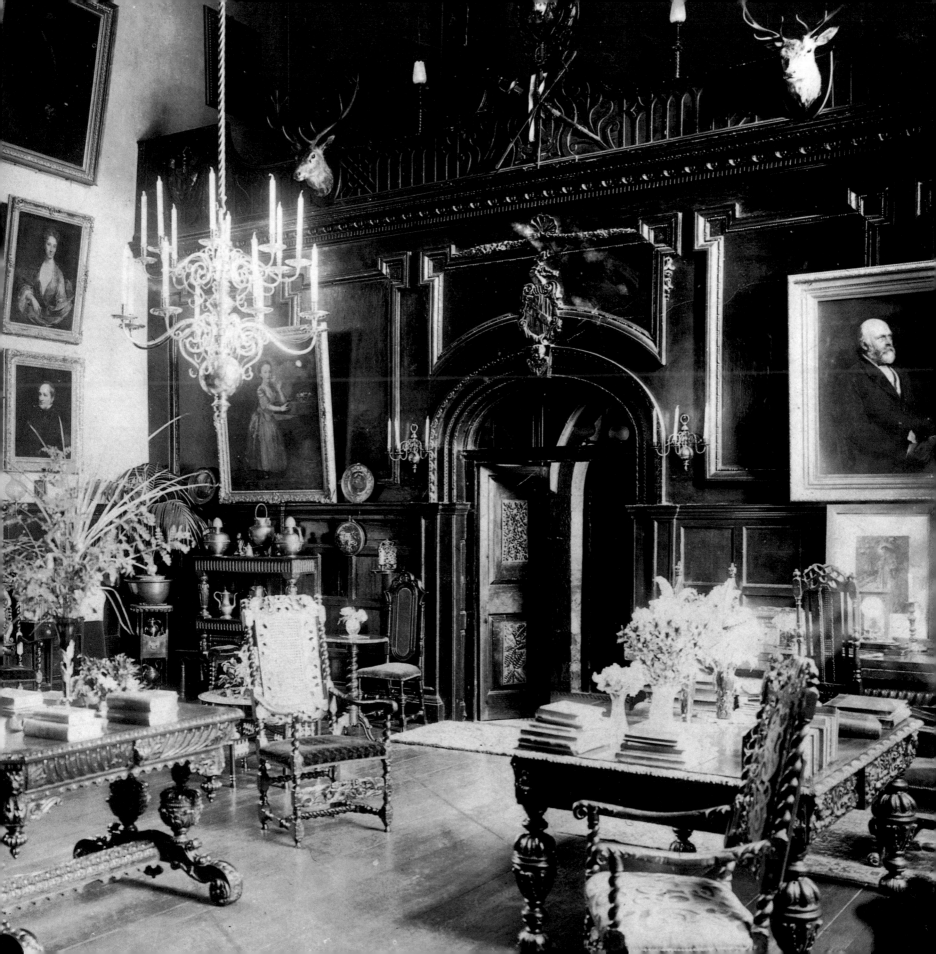

The first known description of Clevedon Court is to be found in a survey of the manor taken in 1629. 'There is also scituate upon the said demaynes a fayre auncient and large stone house, stronglie built and pleasantlie scituate, conteyning many faire rooms, howses of office, and other buildings, with two gardens, an orchard, a fayre court, a strong and large barne, and other out houses, besides 60 acres of wood and coppice of 30 or 40 yeres not valuewed.' When this was written, the house had already stood for over three hundred years, having been built *c.* 1320 by Sir John de Clevedon as an extension to even earlier buildings, the oldest of which, the Tower at the north-east corner of the house, dated back to the middle of the Thirteenth Century and was all that remained of a fort built as a protection against invaders from Wales. Sir John's house, which stands today almost unchanged, was a manor house built around a Great Hall, typical of its date except in one respect. Manor houses of the period were almost invariably built next to the parish church. Not so in the case of Clevedon, where St Andrew's church is two miles away. Sir John therefore incorporated into his house a hanging Chapel on the first floor.

The male line of the de Clevedon family came to an end in 1376, and after that Clevedon Court passed to the Northamptonshire family of Wake, who were the owners when the above description was written. At the turn of the Eighteenth Century, it was bought by a Bristol merchant, Sir Abraham Elton, who had built up an immense fortune through a variety of businesses: shipping, property, a glassworks, mining and the slave trade. The Eltons were to remain at Clevedon for the next two hundred and fifty years, each of them making their own contribution to the development of the house. Sir Abraham II, for example, gave the Great Hall a new timber roof and added a coved ceiling. Sir Abraham IV added a few touches of Gothic to the old house, while Sir Abraham V and his wife much improved the grounds, laying out romantic walks and vistas. Their son, Sir Charles Elton, who inherited in 1842, was a poet and classical scholar, a friend of Thackeray, John Clare, Charles Lamb, Robert Southey and Samuel Taylor Coleridge. He was a regular contributor to the *London Magazine* and made Clevedon a centre of literary life. But it is his great-nephew with whom Clevedon is perhaps best associated, Sir Edmund Harry Elton. Landscape artist, mechanic, Captain of the Fire Brigade, photographer, inventor (of the Elton instantaneously detachable dress guard clip to keep ladies' skirts out of their bicycle wheels, and the Elton Rim Brake, one of the first forked bicycle brakes applied to the rim of the wheel instead of the tyre) Sir Edmund was a celebrated potter, the creator of Elton Ware, which at one time enjoyed enormous popularity in America where it was marketed by Tiffany and Company. He has been known forever after as the Potter Baronet.

Sir Edmund's grandson, the late Sir Arthur Hallam Elton, was himself a remarkable man. Having acquired a passion for the cinema while at Cambridge, where he was film critic for Granta, he became a scriptwriter for Gainsborough Films in 1927. Four years later he was recruited by John Grierson for the Empire Marketing Board film unit, and went on to become one of the pioneers of the British documentary film movement. On inheriting Clevedon in 1951, he devoted much of his time to its restoration, but the cost of this, together with that of death duties, made it a necessity to approach the National Trust. The house was handed over in 1960.

The Potter Baronet, photographed in 1886 by E.H. Hayell, with one of his Elton Ware vases. On the left is George Masters, a hunchbacked village boy trained by Sir Edmund.

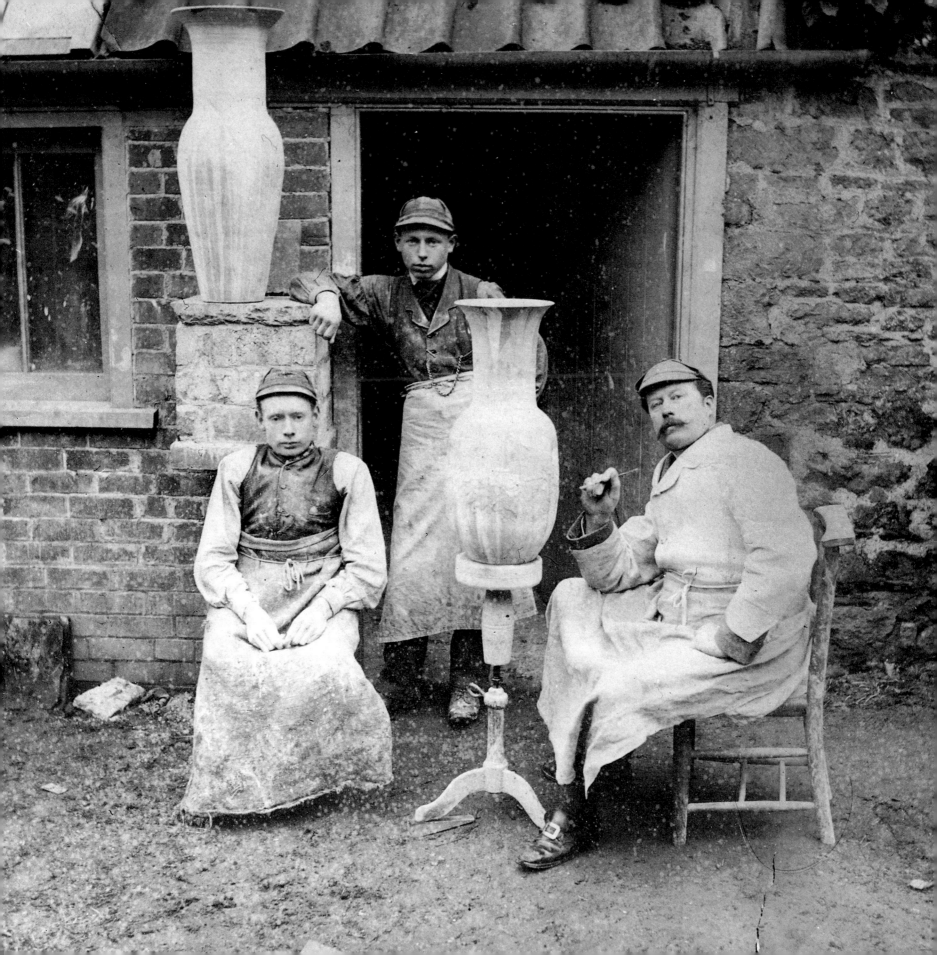

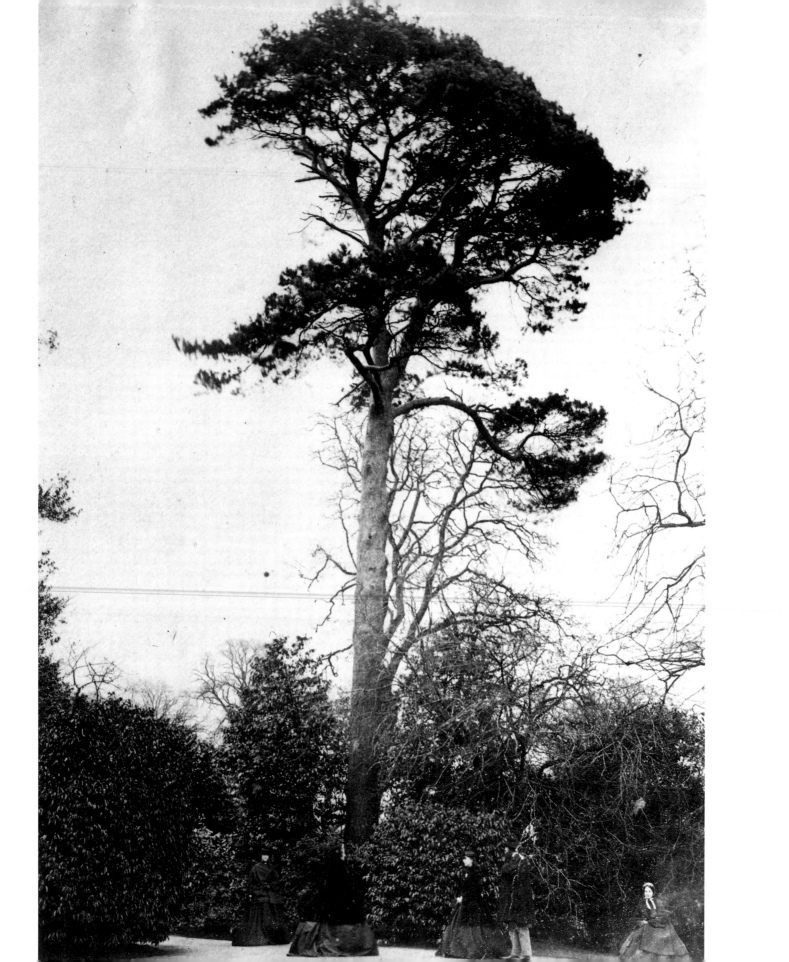

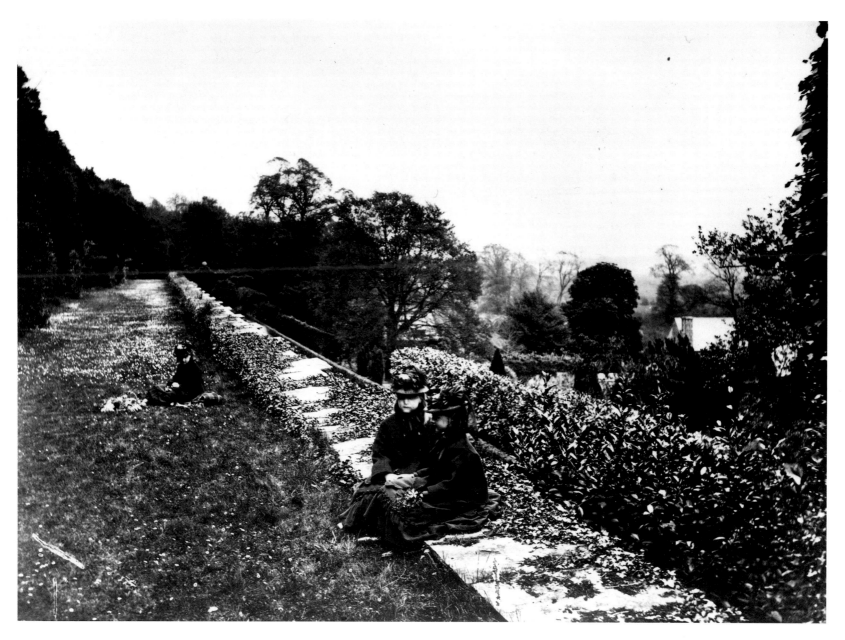

Above: The three granddaughters of Sir Arthur Hallam Elton photographed on the top terrace at Clevedon in 1873 by Goodfellow of Bristol. They are dressed in mourning for their grandmother, Dame Rhoda Elton.

Left: An early photograph by Goodfellow of Bristol showing a group of people under a cedar tree in the garden at Clevedon, dated 1874.

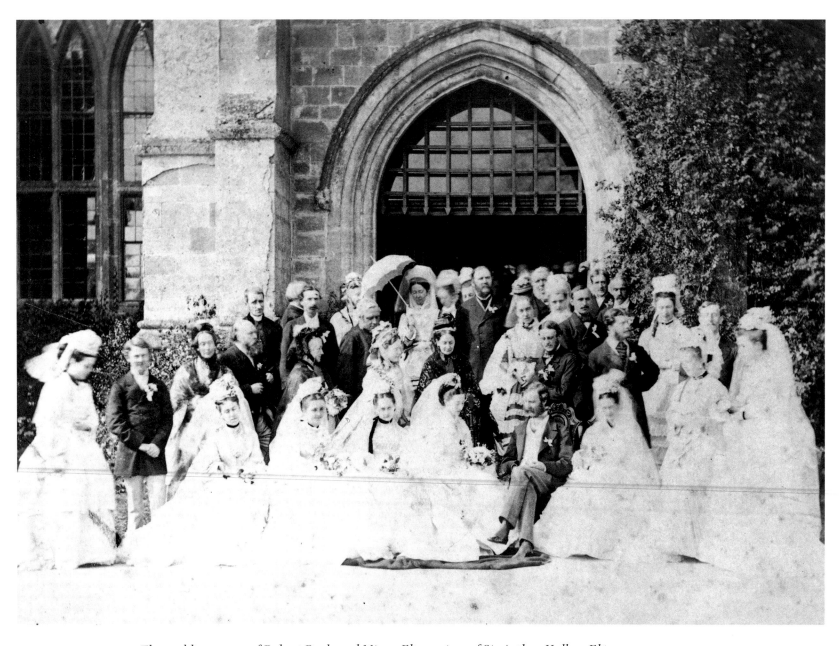

The wedding group of Robert Boyle and Minna Elton, niece of Sir Arthur Hallam Elton,
photographed by Goodfellow of Bristol in April, 1873.

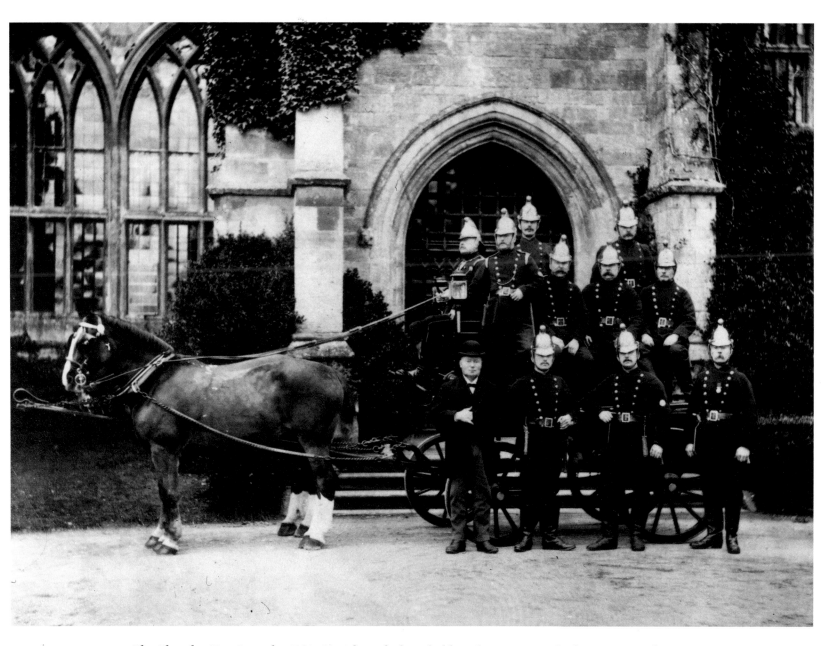

The Clevedon Fire Brigade, 1883. Sir Edmund Elton, holding the reins, was the first captain. The photograph was taken by Edwin Henry Hayell, a well-known photographer in the district.

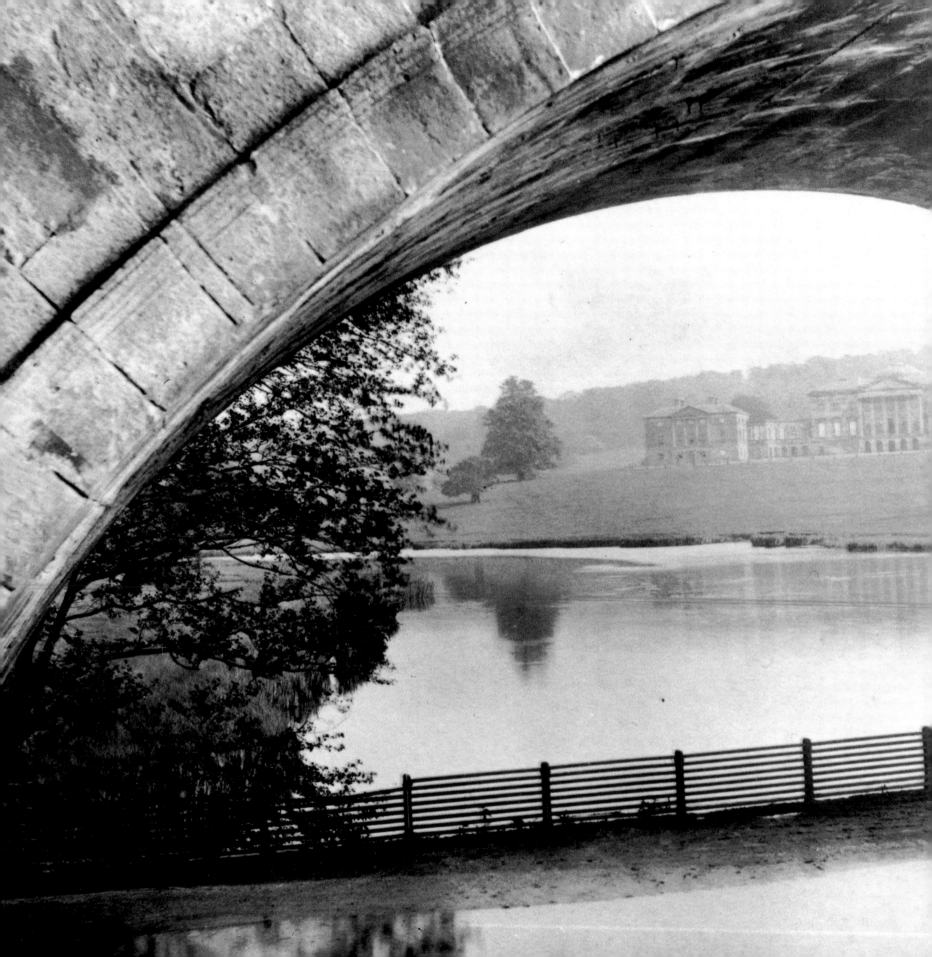

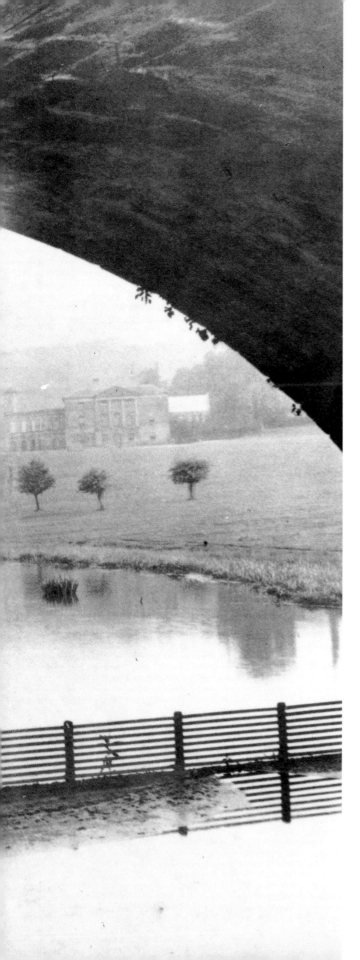

KEDLESTON HALL

DERBYSHIRE

The north front from the arch of the Adam bridge.

When Robert Adam returned to England after a trip to Italy in the winter of 1757–8, he was determined to take London by storm, and lost no time in 'paying his respects to the great', 'putting on a face of brass' and 'trudging doggedly from one nobleman's ante-room to another'. Among those he met, in December 1758, was Sir Nathaniel Curzon, who had recently begun work on the building of a great house, to designs by Matthew Brettingham, on his newly inherited estate at Kedleston in Derbyshire. Soon after the meeting, at which Adam showed his potential patron his latest drawings promoting a new style of architecture, he wrote to his brother James to tell him how Sir Nathaniel was 'struck all of a heap with wonder and amaze and every new drawing he saw made him grieve at his previous engagement with Brettingham. He carried me home in his chariot about three and kept me to four seeing said Brett's designs, and asking my opinion. I proposed alterations and desired he might call them his own fancys. I went back on Saturday evening at six o'clock and sat two hours with him and his lady . . . I revised all his plans and got entire management of his grounds put into my hands with full powers as to temples, bridges, seats and cascades. So that as it only is seven miles round you may guess the play of genius and scope for invention, a noble piece of water, a man resolved to spare no expense with 10,000 a year, good tempered and having taste himself for the arts and little for game.'

A year and a half later Adam was given the sole direction of the house as well, and the result is one of his masterpieces. Indeed the north front has been described as 'the greatest Palladian façade in Britain, and with few rivals anywhere in the world'. Inside are two of the grandest interiors in England, each one a testament to the fascination of the eighteenth-century aristocrat for the architecture of the ancients. The Hall, 67 feet long by 42 feet wide, was based on the Egyptian Hall of Vitruvius, and is set round with twenty enormous Corinthian columns 'proportioned,' wrote Sir Nathaniel in his guide to the house, 'from the three columns in the Campo Vicino in Rome.' The Saloon, a huge domed rotunda rising to a height of 62 feet and top-lit, was inspired by the Pantheon in Rome. Throughout the house, at almost every turn, there is some detail derived from a monument of antiquity.

Kedleston's most famous son was George Nathaniel Curzon, the great-great-grandson of its builder, who had a distinguished career in government, serving as Viceroy of India from 1899 to 1905 and becoming Foreign Secretary in 1917. He inherited his ancestor's love of ancient buildings and bought and restored Tattershall Castle in Lincolnshire and Bodiam Castle in Sussex, both of which he gave to the National Trust. When he finally took over Kedleston in 1916, he lavished his attention on it. 'He made the most elaborate plans,' wrote his second wife, Grace, in her memoirs, 'for new bathrooms and electric lights and central heating and telephones, and everything that could bring it up to date without affecting its essential character . . . He went into every minute detail of the plans, down to the last bath-tap and electric light switch. He even used to get into the new baths – lined first of all with copies of *The Times* – in order to discover if they were the right shape from inside.' In spite of all the improvements, however, Kedleston to her was always rather forbidding. 'I always thought it needed a warm sun to bring its frozen beauty to life. The vast, splendid Hall, the long galleries, the tall, cold rooms with their great windows looking out over the Derbyshire Dales, would have come into their own under a hot blue sky with strong sunlight to warm them. If only it had been built at Genoa or Naples!' Kedleston became the property of the National Trust in 1987 when it was handed over by George Nathaniel's nephew, the 3rd Viscount Scarsdale.

The Beech Avenue, 1885.

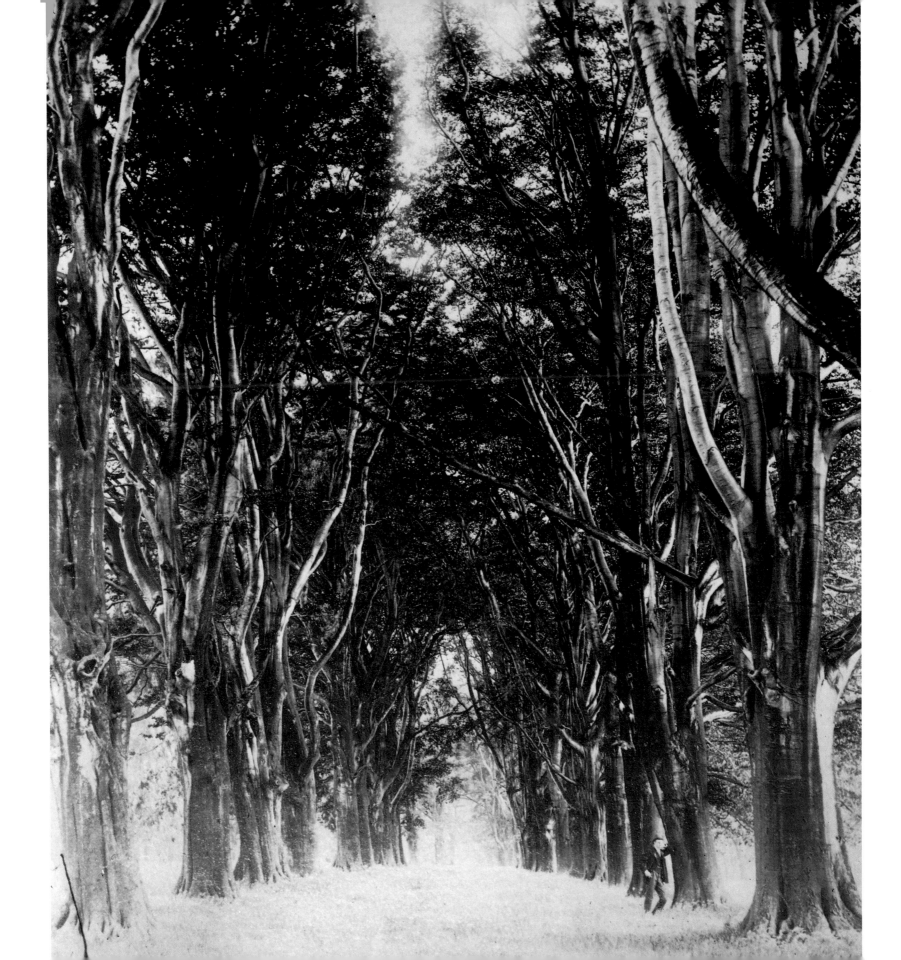

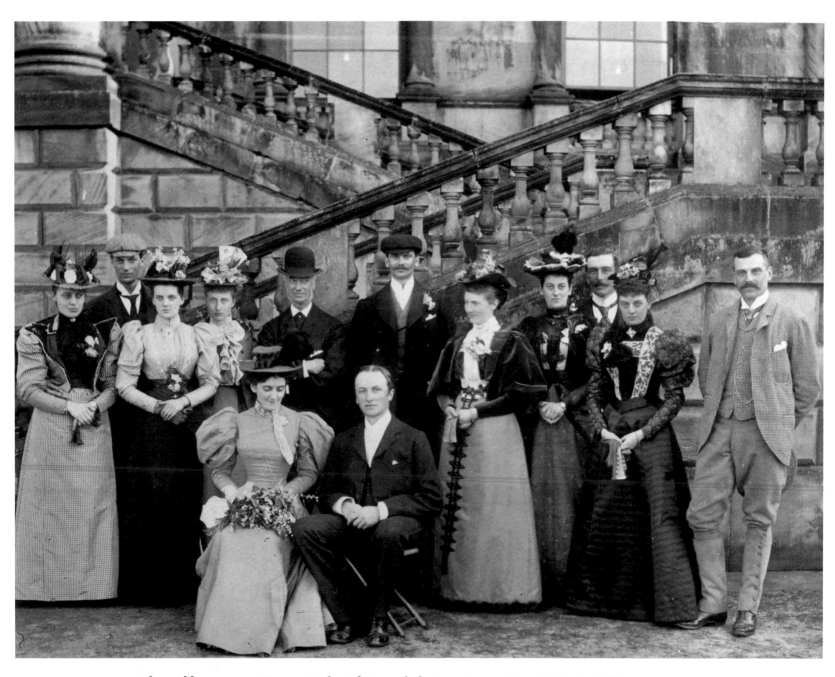

The wedding group at George Nathaniel Curzon's first marriage to Mary Victoria, 1895.
Left to right: (Standing) Geraldine, Frank, Margaret, Lilian, Lord Scarsdale, Asheton, Sophy
Ellie, J. Milier, Evey, Atty. (Seated) Mary Victoria Curzon, George Nathaniel Curzon.

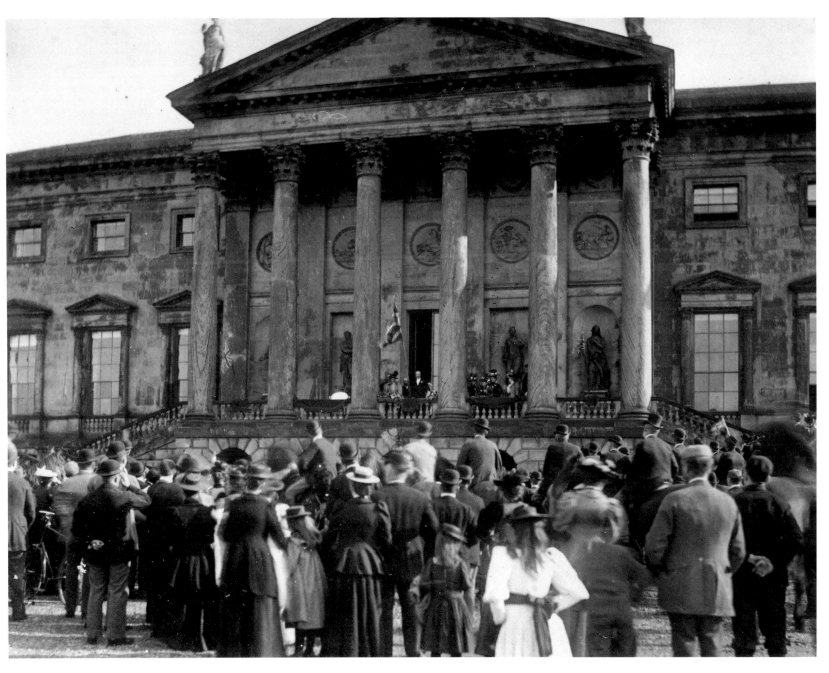

George Nathaniel Curzon addressing the tenants on the day of his wedding.

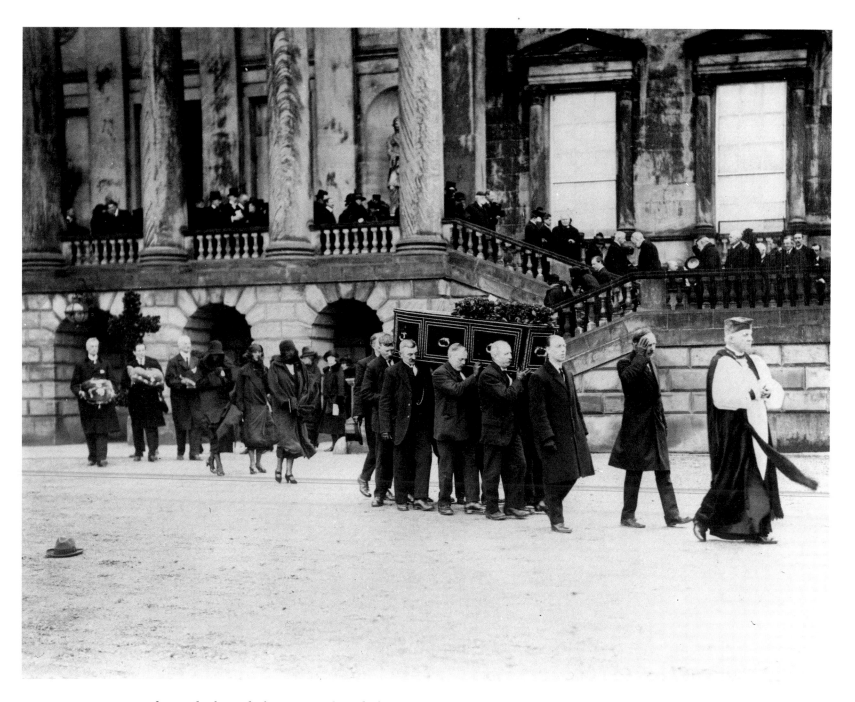

Above: The funeral of George Nathaniel, then Marquis Curzon of Kedleston, 1925.

Opposite: The north front.

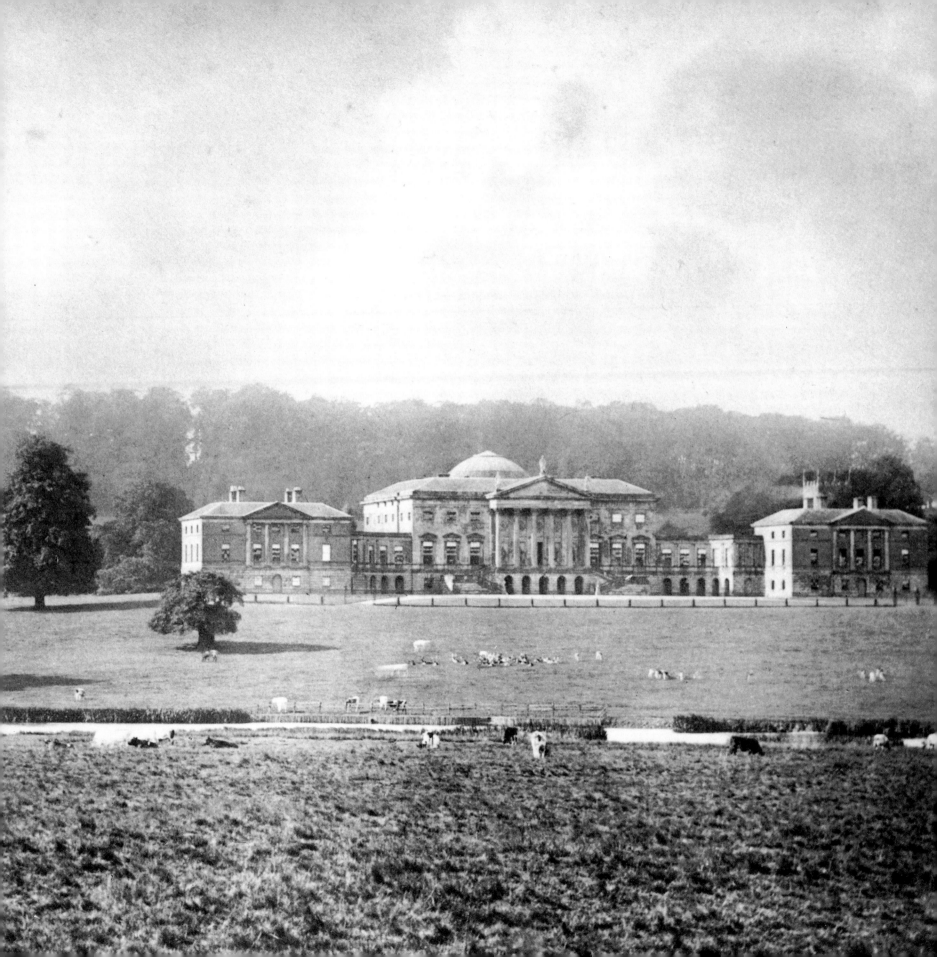

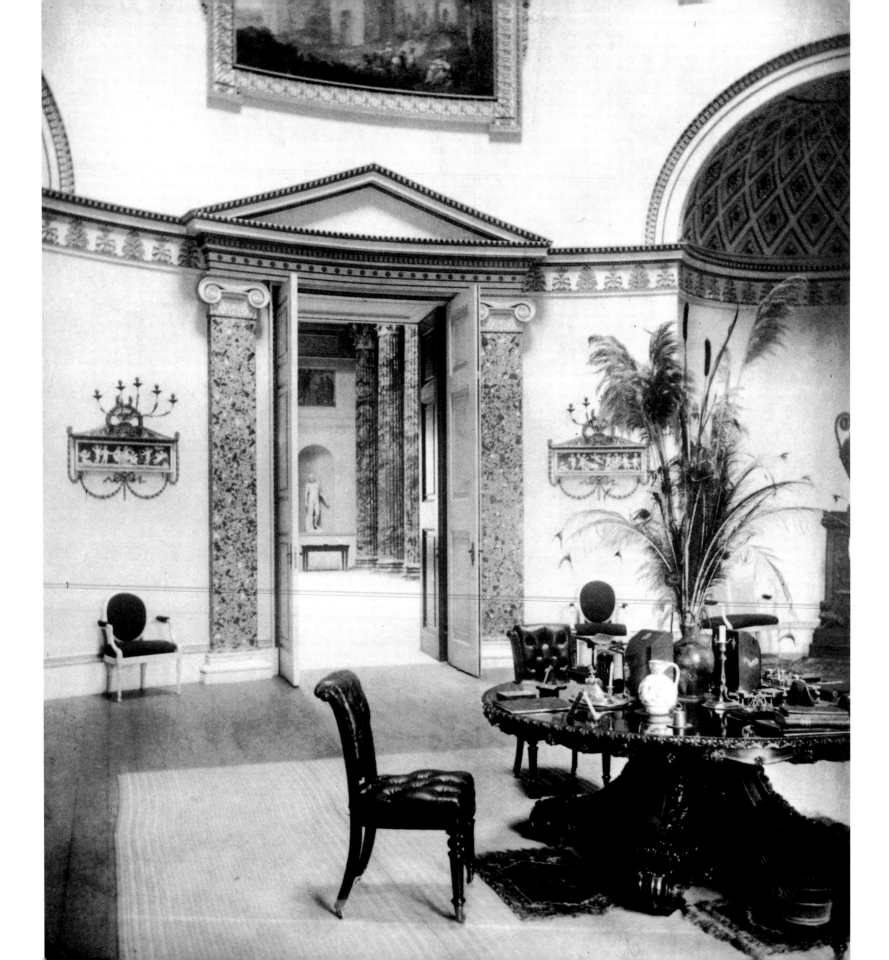

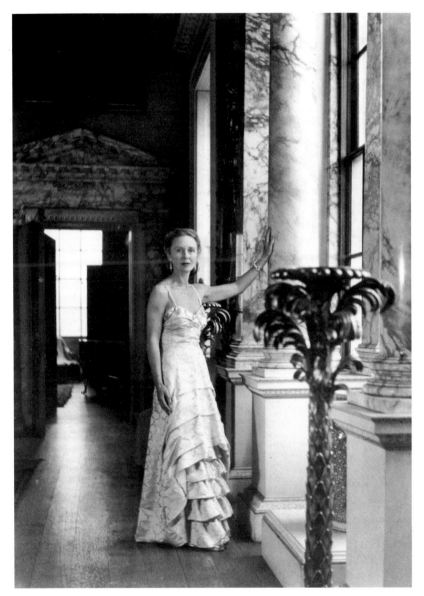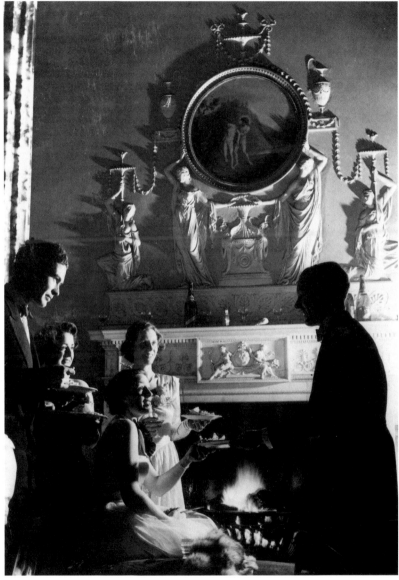

Above left: Ottilie, Lady Scarsdale, 2nd wife of the 2nd Viscount Scarsdale photographed in the Drawing Room, 1949.

Above right: The Hunt Ball, 1955. Breakfast in the Hall.

Left: The Saloon, 1890.

Overleaf: The new Hispano Suiza, 1925.

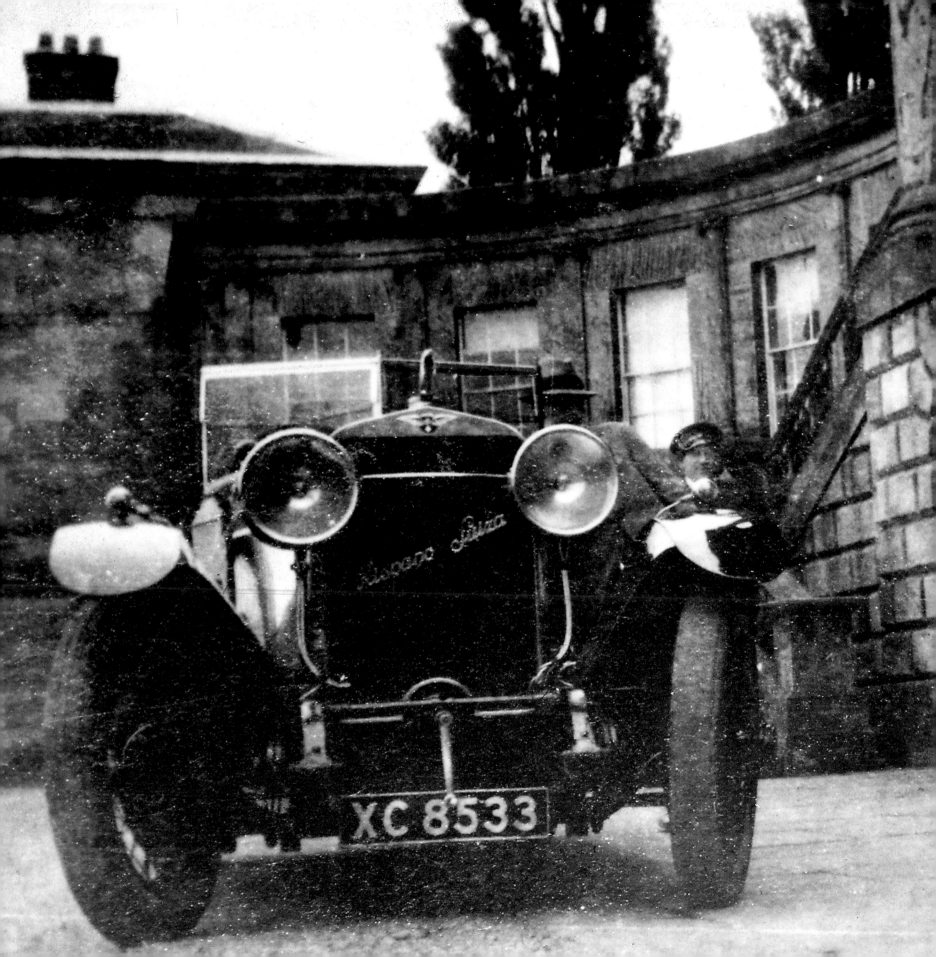

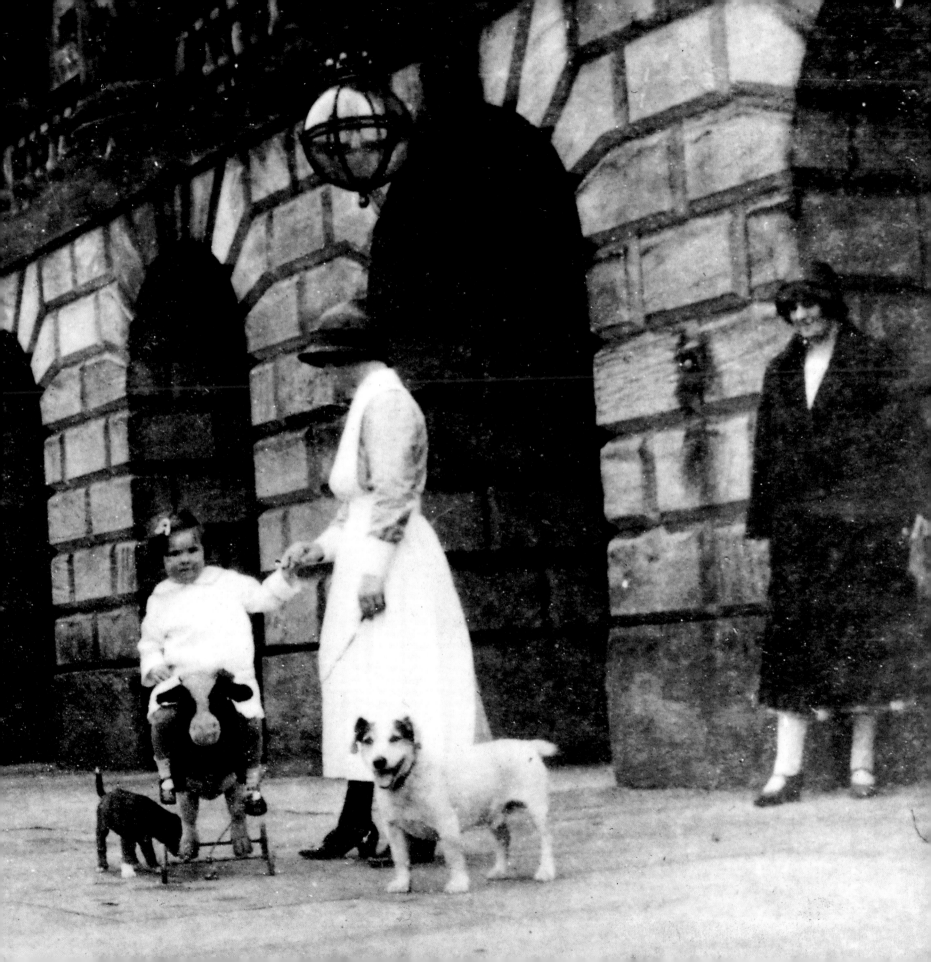

ACKNOWLEDGEMENTS

For their help and cooperation in the creation of this book I am particularly grateful to the following: Ms Rosamund Griffin, Sir Ralph Verney, Ms Francesca Scoones, Lord Egremont, Mr Bob Lassam, Mr Michael Sandford, Mr Hugh Dixon, Mr Andrew Barber, Mr Jonathan Marsden, Mr Eric Smith, Mr Tony Mitchell, Mr Jacob Rothschild, Mr Geoffrey Trevelyan, Ms Alison McCann, Ms Anthea Palmer, Canon Peter and Lady Althea Eliot, Mrs Patricia Jennings, Viscount Scarsdale, Michael Holroyd, Ms Susie Cullinan, Lady Elton, Mr John Chessyre, Mr Leslie Harris, Mrs Christopher Hussey, Mr Henry Harpur-Crewe, Mr Henry Hoare, Mr Aidan and Lady Victoria Cuthbert, the Duke and Duchess of Devonshire, Mr Gervase Jackson-Stops, Mr Mark Bainbridge, Ms Gillian Young.

I would also like to add a special thanks to James Lees-Milne for allowing me to quote extensively from his diaries, and to Bob Ireland for taking so much time and trouble with the printing of the photographs.

INDEX